CHIPS & POP

———

CHIPS

[ROBERT BARNARD

DAVE COSGRAVE

JENNIFER WELSH]

& POP

decoding the

nexus generation

[MALCOLM LESTER BOOKS

Copyright © 1998 by d~Code.

No part of this publication may be reproduced, stored in a
retrieval system, or transmitted, in any form or by any means,
without the prior written permission of the publisher or, in the
case of photocopying or other reprographic copying, a licence
from CANCOPY (Canadian Copyright Licensing Agency),
6 Adelaide Street East, Suite 900, Toronto, Ontario M5C 1H6.

Canadian Cataloguing in Publication Data

Barnard, Robert, 1967–
    Chips & pop : decoding the nexus generation

Includes bibliographical references and index.
ISBN 1-894121-08-2

1. Generation X – Canada.   2. Young consumers – Canada.
3. Young adults – Employment – Canada.   4. Young adults – Canada.
I. Cosgrave, Dave, 1967–   .   II. Welsh, Jennifer, 1965–   .
III. Title.   IV. Title: Chips and pop.

HF5415.33.C3B37 1998   305.242′0971   C98-931765-X

Editor: Janice Weaver
Book design: Gordon Robertson

∂ - c ◉ ◻ ᴇ
401 Richmond Street West, Suite 251
Toronto, Ontario M5V 3A8

Malcolm Lester Books
25 Isabella Street, Toronto, Ontario M4Y 1M7

Printed and bound in Canada
98 99 00 01 5 4 3 2 1

CONTENTS

_____

INTRODUCTION

———

Chips & Pop is a book about decoding the Nexus Generation, that group of Canadians born between the early sixties and the late seventies. If this is your first encounter with the Nexus Generation, you are probably not alone. We introduced the phrase only in 1996, about a year and a half after we created it at d~Code. d~Code is a consulting firm that combines the best elements of advertising agencies, public-policy think-tanks, research firms, and strategy consultants. Since 1994, we have worked with the private, public, and not-for-profit sectors to help them understand the Nexus Generation and develop innovative ideas and strategies to effectively connect with it. Our work with this age group—which we had simply been calling "the generation"—led us to some conclusions that seemed to counter the conventional wisdom about young Canadians. Granted, they were, and are, a difficult group to understand. But what understanding there was could be best described as "pop-culturesque," and more often than not was traceable to the famous novel *Generation X*. You're probably familiar with the stereotypes that novel introduced: GenXers are slack, aimless, marginalized. We knew that there was much more to say about this generation than even the most generous interpretations of *Generation X* would allow for. So we introduced the term *Nexus Generation*.

The word *nexus* means link or bridge. We chose it because we believe, for two reasons, that the Nexus Generation is uniquely positioned to play some key bridging roles in society. First, it is sandwiched between the demographic bulge known as the Baby Boom (those born and raised during the two decades after the Second World War), and the Boomers' children, known as the Echo Generation (those born between the eighties and the present). The pace of societal change over the past few decades has left a significant generation gap between these two groups, and Nexus is poised to mitigate any tension they may feel.

Second, the Nexus Generation sits right in the middle of our society's shift from the assembly-line Industrial Age to the data-driven Information Age. The onset of the Information Age corresponds to Nexus' earliest days, and today members of this generation are the stewards of change in many of our key institutions. In a broad sense, Nexus is a generation that will bridge the present and the future.

We introduce the idea of Nexus fully aware of the perils of slapping labels on people, particularly on a highly diverse group of young people. Generalization—and its more malevolent next of kin, the stereotype—can cause problems for all of us. But generational perspectives *are* important. Creating frameworks and identifying both the differences and commonalties between us helps to make sense of an increasingly complex world. As we approach the new millennium, we have in Canada multiple generations attempting to coexist, each with distinct perspectives and needs.

Unfortunately, generational perspectives most often focus on how people are different, not how they are the same. Intergenerational cooperation, a necessary condition of tackling society's most pressing problems, is built on understanding both sameness and difference. In *Chips & Pop,* we share with you all we've learned about

2

Nexus, and we introduce a way of thinking about generations that helps foster this understanding.

This book is divided into two sections. Section I (Chapters 1 to 3) begins with a look back at the origins of the term *Generation X* and its accompanying stereotypes and myths. It then turns to examine Nexus' impressionable early years, and in particular how the parallel emergence of computer "chips" and "pop" culture has served to shape the generation. Finally, it explores Nexus' current relationship with some key societal institutions, such as the state, the community, and the family.

Section II (Chapters 4 to 6) builds on these foundations, providing guidance for those who interact with Nexus as marketers, employers, human-resource specialists, community leaders, and policy makers. If you are part of Nexus, or have Nexus-aged children, we expect you will find insights and guidance here as well. We do not, however, suggest that you read only those parts of Section II that relate to your specific vocation. Nexus is best understood from a holistic point of view, one that considers its roles as a consumer, an employee, and a citizen.

Our starting place at d~Code is Nexus itself—not any particular sector or business function. In fact, we believe "the generation is the consultant." To help us with our work, we tap in to a network of more than 150 "d~Coders" from across North America, facilitating both real and virtual interaction. d~Coders are multi-talented professionals with diverse educational, social, cultural, regional, and economic backgrounds. Individual members of our d~Code network are chosen based on their experience, powers of observation, communication skills, and creative potential. Together, they serve as the "idea engine" for our work with our clients.

d~Code has been building intellectual capital based on Nexus for the past four years. Through our consulting work, our participation in both quantitative and qualitative research, and our monitoring of Nexus culture, we have an acute sense of *what's going on*. We've been doing nothing but tracking the icons, attitudes, and expectations of Nexus in its anxious search to find its place in a changing economy and a changing society.

Over the years, d~Code has developed a new Nexus deodorant, designed listener-attraction strategies for a top Canadian radio station, created marketing ideas for a telephone company, shaped human-resource attraction and retention policies for the technology and financial-services sectors, and worked with governments in areas such as health, the environment, multiculturalism, and national unity.

These three elements—our network, our intellectual capital, and our projects—have allowed us to dive deep and see firsthand what makes Nexus tick.

[A Note about Research]

In addition to our own work and experience, *Chips & Pop* draws largely on polling data from respected national firms such as the Angus Reid Group, Environics, the J. C. Williams Group, the Print Measurement Bureau, and the Strategic Counsel, as well as Statistics Canada. We make frequent reference throughout to a report entitled *Building Bridges: New Perspectives on the Nexus Generation,* the result of a partnership between d~Code, Angus Reid, and the Royal Bank Financial Group in the summer of 1997. This report marked an important milestone in our understanding of Nexus, and served as an inspiration for this book.

We also interviewed a number of business and organizational leaders from each of the three sectors we work in, to provide additional "real world" perspectives on the challenges and opportunities posed by the Nexus Generation. These are rounded off by observations furnished by many of our d~Coders, whom we refer to throughout *Chips & Pop* by their first names and the places they live.

A final note on our use of language. "We" is used in reference to the authors and/or d~Code, while "the generation" refers to Nexus. That having been said, "we" owe those from "the generation" that we've had the pleasure to work with many thanks in helping make *Chips & Pop* a reality.

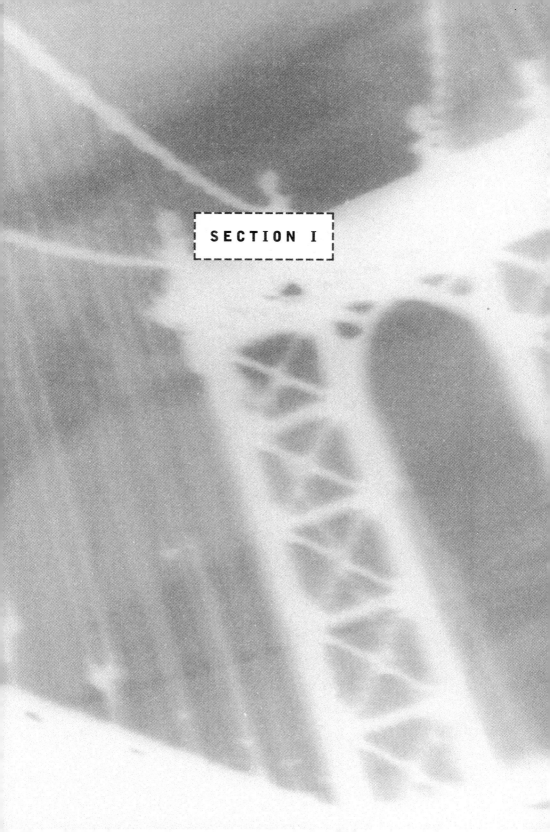

SECTION I

THE STEREOTYPES OF GENERATION X

In the novel *Generation X: Tales for an Accelerated Culture,*[1] Douglas Coupland's fictional characters assemble in the California desert to escape mainstream society. The dissatisfaction they feel with their own lives is matched only by their apparent, if not deliberate, ambivalence towards doing anything about it. They instead prefer to lay blame on others, and lament that they are simply members of an unfortunate generation born a little too late. "We live small lives on the periphery; we are marginalized and there is a great deal in which we choose not to participate" reveals the story's protagonist, Andy. Aimless, slack, apathetic—these adjectives have become the hallmarks of Generation X.

Why was Coupland's bleak, fictional snapshot of a generation taken so seriously? Why have many of these notions persisted for so long? And why are these labels passed on to subsequent groups of young people, as a sort of inheritance for anyone who turns sixteen?

In this chapter, we'll address these questions and take a hard look at the stereotypes that dog Generation X. We'll explore the multiple definitions that exist for Generation X today, and we'll speculate about its future. But what we can't do is provide a *definitive* answer to the question of who or what it is. Since the phrase

Generation X entered the lexicon, its definition has been distorted, its boundaries stretched or contracted, and its meaning confused. The term has long since relinquished any claim to being a useful descriptor, if ever it had any. Our aim is to put a new stamp on the generation and call it Nexus, a term that reveals much more about the people it stands to represent than the letter *x*.

[What's in a Name?]

Just what is *x*? We know it as a seldom-used letter in the alphabet, as well as a stand-in for mathematical variables and unknowns. Our own personal favourite definition of *x*, compliments of the office dictionary, is a "signature for the illiterate." As far as we can tell, the term *Generation X* first came into use in 1964, as the title of a British self-improvement manual for young adults. Punk-rock star Billy Idol probably never read that book, but he did borrow the term to name his late seventies punk-rock outfit. Punk-lore has it that the band Generation X was genuinely despised by its own fans (who often spat on Idol and his mates),[2] though its self-titled debut album enjoyed a modest success on the charts. By 1981, this Generation X had all but disappeared.

A decade later, Douglas Coupland dusted off the phrase and, intentionally or not, attached it to a generation. Generation X has served Coupland far better than it ever did Idol—today it is virtually a household term. But it is interesting to note that although it's a book whose margins are lined with definitions of such obscure notions as "veal-fattening pens" and "Boomer envy," *Generation X* never really defines who its namesake is supposed to be. The term is given only a passing reference in the text—"a generation purposely hiding itself"—though we gather from the flap copy that the generation in question was born between the late fifties and late sixties.

By Coupland's original definition then, Generation Xers are today somewhere between thirty and forty years old. In our experience, quadragenarians purporting to be GenXers are decidedly rare; most people beyond thirty-five tend more than happily to align themselves with the Baby Boom Generation, better known as the Boomers.

Canada's most famous demographer, David Foot, offers a similarly mature and even more narrow definition of Xers: those born between 1960 and 1966.[3] In fact, Foot does not consider GenX a distinct cohort at all, but rather a small, if not unfortunate, group at the trailing edge of the Baby Boom. That's right. According to Foot, GenXers are "late Boomers," not late bloomers. We have encountered some self-proclaimed GenXers who would find this an unpalatable association, to say the least.

At the other end of the scale, definitions for GenX have emerged that include people far younger than Coupland surely ever intended. In his book *Sex in the Snow: Canadian Social Values at the End of the Millennium,*[4] pollster Michael Adams defines GenXers as those individuals born between 1968 and 1982, making the youngest Xer seventeen today. There is nothing wrong with Adams's segmentation—quite the contrary, in fact. He begins with the premise that demography is not destiny, and lets the data guide him in defining generations and the sub-groups he call tribes. His use of the term *Generation X* may be confusing, but his findings tell us a great deal. His data show that young Canadians are "the most complex of generations," exhibiting a wide variation in attitudes and values. The complexity and elusiveness of this group is part of the reason the letter *x* has been used for so long to describe them.

Beat the Champ

As a tag, Generation X's long run at the top has not been without challengers, and we are not the first to propose alternatives. Post-Boomers have also been referred to as the Schizophrenic Generation, the Swing Generation, the Paradox Generation, and Generation Why, but these definitions essentially restate the problem: no one really seems to understand who these people are. Generational historians William Strauss and Neil Howe call it the 13th Gen, in reference to the number of birth cohorts that have emerged since the founding of America.[5] (Just this generation's luck to be number thirteen.) But of all the candidates—mathematical unknowns, unlucky numbers, question marks—none can hold a candle to what we think of as a Boom. Deferring once again to the office dictionary, a boom is something "deep, sustained, prosperous, progressive and popular." No wonder young people are holding out for something better. Generation X has persisted, though largely for lack of a better term.

Safety in Numbers

The size of Generation X is also a point of contention and confusion. Obviously, size is a function of how you choose your boundaries—there are more of Adams's GenXers (6.8 million), for example, than there are of Foot's (2.6 million). Marketer Karen Ritchie chooses an even broader definition in her book *Marketing to Generation X*,[6] and shows that (at least in the United States) it is actually a larger generation than the Baby Boom, making it the biggest of all time.

But the size of a generation also has implications beyond the realm of marketing. Demographers like Foot tend to attribute much of an individual's fortunes to the size of his or her cohort. One of Foot's tenets is that there are clear benefits to being part of a smaller generation, or at the front of the line of a larger one. Members of large cohorts ultimately compete for attention in public schools, spots on midget hockey teams, scholarships at the best universities, entry-level jobs, and executive-track positions. Those at the front end of the Baby Boom, in other words, were merely lucky, while those in the middle benefited from a concurrent expansionary phase—the Boom was so big that society made room for them. But by the time the back end of the Boom hit the front of the line, there were no spots left and no resources to create any more. Remember, these back-end Boomers are Foot's Generation X. He claims that its size and position have been at the root of many of its troubles.

The converse is also supposed to be true: members of smaller cohorts should have a relatively easy time of things. For example, though the name given to the Bust Generation implies something entirely different, Foot suggests that members of this relatively small cohort (whom he defines as those born between 1967 to 1979) can expect smooth sailing, at least for the remainder of the century. Interestingly, he also predicts a "Gen-X Two"—yet another indefinite term—made up of the trailing edge of the Echo Generation, the Boomers' kids. Only time will tell if this sequel term is as inaccurate as the original.

On the other hand, conventional demographic wisdom also suggests that, *en masse*, larger generations carry more clout and ultimately have a greater impact on society. As Foot points out, "When [the Boomers] get interested in a particular product or idea, we all have to sit up and take notice. . . ."[7] It is true that as the Boomers move towards retirement age, society will change to reflect this significant demographic shift. Governments will revise programs and policies and the private sector will react with new products and services to accommodate them. As we'll see, there are signs of this trend already. Just look at the government's most likely solution to the impending Canada Pension Plan crisis: maintain benefits while raising contributions. Policy makers must be banking on Generation X being too small to kick up any sort of a fuss. Given all of the different interpretations of how big Generation X really is, this is a dangerous assumption to make.

[A Grain of Truth]

Definitions aside, why is it that Coupland's fictional account of Generation X has been taken so literally? Why have the stereotypes stuck for so long? Well, Coupland's contemporaries are themselves partly to blame. The release of the book coincided with an economically gloomy time, particularly for young people. Many took comfort in Coupland's stories, told in a familiar and non-threatening way. *Generation X* was hoisted to the top of the best-seller list by young buyers—a novelty in the publishing industry—and hordes of enthusiastic "followers" attended Coupland's lectures and talks. Members of other generations observing the scene, particularly the Boomers, must have concluded that *Generation X* was not only a novel, but also a phenomenon. Coupland's work was meant only to tell stories of a generation, but many took it to be a representational portrait.

Of course, complaints from "old" people about the attitudes of "young" people are nothing new. The Greek poet Hesiod, for example, wrote of the frivolity and recklessness of youth as far back as the eighth century BC, and George Bernard Shaw noted that "youth is wasted on the young."[8] In each and every episode of "Scooby-Doo," the bad guys blame their downfall on "those meddling kids." Clearly, some of the lingering myths of GenX are really just the long-standing myths of youth.

But others seem to owe their origins to the particular circumstances of post-Boomer youth. Just try growing up in the shadow of what is *still* commonly considered the largest generation of all time. In bemoaning the attitudes and actions of youth, many Boomers conveniently forget the fortunate circumstances of their own formative years. Theirs was a time of uninterrupted and unprecedented economic growth, relative peace, and social liberation. Things were not so rosy for those of Generation X, yet Boomers often expect them to be just as successful and well adjusted as they are.

There are also theories to suggest that the troubles of today's young people owe a lot to the broader conditions of the postmodern age—a sort of Generation X syndrome. In *Generation on Hold*,[9] sociologists James Côté and Anton Allahar suggest that modern social and economic conditions have tended to marginalize youth and deprive them of the necessary opportunities to form healthy adult identities. These opportunities, which include finding a job, moving away from home, and starting a family, are restricted for many. Côté and Allahar also argue that adolescence is an artificial life stage, not a biological or even a historical one, in which many contemporary youth become trapped. Thus, stuck in adolescence, while at the same time frozen by a tyranny of educational, occupational, and spiritual choice, many youth appear to be aimless, if not helpless, members of society.

So just how many GenXers are there who fit this description? Michael Adams provides us with some clues. *Sex in the Snow* identifies a segment of young Canadians called the Aimless Dependents, whose members seem to fit the standard Generation X profile. They take a decidedly unemotional approach to life, and feel that "everything has evolved too quickly, often leaving them behind."[10] According to Adams, they are also prone to anger and resentment and are the likely culprits behind such events as the Montreal and Vancouver Stanley Cup riots earlier this decade. These Aimless Dependents make up a little more than a quarter of Adams's total youth sample.

If you think the size of this segment of disengaged youth is extraordinary large, think again. Adams believes that the Aimless Dependents are the generational descendants of what he calls the

Disengaged Darwinist segment of the Boomers. In other words, these two segments share a similar world-view. Like the Aimless Dependents, Disengaged Darwinists tend to be angry, lacking in confidence, and intimidated by change. Just think of Al Bundy from "Married with Children." But where Aimless Dependents make up 27 per cent of Generation X, the Disengaged Darwinists actually account for 41 per cent of Boomers. Perhaps the media should turn its attention to them?

But the media, it seems, is obsessed with a relatively small segment of Canadian youth. Since 1992, the bulk of articles written on Generation X have focused on how tough a time Xers are having, how they are unable to cope or are unwilling to pay their dues. To believe the media would be to think that helping Generation X had become almost a charitable cause, with governments and big business guilting each other into handing out money and jobs to save a helpless bunch of kids. Contrast this with the media attention showered on the Boomers: they are turning fifty, they are closing in on retirement, they are going to change *everything*. Rick Mercer, designated political humorist of "This Hour Has 22 Minutes," puts it this way: "Of course, anyone with the misfortune of being born after the baby boom has to look forward to a lifetime of hearing about baby boomer milestones. Turning fifty will be a joke compared to turning sixty."[11]

Not all the media attention paid to youth is like this. In 1997, the *Toronto Star* featured a series of articles called "1000 Voices: Lives on Hold,"[12] which was aimed at providing a better understanding of the eighteen- to thirty-year-old generation. The *Star* interviewed a thousand people from this group, and they openly articulated their problems, struggles, and concerns—many of which centred on work. But when it came time to suggest solutions, whom did they poll? Business leaders, government officials, consultants, university presidents, and social activists—everyone but the young people affected by the problems. Of course, if we believe the Generation X stereotypes, they would have had little to say in the first place.

What will become of Generation X is difficult to say. Coupland himself has attempted to euthanize this aging phrase, but seven years and six books later, he is still most revered for having created it. The *New York Times* actually ran its obituary in June 1995, but for the most part, it is the mass media that continues to give it life. As recently as June 1997, Generation X still rated a cover story in *Time* magazine. Despite all of its shortcomings and confusion, the term *Generation X* refuses to go away.

[The Generation Formerly Known As X]

As we stated up front, our aim is to give a new definition to young Canadians. We hope we have made a case for doing so based on the confused and empty meaning of the old one. We introduce the term *nexus* as an alternative because it has a clear and descriptive meaning. The Nexus Generation is a distinct group of people growing up at a unique point in history, sandwiched between two significant generations, linking an exciting future to an important past. It is not a small generation, nor is it insignificant. We also think understanding Nexus is good for everyone.

We'll begin by describing Nexus' boundaries. By definition, this generation—those born between the early sixties and late seventies—has no "hard edges." It is a generation based on formative experiences and pivotal events rather than specific birthdates or cohort size. Essentially, you are Nexus if you first felt the effects of the computer chip and global media at some point during your formative years. This means you could have encountered a PC for the first time in university or mastered Pong (the original video game) at the age of seven. You could be Nexus if you watched live CNN coverage of the Gulf War at high school, saw the space shuttle *Challenger* blow up in grade school, or were the first thirteen-year-old kid in your neighbourhood with cable TV and a remote control.

The Nexus Generation in Canada numbers *just under* eight million, and accounts for *just over* 25 per cent of the population[13]—no small generation by any standards. Does this mean that individual members of Nexus will have a tough time? We know that many already have. But to refer to Michael Adams once again, demography need not be destiny. David Foot's argument on the advantages and disadvantages of relative size presupposes that the overall supply of opportunity is fixed. While Canada's economic recovery has not been as kind to youth as it has to other demographic groups, employment opportunities *are* being created in the critical new-economy industries that Nexus is well prepared for—computers, information technology, and communications, to name just a few. At the same time, governments are getting their financial houses in order, taking pressure off interest rates, and creating a better overall entrepreneurial environment. Furthermore, Nexus' field of view when it comes to opportunity is broader than that of other generations. It is a well-informed and mobile group that has few reservations about changing cities, countries, or industries to get to where the opportunities are.

Just how accurate are the stereotypes? We know there is a segment of Nexus that has been marginalized and has not coped well with the challenges it has faced. The size of this segment is not insignificant; since 1990, the ranks of the young and unemployed have remained stubbornly large. Even more difficult to quantify are the many young people who are underemployed—a condition that leaves them both unsatisfied in the present and underqualified for the future. And while Nexus might be the most educated generation to date, more than half its members still do not hold university or college degrees—seemingly the ticket to securing meaningful, rewarding employment and a stable, satisfying life. This segment should be of concern to policy makers, but we think the "Generation X as charity case" stereotype is damaging, to say the least. For one, it is demotivating. If you consistently tell people they are charity cases, they begin to believe it is true. It also gets in the way of the kind of innovative problem-solving that is required to help the segment of Nexus Canadians that needs it most, distorting the real problems and hiding the really good answers.

The stereotypes also mask the significant diversity within Nexus. To tar the entire generation with the same brush is to overlook one of its most distinct characteristics: diversity. As we will show, diversity is emerging as one of the most valuable assets an organization can have. And Nexus' intrinsic diversity also makes for good citizens in our increasingly global society.

In the broadest sense, the GenX stereotypes prevent the generation from getting any respect. Popular commentaries on demographics often exclude people in the twenty- to thirty-year-old range when referencing who the players of the millennium will be. We hear about the Boomers and their Echo children, most of whom are under eighteen, but we hear very little about Nexus, the generation in the middle.

A Generation Sandwich

Speaking of the Echo, it's important *not* to confuse it with Nexus. These post-Nexus youngsters are being born into a world where technology and global media are already commonplace. In his book *Growing Up Digital,*[14] Don Tapscott calls this group the Net Generation (though, predictably, there are other contenders for this title, too). We like Tapscott's method of defining generations because it marries traditional demographics with concurrent technological and social trends. Tapscott asserts that the Net Generation, or N-Gen, will be a driving force in the next century, owing to its sheer size and its unique set of characteristics. He is probably right. The digital up-bringing of these young people will be a powerful and defining force.

N-Geners do bear similarities to Nexus, particularly in terms of their relationship with technology. But unlike Nexus, the Net Generation will never know the world that predated the computer chip and its various related technologies. Nexus recalls what it was like to tune a television with "rabbit-ears," to do long division by hand, or to actually look after a vinyl record—just like the Boomers do. In this regard, Nexus functions like a sneak preview of coming generations. The Boomers can look to Nexus to help them understand their young kids, and to help them adapt the workplace to accommodate new ways of learning and creating.

On the other hand, Nexus also identifies in some important ways with the Boomers. Both groups feel uneasy about the apparent erosion of our universal health, education, and welfare systems. And while the families that Nexus grew up in were, on average, smaller than those of the Boomers, it still has big plans when it comes to long-term relationships and kids. Perhaps the most recent profound experience shared by Nexus and the Boomers was the collective pain felt when our men's hockey team failed to bring home Olympic gold in 1998. Together, the generations waxed nostalgic about the better days of "our" game, remembering Paul Henderson's goal in 1972 and Wayne Gretzky's clutch pass to Mario Lemieux in 1988 to bring home what was then called the Canada Cup.

The Missing Link

The "sandwich" position of Nexus will be critical, since some observers predict that we are racing towards a generational "clash of the titans." In his book *YouthQuake*, author Ezra Levant issues a PG-35 warning to parents to read the book only in the company of their children because its contents "may be unsettling."[15] Levant thinks the Boomers will eventually face the stiff wrath of younger Canadians over issues such as Canada's failing pension plan and the national debt. Don Tapscott goes so far as to do some scenario planning about the sort of relationship that might emerge between the Boomers and their Net Generation kids. He explores the possibilities that the Net Generation's digitally inspired culture might be too much for the Boomers to take, but that N-Geners won't take no for an answer. Fortunately, only two of his four future scenarios are bad, and only one catastrophic.

But these predictions of intergenerational strife overlook one very important group: the Nexus Generation, positioned smack-dab in the middle. Nexus has significant demographic muscle of its own (there are close to eight million of them, after all), and it understands technology and its implications better than the Net Generation. Also, where the Net Generation is *expected* to invade institutions with its new ways of thinking and doing things, Nexus is *already* there. Nexus is a link between the two generations and will mitigate any conflict between them.

Myth-Debunking Unit

As you are surely beginning to see, our story when it comes to Nexus is vastly different from Coupland's *Generation X*. For starters, it is not fiction. Our understanding is based on years of interacting with real people from the generation, and on working with keen observers of its attributes and trends. It is built on hard data, as well as our exposure to a variety of organizations faced with tough Nexus challenges. While we are aware of the dangers of generalization, we will make here the first of many observations: the Nexus Generation tends to defy conventional Generation X wisdom. Following are some alternative words that can be used to describe the Nexus Generation, words we'll refer to throughout this book.

Aimless or Driven?

Often thought of as lacking clear goals or aspirations, Nexus is in reality a generation that both knows what it wants and feels in control. Recent national survey data indicate that more than half feel strongly that *they* are the ones in control of their own lives, not anyone else.[16] Many espouse the entrepreneurial spirit, because they want both to be closer to the action and to better self-direct their careers. They are also proactive retirement planners—the Nexus Generation in Canada holds substantial financial assets despite the fact that many of its members have only just embarked on their careers. Far from fatalistic, most disagree with the statement that "at any moment things could fall apart in their lives." Pollster Allan Gregg refers to Canadians eighteen to twenty-nine as a "take-charge generation with both the tools and inclination to forge a life without the traditional Canadian social safety net."[17]

Apathetic or Optimistic?

The adage that the post–Boomers will be the first generation worse off than their parents is simply not true—at least Nexus doesn't think so. Only one in five would agree with this prediction.[18] When it comes to Canada's unemployment problem, Nexus is likely to be less anxious or worried about unemployment than those aged fifty to sixty-four,[19] a striking result given an apparent crisis in youth unemployment. Nexus members are confident in their own ability to pull through. Almost half believe they will meet or exceed their career expectations, and that they will bequeath to their children a better world.[20] Members of Nexus are also optimistic about their abilities to achieve the work-life balance that seemed to elude the yuppies of the 1980s. And though not all are interested in marriage today, those that are are determined to marry for life.

Disloyal or Savvy?

Human-resource managers we talk to often complain that members of the Nexus Generation are disloyal, impatient, and unwilling to pay their dues. But Nexus is simply being realistic, if not savvy— those in the generation understand better than anyone that the idea of lifetime employment is dead. A large proportion of Nexus is comfortable with the notion of multiple careers in a lifetime. Leading a new trend towards "free agency," Nexus remains in work relationships only as long as the fit between employee and employer is mutually beneficial. Once learning curves flatten, growth in responsibility fades, or tasks become predictable, members of Nexus will "protest with their feet" and go elsewhere.

Slack or Strategic?

Coupland's GenXers preferred meaningless no-brainier "McJobs" to meaningful employment. Slackers, you say? We don't think so. Nexus members have been in the workforce for a long time. Many got their first part-time jobs as teenagers, to help out with finances after a family split or to earn a few spare bucks to buy the things television ads told them they "had" to have. Still others found the need to supplement their incomes to offset rising tuition costs. Today, members of the generation work just as many hours as anyone—they have learned to value work experience in any form. Even among those who primarily work part time, only a handful say that they are doing it "just for the money."[21] To Nexus, work has come to mean much more.

Cynical or Sceptical?

What's the difference? Cynicism implies bitterness and mockery, whereas scepticism is a healthy questioning of "truths" to get at better "truths." Nexus has plenty of reason to be sceptical, particularly towards the traditional institutions that it deems to have acted irresponsibly. The generation has access to the information and the critical-reasoning skills that lead it to ask some tough questions: Should I get married? Why go to church? Is university the right choice? The explosion of information has also meant an explosion of choice. Institutions must continuously work to maintain their relevance to Nexus.

Trapped or Adaptable?

True, many from Nexus have stayed in school or lived with their parents well into their twenties or even thirties. Does this mean Nexus is trapped? Not at all—it is merely adapting to change. In fact, Nexus is more comfortable with change than other generations, and actually craves change and variety in the workplace. A more transient generation than any before it, Nexus is able to create temporary support structures through real or virtual communities. Nexus will continue to draw on this important coping mechanism as we enter the millennium.

[Conclusion]

Now that we've put aside the term *Generation X* and introduced you to the Nexus Generation, it's time to turn our attention to how this group got to be this way. If you're not part of Nexus but these generational attributes sound awfully familiar, we're not surprised. Nexus is not from another planet. But as we will show in Chapter 2, Nexus did grow up during a time when things on *this planet* were significantly changing. If Nexus' generational attributes seem a little different, it's because of the environment that shaped its formative years.

THE MAKING OF A GENERATION

Occasionally, identical twins suffer the extreme misfortune of being separated at birth. Raised by different parents in separate environments, they often experience radically divergent circumstances. Fate sometimes brings these people together again, and their teary reunions become glorious media events. But these reunions also provide opportunities for science to solve one of its greatest and most persistent debates: Is it nature or nurture? Are we products of our environment or merely expressions of a predetermined biological code? Identical twins, when raised apart, constitute the perfect "controlled experiment" for helping resolve this question.

There are no such experiments when it comes to generations, but a similar debate exists. Are a generation's characteristics simply reflections of plain old human nature, or do environmental factors play a stronger mitigating role? Generations are made up of people, after all, with *almost* identical DNA. They have little choice but to be born and to die and to go through a variety of fairly predictable life-stages in between. A twenty-five-year-old, some would say, is always a twenty-five-year-old, regardless of the generation she is a part of.

On the other hand, it is not difficult to imagine that children who grew up during the Great Depression would be significantly different as adults from those raised during the excesses of the 1980s. Similarly, a generation raised during the Vietnam conflict might have more in common with the 1914–18 cohort than it would with a generation spared the experience of war.

At d~Code, we think there is no right or wrong answer to this nature vs. nurture question. Simply put, generations have similarities and they have differences. We like to use a biological analogy to illustrate this point. Generations can be thought to possess *generational genes* that account for the many similarities between them. These genes influence different generations in a consistent manner, regardless of the era or the environment in which the generations are raised. The differences between generations can be thought of as a result of *generational conditioning*. Just as a child's environment shapes who she will become, a unique set of experiences spanning each generation's formative years (roughly birth to the age of eighteen) condition it and help to shape its unique set of values.

In this chapter, we explore the concepts of generational genes and generational conditioning a little further. We also discuss the specific circumstances and events that marked Nexus' early years. In particular, we show how Nexus' unique position relative to the Information Revolution, globalization, and a range of other conditioning experiences has resulted in its signature set of generational attributes.

[Darwin 101]

Most of us learn a little bit of genetics in high school, particularly how certain human traits (thanks to some funny thing called a double helix) are fixed at conception. If both of our parents have brown eyes, for example, the likelihood of our eyes being blue is exactly zero. Similarly, if our blood is type A negative, then at least one of our parents must have passed on to us a gene that tells our bodies to produce this kind of blood. Sometimes these genes are "expressed," meaning they produce a particular effect, and sometimes they "recede," meaning they produce an effect in some but not others. Boys studying genetics sometimes learn about irony as well, since male baldness is caused by a recessive gene passed on to them by their mothers.

But aside from the few examples we learn in biology class, where do all the other million or so human traits come from? If you were to ask a "psychological Darwinist," or a "behavioural geneticist," he might go so far as to say that *all* of human behaviour is genetic. As we speak, billions of dollars are being spent mapping the human genome, the sum of all our genetic material, with hopes of pinpointing the chemical combinations responsible for not only how we look or how we fight disease, but also how we act and behave. A recent *New Yorker* article took social Darwinism to extremes in offering an "evolutionary" explanation for the philanderings of certain American presidents.

[Psych 202]

We might also have learned a thing or two about psychology in high school. Most of us were taught the conventional psychological wisdom, inspired by eighteenth-century philosopher David Hume and contemporary psychologist B. F. Skinner, where the human mind starts as a blank slate whose form and function are mostly determined by external factors. From the first moments after birth (or perhaps even before), we begin to associate our experiences and to understand the cause-and-effect relationships between them. Individual behaviours are influenced or reinforced by their consequences—we cry and our parents comfort us, we misbehave and our parents become angry, we are successful and society rewards us.

In the extreme, a serial killer's actions might derive from a lack of physical contact as a child. Ultimately, these experiences constitute a unique view of the world, and a highly individual set of behaviours to go with it.

Today there is a growing body of scientific evidence that is reinforcing the importance of early childhood experiences. Fraser Mustard, founding president of the Canadian Institute for Advanced Research, suggests that "there are specific windows of opportunity in our development where it is critical that the cells in our brains (or neurons) receive a particular variety of stimulus so that they can be properly 'wired' together." Experiments on cats show that if the cortex of the brain does not receive stimulae from the eye during the early stages of their development, the abilities of these animals to see is permanently and irreparably impaired.[1] More complex human traits and behaviours, such as the propensity to cry during movies or to succumb to "road rage" while behind the wheel, are ultimately expressions of brain functioning—where did they come from if not past experience?

If your high-school education did not resolve the nature-nurture debate for you, you need not question the quality of your instruction just yet. It turns out that the "best" answer, thanks largely to studies of our unfortunate identical twins, is that both contribute in nearly equal parts to how people behave.[2] Interestingly, many quirky or idiosyncratic behaviours turn out to be genetic, such as a predilection for giggling or a sweet tooth. But a great many of our human qualities—a full 50 per cent, in fact—derive from the environment around us, not our genetic legacy. Behaviours, attributes, and values are most fully understood by drawing on the best of both worlds. This is essentially d~Code's approach to generations. Our aim is to understand where age-old *generational genes* have expressed themselves in Nexus, and where *generational conditioning* has made Nexus unique.

[It's in Your Genes]

One of the more common responses we get to our work on Nexus is, "Hey, I was just like that when I was twenty-five." Of course you were. Truth is, quite a bit of what we know about Nexus is built on basic human nature. Many Nexus attributes relate to the fact that members of this generation are still relatively young and their generational genes are just kicking in. Our aim in this book is not to provide an exhaustive summary of human behaviour, but we do want to touch on four generational genes—rebelliousness, recklessness, naïveté, and the search for stability—which form the basis of what are a fairly standard set of youth behaviours and compulsions.

Every young generation tends to feel misunderstood or misrepresented. This feeling often translates into a questioning of traditional authority or the creation of new forms of expression. The sixties, for example, were a rebellious era marked by both defiance and creativity—dodging the draft, marrying someone from another ethnic group, making psychedelic music. For Boomers, rebelliousness was epitomized by the likes of James Dean, Jimi Hendrix, and John Belushi.

Interestingly, recklessness was the other hallmark of this particular group of rebels. Where rebelliousness is an outward expression, recklessness has an internal, individual focus. Icons Dean, Hendrix, and Belushi, for example, all suffered what were essentially self-inflicted, premature deaths. Recklessness manifests itself as a kind of invincibility. Young people have always suffered from the delusion that sickness and death are conditions for old people to obsess over, not them. They need not think about their health just yet. This feeling of invincibility is responsible for a fundamental disconnection in their thinking—behavioural choices made today are de-linked from health outcomes tomorrow. The Boomers engaged in "free love" and indulged in LSD. Today many within Nexus smoke cigarettes, abuse drugs and alcohol, and practise unsafe sex, despite the fact that they are members of the most well-informed generation to date.

Young people also tend to be strongly influenced by the naïveté gene. Although it's often thought of as a negative trait, we think that naïveté helps young people to be more pioneering and more able to cope with change than their parents. For young people, most traditions and routines have yet to take hold—they simply don't know any better. Naïveté also leads us to unabashedly question that which we do not understand. The Boomers openly questioned barriers to civil rights and sexual equality, for example, because they just didn't make sense. Nexus questions contemporary institutions for the same reason.

The fates of Nexus contemporaries River Phoenix, Kurt Cobain, and Chris Farley bear striking resemblance to those of Dean, Hendrix, and Belushi. A brash but troubled young movie star, a musical visionary, and a large but lovable comic genius. These two groups of young cultural icons were carriers of the same generational genes. For the average Nexus person, rebellion may mean becoming a professional computer hacker or choosing to pass on a university education. Recklessness may mean quitting a perfectly good job to start a risky new business or trying extreme heli-skiing in British Columbia. Naïveté means travelling alone through dangerous parts of Africa or tearing apart a piece of new technology to see how it works. These are simply the expressions of generational genes placed in a slightly different context.

The final generational gene to consider here is the search for stability gene, the one that ultimately makes most people from any generation try to "find themselves" and *grow up*. This gene prompts us to trade in some of our rebellious individuality for committed, life-long relationships. People begin to succumb to routines and to uphold their own "modified" traditions. They begin to give up their more reckless behaviours and start to seek asylum from change, wherever possible. The stability gene prompts people to *settle down*. Though some would deny it, this is just what the Boomers have done. They *were* the hippies, the flower children, and the "peace-niks" of the sixties. They *became* the suburban, mini-van–driving materialists that were notorious in the eighties. Will Nexus also trade its youth-hostel cards for American Express cards and its backpacks for briefcases? We are not sure. This depends on your definition of stability. As we will point out in subsequent chapters, Nexus is redefining what stability means.

[Skipping a Generation]

Certain cancers have been traced to particular genes that skip generations. That is, a grandfather and a granddaughter might become afflicted with cancer while a mother might not, though they all carry the same gene. One interesting theory suggests that generational genes also act in this manner, skipping four generations at a time.

In their book *Generations, A History of America's Future, 1584–2069*,[3] Neil Howe and William Strauss show how America has gone through five historical cycles, each comprising four eras and a corresponding generation. They suggest that four distinct generational personalities, which they describe as Idealist, Reactive, Civic, and Adaptive, emerge in order in each of the cycles. In the present cycle, for example, the Boomers are the Idealists—righteous and principled, but prone to arrogance—while Nexus members are Reactive—lonely and troubled, though savvy and practical. If Howe and Strauss are correct, then Nexus is most likely to resemble generations of the 1920s or 1820s. Interestingly, the 1920s saw the rise of a talented young author, F. Scott Fitzgerald, regarded at the time as the voice of a younger or "lost" generation. According to Howe and Strauss's prediction, another talented young author, Douglas Coupland, emerged some seventy years later and became the voice of yet another collection of the young and the misunderstood.

It is interesting to note that in Howe and Strauss's theory, these generational personalities are very much tied to the history of their era. The Boomers, they suggest, are the way they are because they grew up during an "Outer Driven Era" characterized by high fertility rates and steady economic growth. Nexus, on the other hand, grew up during an "Awakening Era" marked by falling fertility rates and foundering economies. The mood during this era is largely of one challenging existing values and the institutions that harbour them. So is the cart pushing or pulling the horse? In a way, Howe and Strauss are suggesting that the formation of a generation's character mimics more complex biological systems: one part destiny, one part circumstance, with one feeding and conditioning the other.

[Chips & Pop:
Conditioning Experiences]

Another of the more frequent comments we hear at d~Code is, "Boy, you really understand my kids. . . . Their approach to life is far different than mine was at the same age." No, they are not talking about pre-teens. They are talking about their adult, Nexus-aged children. We sometimes hear cases of the apparent aimlessness and lack of motivation discussed in Chapter 1, but just as often, parents are proud—even in awe—of the things their kids have done, the chances they have taken, or simply the way they are.

We have been told stories of corporate executives dramatically shifting their careers, inspired by their twenty-year-old children who understand the work-life balance better than they do. We hear stories from mothers who delight in the courageous career, family, and life choices that their thirty-year-old daughters are making, choices formerly impossible or unheard of for women to make. These distinct Nexus characteristics are the results of extensive generational conditioning.

Of course, Nexus is not the first (or last) generation to have unique, evolutionary qualities as a result of its formative experiences. The children and young adults of the Great Depression, as we have suggested, will forever have visions of scarcity, hunger, and hopelessness etched in their minds. Similarly, those who grew up during either world war will not soon forget the death, disorder, and chaos associated with them. An entire generation of Germans, mindful of the social discontent and uncertainty caused by rising prices in the 1930s, is to this day hypersensitive to inflation. The German Central Bank's sole mandate ever since has been to keep prices stable.

We conducted an informal poll of our own parents to help illustrate this point. One of our moms is terrified of thunderstorms because they remind her of the bombing raids in the Second World War. One of our dads, who experienced rationing during that same war, spreads butter on his toast as if it were going out of style. None of them has his or her credit cards "maxed out" the way we do (why be in debt if you don't have to be?), and three out of five do not use (or trust) electronic banking.

While Nexus might have been spared the horror of conventional war and the squalor of all-out depression during its formative years, it *has* grown up in a time of serious revolution. Since the 1970s, roughly when the leading edge of Nexus became aware of what was going on around it, the world has erased and redrawn political borders, knocked down and erected new walls, and crumbled and relaid the foundations of family, morality, and community.

Perhaps the most significant revolution, in terms of its speed and scope, has been the technological one. It has led to the advent of the personal computer, facilitated the proliferation of media, and laid the foundations of globalization.

Of course, Nexus cannot solely lay claim to any of this history or to its effects—we know that most of you will at least remember all of these important events. The key difference is that Nexus experienced them during its formative years. The young generation was, in effect, nurtured by the broader social environment of the late sixties, seventies, and early eighties. The technological revolution has for Nexus been a pivotal experience. The collective neurons of the generation are "hard wired," such that it has an intimate relationship with modern technology.

Beyond the computer chip, media-driven pop culture, and globalization, a number of other conditioning experiences have contributed to Nexus' attributes. These relate to the flux in our political, social, and environmental systems, which has been evident since the early seventies. It is important to note that while many of these experiences have little or nothing to do with technology or the media, these have played a role in broadcasting them and in some cases amplifying them. To borrow from Marshall McLuhan, the history of Nexus' formative years cannot be uncoupled from the media and technology by which it was delivered.

Chips

Nexus is contemporaneous with the most significant socio-economic shift since society collectively left the farm for the factory. Yes, we are talking about the Information Revolution. We are talking about computers and the Internet and all of the related technologies that allow us to crunch, store, send, and create information of all kinds. This revolution started well before any Nexus members were born, though its most profound effects were felt as they were growing up.

In 1958, the integrated circuit, better known as the computer chip, was born. The transistor, a breakthrough in its own right, had emerged a few years prior as a better means to regulate electric current. Transistors enabled dramatic improvements in the computing machines that existed in those days, but for the most part they remained large, cumbersome, inefficient, and terribly expensive. Researchers at Texas Instruments provided the next key innovation, as they were able to build resistors (devices that restrict the flow of electric current), capacitors (devices that store electrical potential energy), *and* transistors on the same silicon chip—thus the integrated circuit was born. Integrated circuits meant smaller, more efficient, less expensive computing machines. The race was now on to build them.

By most accounts, the first personal computer (PC) did not appear until 1975. Called the Altair 8800, it bore little resemblance to our modern-day machines—no keyboard, no screen, no mouse— just a box with a few switches and flashing lights. Once built (it arrived in pieces), it did little of anything, never mind anything useful. The process of loading in instructions was time-consuming and error filled, and there was no way to preserve any "work" for later. Still, demand for the Altair far outstripped supply, and by the end of that year a few dozen manufacturers of PCs had staked a claim in the marketplace.

One of the earliest devotees of the Altair was a teenaged Bill Gates. He saw in the Altair 8800 not a series of functional limitations or design flaws, but instead an opportunity to make something better. In his own words, he "naively started a company . . . with no time to waste"[4] to design software for the helpless little machine. We could argue that Gates's naïveté gene has made him a fortune.

With the help of a fledgling Microsoft, these first-generation machines brought personal computing one step closer to the masses. Still, the "build it yourself" models tended to be the dominion of the now-famous "techno-geek." If you didn't own a soldering gun, you weren't known by name at the local Radio Shack, and you didn't have a light social schedule, you probably had little to do with computers in those days.

Two companies would soon enter the still-developing PC industry and change everything. The first was Apple, conceived in a garage by two pioneers of the aforementioned techno-geek movement. Apple was (and, to some extent, still is) as much a cult as a computer company. Co-founder Steve Jobs was visionary, idealistic, and charismatic, and Apple's product was alluring and simple to use. Apple was the technologically superior underdog with a noble mission: to put computers on every desktop in America.

The other company was corporate giant IBM. It had been too busy making mainframe computers and Selectric typewriters to notice what was going on with the PC, and had done little in the way of related research or development. Nonetheless, leveraging its relatively unlimited resources, IBM launched its own PC in 1981, four years behind the wildly popular Apple II. IBM's mission was to take market share away from Apple.

Though neither Apple nor IBM is the dominant computer company today (remember Mr. Gates?), their David-versus-Goliath battles in the 1980s helped make PCs cheaper, easier to use, and much more practical. So much so that they began showing up in average workplaces, ordinary homes—even public schools. The school system is where Nexus met the PC head on.

It's not difficult to imagine the allure of PCs to young Nexus. For one thing, rumour had it that you could play games on computers. Pong, the first real video game, had already demonstrated to kids that it was possible to wire a TV screen in such a way that the images could be controlled by the viewer. Several members of our d~Code network remember playing Pong for hours and days on end, despite the fact that it was, in their words, "as crude a game of ball and stick as you could imagine." The PC promised even more control over the screen. On a PC you could not only play games, but also dissect them, probe them, and study them—even change or create them. Twenty-four-year-old David, a Toronto d~Coder, remembers creating a Pac-Man simulation (well before the real thing) by simply typing out characters and "gobbling" them up with the backspace key. A nostalgic Bill Gates notes that computers were for him as a child the lone opportunity to give orders to a big machine and always be obeyed.

But getting access to these early computers was not always easy for Nexus. Most schools invested in only a handful of them to start with, since they had yet to prove to be of any use in education. Offering computing classes meant diverting time, money, and classroom space away from the more traditional and proven disciplines. It was also not clear which department would offer these classes or who would teach them—was it math, science, or business? Denise, an Ottawa d~Coder we spoke to, recalls that "my first teacher was a computer genius who developed a typing program that could count words and track errors." Unfortunately, all she ever learned to do on a computer in his class was type.

Computer science ultimately emerged as a legitimate discipline in high schools, and the PC lab soon held its own next to the chemistry lab. For many of the Nexus Generation, learning about computers was on a par with learning math, science, and English. These early computer-science classes were, however, experiments in collective, non-hierarchical learning. Most often, the instructors in these classes knew little, if anything, beyond what their students knew. There were no textbooks to reference, no proven teaching methods to draw on, and few illustrative cases to study. There was something called a flow chart, a graphical plan laying out the logic of a set of instructions, which teachers pleaded with their students to complete prior to logging on to a machine. Some d~Coders we asked recall hating the idea of doing flow charts because it cut into their time on the machines. To Nexus, learning about computers was not about careful planning. It was about reckless experimentation, baptism by fire, composition at the keyboard. It was about trying to do what the teacher said couldn't, or shouldn't, be done. In the chemistry lab this might have resulted in an explosion. In the PC lab, the worst you could expect was a crash.

For the first time, Nexus was not learning primarily from a teacher or from a book. The computer was now the instructor, providing immediate feedback to the student for being wrong and rewarding correct answers with equal swiftness. The computer, unlike some human instructors, was patient, non-judgemental, and engaging. Nexus could spend hours at the terminal playing, learning, experimenting. Like a dog fetching a ball, the computer was a loyal friend who would never tire of the game.

If you were born into the second half of the Nexus Generation, chances are someone on your block had a computer in the home and that's the first place you ever saw one. If you were lucky, the kid with the computer was you. Using a computer at home had obvious advantages over using one in school. For one, the ratio of machines to users was better. "I'd let the first five people in my room where my computer was; the others had to wait outside," recalls Mike from central Ontario, one of our more fortunate d~Coders. No one was going to ask you to do a flow chart either (unless one of your parents was a teacher), and no one was going to give you flak if you wanted to play a game. But most of the people we asked remember being more resourceful than playful in the early days of computing. One wrote a program to simulate the tossing of a coin, then took bets from his buddies. The scheme wouldn't have worked with a real coin—they were essentially paying him to use his computer. Natasha, raised in Vancouver, remembers creating rudimentary computer graphics by blacking out "pixels" on a low-resolution grid. The process was time-consuming and the results less than brilliant, but Natasha is now a leading graphic designer at the tender age of twenty-three.

It is important to note that the personal computers that most Nexus members cut their teeth on were far different creatures from those of today. Now we flick a switch, pump in a password, and our favourite "apps" appear before us, ready to go. Modern computers are thoughtful and forgiving. They always remind us to save our work (though, not fully trusting, they do it too), and thanks to a feature called Undo, they allow us to turn back the clock on our most serious, not to mention stupid, mistakes. Should we misplace something, they will leave no "bit" unturned in helping us to find it. Should we get lost, help is on the way.

Early machines were far less self-sufficient and far less gentle. First, they needed to be hand-fed an operating system to tell them how they were supposed to work. If you wanted them to do anything beyond that, they demanded an additional set of instructions. A few programs existed that were of interest, and these you could patiently up-load with a standard audiotape deck. But the young computer industry would not figure out, at least for a few years anyway, how important software really was. In the early days of the PC, if you wanted a program, you programmed it yourself.

Compared with the computers of today, early machines suffered from poor long- and short-term memory. "Hot" machines might have had a few thousand bytes of readily available memory, and perhaps one hundred times that in storage capacity. One of the authors, an aspiring computer pioneer, recollects setting out to program a Dungeons and Dragons–like fantasy game on a 1K computer. He didn't get very far, but it forced him to think of ways to use the memory more efficiently. Today, machines carry memory that is greater by three or four orders of magnitude, while the cost of manufacturing has fallen through the floor. Now we waste memory because it's easy to get more.

Even as early PCs became more powerful, using them remained, for many, counter-intuitive. Natalie, a d~Coder from Halifax, always wondered "why Shift-F7 was ever chosen as the way to get the things to print?" She also could never remember the command to copy a file from one place to another, remarking that "if you got one back-slash or colon or letter wrong, it wouldn't work."

Was Nexus complaining? Certainly not. Members of this generation gladly learned to use computers on their own terms—learning their language, working within their limits, understanding their idiosyncrasies. Nexus was not only playing games, but also creating art, devising simulations, and solving problems. In Nexus' day, the solution was not "buy a faster machine" or "get a new piece of software," but make do with what you have, improvise, innovate.

Nexus is clearly not the only generation to understand computers, though the nature of that understanding is different. Members of Tapscott's Net Generation, immersed from day one into a silicon world, take computers for granted. Theirs is a world of information—colourful, interactive, and hyper-linked—coming at them at faster speeds and in greater quantities all the time, thanks to Moore's Law (which maintains that computers get twice as fast and halve in price every six months). They are more likely to be aware of the most powerful Internet search engine, the coolest Java applications, or the most innovative site on the Web than they are of the inner workings of a machine. Any interface that isn't fully "point and click" isn't worth bothering with at all.

The Boomers, though it has taken some time, are also on board with the Information Age. Though computer literacy studies for years showed sharp declines beginning at age thirty-five, this is beginning to change. Many Boomers now have Internet-linked computers on their desks at work—if not at home—and are discovering the convenience of e-mail and the power of the Web, thanks to corporate-sponsored training or coaching from their kids. But for most Boomers, getting wired has been merely a reaction to what is going on in the world. While there is probably not a single Boomer who would tell you that Microsoft Excel isn't a giant improvement over pencil, paper, and ledger, few would say that the Information Revolution has fundamentally altered, or become an intrinsic part of, their lives. In marketing speak, they are at best "mature users," while Nexus members are the "early adopters."

To grasp Nexus' relationship with the PC, think of the person you know best in the world, the one you know almost as well as you know yourself. Aside from a partner or a spouse, this person is most often a sibling, a childhood friend, perhaps a son or a daughter. They are often people you've known *from the beginning*. You've either grown up with them, or watched and helped them grow. You've charted their progress and noted their milestones; you know where they are headed. You don't just know them, you know them inside and out. This is how Nexus understands the PC.

Pop

The year 1958 boasted another important first for the Information Age. Scientists were able to bounce a radio broadcast off a rocket ship and back down to earth, demonstrating the scientific principles that ultimately led to satellite communication. Modern media—global, instant, omnipresent—owes much to satellite technologies that allow us to fling Technicolor images and high-fidelity sound from one side of the planet to the other in close-to-real time.

The profound effects of television had, of course, already rippled across North American society by the late fifties. Television

41

sets, now more likely to be found in the home than not, were fast replacing the radio as the social hub of the household. Families delighted in seeing familiar and comfortable portraits of themselves, and at the same time were fascinated by the bells and whistles of this still relatively new medium. By the late fifties, television had begun to fundamentally alter the nature of North American culture. Television was *the* defining media for the Boomers.

In the meantime, the next media innovation was simmering in the background. The precursor to modern cable television—called community antennae television, or CATV—had been invented in the 1940s by a small-town appliance salesman eager to sell more sets. By installing a tall antenna at the top of a local hill and running wires from it back to his shop, he was able to pull in distant broadcast signals, thus appeasing customer demand for more programming. When one final innovation was added to the mix—namely, coaxial cables capable of delivering multiple signals to the same television—the loop was complete. Cable television had arrived.

Urban centres were quick to adopt the innovations of these more remote communities. Owing to the popularity of television, the roofs of many apartment buildings had become "forests" of television antennae. The consolidation of these antennae and the delivery of signals by coaxial cable solved this aesthetic problem, though people soon realized that the true power of cable television lay in its ability to vastly increase the number of television stations available to them. By the mid-fifties, experiments in relaying signals across the country by microwave had begun. A city like Ottawa, which might have had two or three stations, could double its available content by importing signals from Toronto, Montreal, or Buffalo.

The third and most important media innovation for Nexus brings us back to our reflective rocket ship. By 1962, permanent satellites had been launched into orbit, and the first sounds and images began making transatlantic "flights." In 1964, the Olympic Games in Tokyo were telecast live by satellite across the globe. By 1968, the global "satellite loop" had been closed, meaning that satellite transmissions could, in theory, reach anywhere on earth. Thanks to the satellite, media by the 1970s was poised to become truly global in its content and its reach.

The impact of increased (and increasingly global) television content was first felt in North American living rooms. The "big three" networks had been providing squeaky-clean programming (i.e., "Father Knows Best," 1954–60), sponsored by squeaky-clean sponsors (often manufacturers of soap and detergents), that targeted the family as a unit. Families would somehow agree on what to watch and when to watch it, and proceed to do so in peaceful harmony.

Satellite-fed, multi-channel cable television quickly exposed and shattered these fragile family-viewing coalitions. Mom didn't want to watch "Hockey Night in Canada" if she didn't have to. Sons and daughters could finally admit just how boring Lawrence Welk and his bubbles really were. Father must have felt his tenuous control over the set slip. Fortunately, many families later invested in additional technologies—the second set, the remote control, and the VCR—that helped them avoid all-out domestic violence.

By 1970, close to a third of North American households had purchased a second television. For young Nexus, this meant the freedom to choose what to watch and the luxury of watching it without *being* watched. It also meant that these earliest members of the Nexus Generation, some now a mature five or six years old, were targeted by programmers and advertisers alike. It started with Saturday morning cartoons, which Nexus would sneak downstairs to watch while Mom and Dad slept in. Jared, a thirty-year-old d~Coder from Alberta, remembers that early cartoons were both entertaining and educational. "The line-up started with 'Professor

Kitzel,' then we made cereal, then came 'Scooby-Doo' and 'Rocket Robin Hood.'" The first of these used every kid's fascination with the time machine to teach lessons in history, the second always had a "moral to the story," and the third retold a classic tale in an innovative way. But cartoons soon devolved into the fantastic, non-linear, monster-infested, low-quality animation variety we see today. According to marketing analyst Karen Ritchie, this type of programming is in reality a thinly disguised plot to sell toys and other goods. As she puts it, these advertisers "helped create for many children a dissatisfaction with their basic circumstances as they pitched toys, games, and candy to rich and poor alike, suggesting that friends would admire you, your family would be happy, your grades would improve and your teeth would never have cavities if only your parents would buy Brand X."[5]

The remote control was, depending whom you ask, either the most important or the most annoying improvement to television during Nexus' formative years. *Control* is, of course, the operative word in *remote control*, because only the one pushing the buttons enjoys the response. Most of us love to participate in "channel surfing," but few of us enjoy being mere spectators to the sport.

For young Nexus, channel surfing was indeed a sport. The name of the game was to race around the dial as fast as possible, distinguishing programs of merit from those with none, and avoiding any commercial "land-mines" along the way. Nexus soon grew able to process all of this information in the span of a few frames. Hair-trigger thumbs would signal a change in channel at the first sight of a box of Tide, a receding hairline, or a Lawrence Welk bubble. Anything that appeared attractive would warrant a brief pause in the game, time to take it in and file it away for the next time around the dial. The hair-trigger thumb, cross-trained on early video games and connected to a vast neural database of images, sounds, and styles, became one of Nexus' most potent weapons.

According to many d~Coders, the best way to dis-empower Nexus is to remove the batteries from the remote.

Even with two remote-control-driven televisions in the home, there was still too much for any one person to watch. With the dozen or so channels available to the average home in the seventies, hundreds of programs were available in any given week. Thankfully, another technology intervened: videotape recorders became commercially available in the mid-seventies, meaning that machines could now watch programs for you. Everyone in the family loved the VCR, making it the fastest growing home appliance of all time, but Nexus had a special relationship with it. For one thing, Nexus knew how to program it. This meant not having to weigh the costs of doing other things against missing favourite programs. Nexus could hang with friends, play video games, program a computer, or do nothing at all, confident that the VCR was taping the best shows for later. Good thing, since many members of the generation we asked remember there being much more good stuff to watch back then.

Television really did start to get interesting in the seventies. The networks, fresh from the discovery that the family viewing market could be subdivided into smaller, more targetable groups, were creating a diversity of programming choices. Single-sponsor advertising had long since been abandoned in favour of multiple sponsors, which spread out the potential risk of offending viewers. This meant that traditionally antiseptic programming, the kind where married adults slept in separate beds (i.e., "The Dick Van Dyke Show," 1961–66), could be replaced with more true-to-life scenarios, where single mothers raised children ("One Day at a Time," 1974–84) and homophobic, middle-aged white men made racial slurs ("All in the Family," 1971–80). Television was no longer some moral fantasy land or benchmark for family values. For Nexus, television began to reflect real life.

Television became really "real" with the launch of CNN in 1980 (it was available in most of Canada by 1985). The twenty-four-hour cable-news outlet was wholly dependent on the satellite for not only broadcast purposes, but also content. A flash flood in Egypt, a bloody riot in Northern Ireland, a famine in Ethiopia—this was CNN's product and the network needed it in real time, around the clock. CNN and the television satellite made the world a much smaller place. It broadened the scope of our compassion, as our hearts went out to images of people suffering in far-away places. For the Nexus Generation, CNN provided the earliest glimpses of what was going on globally without having to wait. It is reported that during the Gulf War, a senior U.S. intelligence officer said in a briefing to his boss, "I'm only fifteen minutes ahead of what CNN has."

Many of the more notable events in recent history might as well have included the footnote "as seen on TV." The Gulf War, the fall of the Berlin Wall, the Tiananmen Square massacre—each a Nexus formative experience in its own right—were fed to us by CNN. Two of the three authors of this book bonded for the first time while watching O. J. Simpson's Bronco chase on television. Just about every d~Coder we talked to remembers where they were when it happened, just as Boomers remember where they were when J.F.K. was assassinated.

One further innovation in television content stands out as significant to Nexus: the music video. Some members of the generation might remember "Good Rockin' Tonight" on CBC, but the launch of MuchMusic in 1984 really sparked the era of the music video in Canada. Though the Buggles' prediction that video would kill the radio star did not quite prove true (Nexus still loves radio), videos had a huge impact on the music industry and its fans. Videos communicated not just music, but also styles, culture, and "cool." The best bands now had to look good as well as sound good. In fact, the "sounds good" criterion was waived for some acts, who relied more on image than anything else. Dead or Alive, Wham, and

Culture Club all come readily to mind as video-driven bands who might have had trouble in an audio-only world.

Early videos consisted mostly of mock concert footage, complete with "guitar hero" poses and pouty smiles. They gradually evolved into the frenetic, five-frame-per-second sort that hurt a Boomer's head to watch. Nexus liked it, though—it was a bit like channel surfing, except that it was automatic. Video-makers figured out how young people were watching television, and they emulated it in their work.

The 1980s were an interesting time for music in general. The industry was struggling to find contemporary supergroups with wide appeal, as the Beatles and the Rolling Stones had been. With the help of video, music was fragmenting into disco, punk, rap, metal, and pop. In much the same way as expanded choice on television was affecting Nexus' viewing habits, choice in music was affecting the way Nexus listened.

Globalization

The final informational and cultural phenomenon that touched Nexus in its formative years is globalization. While *globalization* is one of the most fashionable buzz-words bombarding Nexus through today's media, it's tough to figure out whether it is a driving force of change, or simply the result of some of the factors we've already touched upon. But regardless of the overuse and ambiguity of the term, there's no doubt that globalization has had some important effects on the Nexus Generation. Two in particular are worth highlighting: access and speed.

To start with, globalization provided Nexus with a range of products and services that were almost unheard of in its parents' generation. Nexus members who were raised on the Prairies might remember the transition from the days when grapefruit could be found in Safeway during only the warm months of the year. Now even an average grocery store has a wall full of exotic fruits and vegetables, like kiwis, cilantro, or mangos. This access to things international—be it CNN, Swatch watches, Sony disc players, or Icelandic pop star Björk—increased exponentially during Nexus' early days.

Global access was also a reflection of the changing ethno-cultural nature of the marketplace—immigration was transforming the very way Canada looked. This was most evident in schools from coast to coast, where third-generation Canadians sat next to the children of immigrants from Asia and Africa. They might even have all played on the same hockey team. Citytv in Toronto was the first media outlet to understand and reflect Canada's diversity. Rather than generic white males with side-parted hair, their talking heads came to represent what society really looked like.

Second, because of advances in technology, Nexus has seen the speed of global transactions accelerate. On the positive side, this means a Nexus backpacker can travel to Spain with nothing more than a plastic bank card. On the negative side, this means he can watch the value of his Canadian dollar fall in real time—second by second. It was, incidentally, during the formative years of this generation—the mid-seventies—that the whole notion of "floating exchange rates" came into being.

In fact, when it comes to speed, Nexus can handle pretty much any velocity. Events and revolutions in its formative years have fundamentally altered expectations about the pace of change. A generation that lived through the evolution from vinyl to 8-track to cassettes to CDs and beyond is unlikely to believe the "established way" will remain the way forever. After all, the supposedly permanent Berlin Wall *did* crumble.

While Canadian Boomers lived through decades of clear distinctions between Left and Right, Nexus has witnessed all political parties drifting towards the same agenda, most often deficit cutting.

Internationally, there has been a similar kind of move towards the mushy centre, as more and more countries around the globe try to create Western-style democracies. Nexus was initially raised on a steady diet of the Soviet Union as the "evil empire," only to witness this system of government and society collapse. Now the president of Russia golfs amicably with the president of the United States—both decked out in their universally recognized polo shirts. Some political commentators have boldly called this convergence the "end of history,"[6] and claim that the victory of Western ways is all but complete.

It's worth remembering, however, that globalization is not all about "convergence" and "homogenization." Social fragmentation has also been its major hallmark. Globalization carries within it polarizing side-effects that Nexus witnessed firsthand. At the global level, the forces of economic integration have not been uniformly beneficial to all parts of the world. In the last twenty years, the chasm between the "haves" and the "have nots" has widened to the point where the term *Third World*—well-known to many Boomers—has become almost meaningless.

Within Canada, Nexus has seen a gradual squeezing out of the middle class, both as an income bracket and as a way of life. This squeeze is driven by the fact that wages within traditional jobs, such as manufacturing, have experienced a downward pressure, while the salaries in professions favoured by globalization have been on the increase. In addition, attempts by the most wealthy to create safe havens—in the form of private schools or "gated communities"—reflect a growing desire on the part of many to protect and reproduce their standard of living.

Nexus: A Transitional Generation

The Industrial Revolution began around 1750 and had largely taken hold by 1880[7]—a span of some 130 years. Over that time, steam gradually replaced muscle as the dominant source of power, iron replaced wood as the key element of manufacturing, and the mass-production factory eclipsed the artisan's shop as the most efficient unit of commercial organization. But for all the economic impact these changes had, their social impacts were even greater. Families were uprooted and torn apart, people abandoned agriculture and converged on the cities, and cottage industries gave way to industrial giants. The profound social effects of the Industrial Revolution took at least two generations to sort themselves out.

Some would argue that we are currently in a post-modern Industrial Age—in other words, the Information Age has yet to fully arrive. Perhaps, but consider the following: the world's richest man, Bill Gates, heads a computer-software company that didn't exist twenty-five years ago in an industry that didn't exist thirty years ago. His company, Microsoft, recently surpassed the quintessential industrial giant General Motors in total market capitalization. Ted Turner, power broker and media visionary, recently upstaged the president of the United States when he offered $1 billion to the United Nations. The centres of power in the United States are no longer Detroit or Chicago, but are instead San Francisco (Silicon Valley), Atlanta (CNN), and Seattle (Microsoft). Our nation's political capital, Ottawa, doubles as our high-tech capital. Emerging economic hotbeds such as Austin, Texas, spontaneously develop, not around oil reserves or transportation hubs, but around "ingenuity reserves" and "intellectual-capital hubs" such as universities and polytechnic institutes. The Information Age may not have fully arrived, but you can hear it coming.

The speed with which the Information Age is descending on us is as important to Nexus as the scope of its changes. Because of this speed, Nexus is the *transitional* generation. Meeting the challenges of the Information Age will require bridging new realities and existing values. It will mean linking the needs of one generation to the hopes of another. It will require that we fill in the gaps between the present and the future. As media guru Douglas Rushkoff says, "[We] need look no further than our own children for reassuring answers to the myriad of uncertainties associated with the collapse of the culture we have grown to know and love."[8] Nexus will always be the "first child" of the Information Age, and the only child to remember both a "before" and an "after."

Hits from the Formative Years

Of course, "chips" and "pop" were not the only forces acting on a young Nexus Generation. As we have suggested, a range of formative experiences spanning the social, political, and economic realms caught the attention of the generation. The seventies, eighties, and early nineties saw their share of hardship, triumph, conflict, grief, and joy. The Nexus Generation watched much of it on television. A history viewed through the television tube is a history where the viewer retains the option of changing the dial. Here are the formative experiences that we think Nexus had no option but to pay attention to. Two important themes—instability and paradox—emerge from these experiences and serve to shape the generation's attitudes today.

The Broken Family and the Ensemble Cast

While Nexus was busy growing up, its parents were taking full advantage of a newly liberalized set of divorce laws in Canada. Close to one-third of Nexus members, in fact, saw their parents divorce. The broken family had a series of effects on Nexus, apart from the obvious emotional pain. "Latch-key" kids babysat themselves, with the help of television and video games. Do-it-yourself kids cooked their own meals and got part-time jobs as soon as they were able, as inflation ate away at their allowances. But one area where Nexus could not go it alone was in replacing the support of an entire parent. As one twenty-eight-year-old d~Coder remembers, "I had two rooms, two sets of keys, two sets of toys, and four parents, but I still felt alone sometimes." What was supposed to be a source of stability for Nexus—the family—became instead a source of stress and instability. As a result, members of this generation developed an ensemble cast of friends to lean on, a sort of surrogate family, many of whom were having the same problems as they were.

At the same time, Hollywood was experimenting with the ensemble cast, and taking full advantage of widespread teen angst. The genre was perfected in *The Breakfast Club* (1985), a film about five mismatched high schoolers who get stuck together in day-long detention, which starred a new wave of brat-packers as the misfit, the geek, the rebel, the jock, and the princess. Many from Nexus, and particularly those from broken homes, identified strongly with the characters in *The Breakfast Club*, and the power of friendship relationships that crossed gender and social lines. Today the most popular Nexus television programs, "Friends," "Seinfeld," and "E.R.," for example, still feature ensemble casts of friends who act as a surrogate family. Media reflects reality, once again.

The Recession Twins

The first recession in 1981 got to the Nexus Generation via its parents. Many of them were laid off, worried about their business prospects, or simply depressed as a result of the economic doldrums of the day. To some parents, the recession of 1981 was a grim reminder of their formative experience—the Great Depression. Downsizing and re-engineering were the dominant business fads, adding to the economic uncertainty felt in many households. Thankfully, things turned around and the mid- to late-eighties were for many a prosperous, if not self-indulgent, period.

The next time a recession hit was 1991, just as the leading edge of Nexus were launching careers. A slightly bitter thirty-one-year-old d~Coder told us that his "guidance teacher pushed him to take a degree in science, because that's what Canada needs." Apparently Canada didn't need too much of it in the early nineties, because the only job he was able to get was digging holes. In fact, the youth job market is only now recovering from these tremors, forcing many individuals in this generation back to school for second and third degrees, grasping for some stability in a turbulent economy. For others, the "Recession Twins" have made them more sanguine than some of their Boomer elders about the promise of endless prosperity.

The Party's Over

When most members of Nexus were kids, Canada had, in Pierre Trudeau, a prime minister who could give the media the finger and get away with it. This was the same media that had created the mania largely responsible for sweeping Trudeau into office in the first place. He began his tenure with a balanced budget, but left behind a debt of more than 200 billion dollars.

Trudeau and company also had an inclination towards large, national projects. One in particular was the patriation of the Constitution in 1982. Jane, a twenty-seven-year-old d~Coder from Manitoba, remembers seeing "Trudeau and the Queen sitting at a big table with a big pen, signing what was supposed to be an important piece of paper." But for Nexus, not much changed on the unity front as a result; the uncertainty over Canada's future has been around for Nexus' entire life.

Everything came to a screeching halt for the Liberal Party of Canada in the summer of 1984. Live on the CBC, a dishevelled John Turner meekly defended his actions around a series of blatant patronage appointments left to him by his former boss, while an articulate and dapper Brian Mulroney fired back, ". . . you had a choice, sir. You had a choice." This marked the beginning of a new era of Conservative rule in Canada. Once again television played an important role in politics and Nexus was watching. Of course, federal patronage appointments were not the only scandals from Nexus' formative years. Grant Devine's Saskatchewan Tories were exposed for diverting public funds for private and party purposes in the eighties. Members of his government are still in court. In New Brunswick, meanwhile, rumours surrounding Richard Hatfield's private life cost the Conservatives every seat in the province.

Everything came to a screeching halt for the Conservative Party of Canada in 1993. Live on the CBC, a ruffled Kim Campbell attempted to defend the actions of her former boss, which, among other things, included spending beyond his means, making patronage appointments, and trumpeting the Meech Lake and Charlottetown accords as the solution to our perpetual unity crisis. In Canada, once-distinct political ideologies were becoming indistinguishable and the party system increasingly ineffective.

Space and the Space Movie

Prior to 1969, travelling by rocket ship to outerworldly destinations was pure fantasy. *Apollo 11* changed all that, as well as the way the Nexus Generation viewed the space movie. *Star Wars* (1977), *Close Encounters of the Third Kind* (1977), and *E.T.* (1982) were more than fantasy to Nexus—they were the future; they were the *present*. Budding astronauts (outfitted with C3-PO action figures, Gertie lunch pails, and digital watches that chimed the *Close Encounters* theme) dreamed of the day when civilians would travel in space. Why not? Technological growth seemed boundless. Machines simply got faster and stronger and smarter all the time. The U.S. space program lost not a single astronaut through the seventies and the first half of the eighties. Shortly after the millennium, Nexus was told, ordinary people would live in space. What would stop us?

The space shuttle *Challenger* blew up in January 1986 and took the "solar wind" out of the sails of our budding astronauts. Technology was fallible and stoppable, and people got hurt badly because of it. Later members of Nexus would remember only the distasteful jokes, but the damage was done. Space movies were now even more real, since they were no longer the only place where rocket ships blew up. Nexus became a generation that is not fearful of technology, but one that holds no illusions about its limits either.

Television Wars and Wars on TV

The Nexus Generation grew up watching people die in the movies and on television. As bullets and blood became Hollywood's hottest commodities, Nexus became less and less easy to shock and impress. Hollywood's answer? More blood and more bullets. Though parents were never quite sure, Nexus knew none of it was real. The original Rambo movie, *First Blood* (1982), was simply about a man pretending to be a cartoon action figure. Nexus understood that violence in the movies and on television was at least once removed from reality.

Nexus watched its only "real" war, the Gulf War (1991), on television. Its images of anti-aircraft fire streaking across the desert sky more closely resembled a video game than anything else Nexus had ever seen. While its parents or grandparents had talked about war as something that took away friends and family, the Gulf War seemed more like a technological demonstration. It was fought and observed at a safe distance, as were other modern conflicts that preceded it, such as the Falkland Islands (1982) and Grenada (1983). Paradoxically, to Nexus war has never equalled sacrifice, and particularly the sacrifice of human life. To this generation, war has always seemed one step removed from reality.

The Nuclear Threat

The nuclear threat made little sense to a generation that had not lived through a major war and did not see the origins of the superpower stand-off. Yet Nexus was raised under the chill of the Cold War, and became accustomed to phrases like "mutually assured destruction." Calculations were made of the number of times the world could be destroyed if existing arsenals were detonated. Doomsday clocks, with minute hands set to only minutes before midnight, seemed to suggest that nuclear war was not an "if" but a "when."

The airing of the famous television movie *The Day After* (1983), about the imagined after-effects of the nuclear bombing of Lawrence, Kansas, led to nightmares and anxiety in many Nexus youth and teens. Chris, a Toronto d~Coder, remembers his teacher warning him to watch it with his parents because it was "bloody terrifying." The teacher also did a full debriefing in class the next day. The movie *War Games*, released in theatres that same year, suggested that breaches in governmental security were possible (thanks to a Nexus-aged hacker) and could kick-start the end of the world.

The swift fall of communism and the retreat from the brink took everyone, including Nexus, by surprise. History, just like technology, was moving incredibly fast, and suddenly the two superpowers were celebrating the dismantling of weapons rather than their creation.

Risky Love and Pharmaceuticals

The widespread acceptance and availability of "the Pill" in the seventies promised a generation of Nexus women unprecedented control over the sexual experience. Free from the fear of unwanted pregnancy, Nexus was poised to be the next "free-loving" generation.

Meanwhile, Nexus boys were watching *Risky Business* (1983) to see just how it was done. It seemed easy enough: all you had to do was wait until the parents left town and sex would find you. Of course, in the words of one of our d~Coders, "it helps if you look like Tom Cruise."

But before another era of free love could be declared, the emergence of AIDS in the early eighties spoiled the fun. AIDS put "the fear of God" back into sex for Nexus, a fear that Nexus' seemingly bashful parents didn't help allay. "My parents never told me a thing about sex—I learned it from that *Risky Business* movie," one d~Coder (who asked to remain nameless) told us. Others got it from health class or from the Judy Bloom novel *Forever* (1984), whose central character called his penis Ralph. Whatever the case, Nexus is a generation that is well informed on the topic of sex, yet fearful of some of its consequences.

Oil, Oil Everywhere . . .

Nexus has two distinct and separate memories when it comes to oil and its formative experiences: the energy crisis in 1973 and the *Exxon Valdez* spill of 1989.

In addition to exposing the vulnerability of North American economies to global forces, the energy crisis created the first widespread acknowledgement of the limits of natural resources. This realization is etched in the collective Nexus mind. Gill, a Toronto d~Coder, tells us that she still "runs around the house flicking off lights" to save energy. While it is probably true that we will run out of oil sometime in the next fifty to one hundred years, known reserves are today greater than they were during the crisis.

In 1989, the *Exxon Valdez* oil tanker ran aground in Prince William Sound, off Alaska, spilling 232,000 barrels of oil. That much oil would have come in handy back in '73. We were told we wouldn't have any; suddenly it was everywhere. Nonetheless, to

Nexus this disaster capped off a decade that produced overflowing landfill sites, acid rain, ozone holes, and poisoned fish.

At the same time, the media had grown fond of "environmental doomsdayism." For example, the front pages of newspapers around the world reported that the Kuwait oil-well fires might take fifty years to extinguish, all the while blanketing the earth in grey clouds and black filth. When the fires were extinguished in a mere six months, the story was hardly reported.

As a result, Nexus is an environmentally conscious generation (witness the Blue Box phenomenon), but it is also sceptical of "radical" environmentalism.

The Church Files

Nexus' formative religious experiences were marked by a decline in the credibility of established religion, corruption and scandal in televangelism, and instances of bizarre cult behaviour. Nexus even observed some religions that practically encouraged their followers to hope for an end to the world.

Most of Nexus will not recall the Catholic Church's unveiling of Vatican II (1965), its long-awaited attempt at liberalization and modernization. The reforms largely failed to bring either Nexus or the Boomers back into the fold. One of the authors does remember when confession became reconciliation, but thought it bizarre that where we had once been swapping secrets with God, we were now talking to a mere mortal.

The mid- to late-eighties proved tough for many of our modern religious icons, the televangelists. Ironically, the various improprieties of Jim Bakker, Jimmy Swaggart, Oral Roberts, and Pat Robertson were exposed by television, the very same medium that created them. Few from Nexus will ever forget the broadcast images of Bakker's heavily made-up wife, Tammy Faye, pathetically pleading his innocence.

The Jonestown mass suicide (1978) also floats around in Nexus' memory as a bizarre instance of devotion gone wrong. Leader Jim Jones and hundreds of his followers moved from San Francisco to Guyana in order to escape what he perceived to be media persecution. When allegations of abuse were levelled against the cult, Jones and his followers perished by drinking cyanide-laced Kool-Aid, shocking the entire world.

[Conclusion]

In this chapter, we have laid a framework for understanding Nexus that considers both its generational genes and its generational conditioning. These two influences led the generation to develop obvious similarities to, as well as distinct differences from, other generations. It bears mention here that the similarities between generations, though most often overlooked, are one of the keys to intergenerational cooperation.

Two common themes that emerge from Nexus' formative experiences are paradox and instability. First, Nexus has been forced to reconcile many seemingly contradictory notions and ideas. It was promised free love and space travel, only to have these promises repealed. It was guaranteed nuclear conflict between two ideological solitudes, but the conflict fizzled and the solitudes converged. Energy scarcity pointed to a potentially "darkened" world, though in the end our reckless use of energy holds an even darker threat. The benefits of many religions seem to Nexus to be realizable only after death. In subsequent chapters, we will see how Nexus' paradoxical conditioning experiences have manifested themselves today.

Second, Nexus has been forced to manufacture stability within increasingly unstable environments. Nexus has survived broken or dysfunctional families and endured economic fortunes tied to business cycles. It has lived under a haze of political uncertainty and a political system increasingly unable to cope with this. Nexus' quest for stability will remain important as it moves into full "adult-hood."

The material in this chapter forms the basis for the rest of the book and the next chapter in particular, where we indicate how Nexus' values have affected its relationships with various traditional and emerging institutions.

THE INSTITUTION OF CHANGE

———

We concluded Chapter 1 with a series of myth-busting statements about the Nexus Generation's confidence, optimism, pragmatism, and adaptability. On average, the generation likes its chances for success in a turbulent and challenging society. But before you conclude that it is sporting some serious rose-coloured glasses, consider that it is also highly realistic, sceptical, and concerned when it comes to the pressing issues of our day. Polls consistently show that jobs, the economy, health care, education, and national unity are top of mind for this generation, and that Nexus has some significant doubts as to the abilities of existing institutions to "fix" what is broken.

In the previous chapter, we touched on the conditioning experiences that have helped to shape Nexus, such as divorce, recession spending, the end of the Cold War, the decline of religion, and, of course, the rise of information technology. In this chapter, we will probe Nexus' attitudes towards several key Canadian institutions— family, community, religion, universities, and the state—and uncover why it has uneasy and uncertain relationships with these "pillars" of our society. This generation is mulling over the idea of family and reworking its definition of community. Many young Canadians, though not all, are ignoring organized religion, as well as looking for alternatives to standard education. Nexus has all but lost confidence in the capacity of the state as a provider of security and stability. The media, as we will show, seems to be the one institution with which Nexus has a stable relationship.

[The Nuclear Family Threat]

In early 1998, our national newspaper, the *Globe and Mail*, ran the headline "Family Values a Big Hit with Boomers' Kids."[1] The article drew from 1995 Statistics Canada data and concluded that members of "Generation X" (though most aren't really the Boomers' kids) hold more conservative family values than their parents or grandparents (confused generational definitions not withstanding). It even went so far as to predict that these values might represent a "social shift of huge proportions."

So how is the institution of family faring with this generation? Is Nexus, as the article suggests, simply reflecting generational genes that have been dormant for a while, or is it altering the notion of family altogether? By "family values," the headline presumably was referring to the traditional familial arrangements of the fifties and sixties (i.e., those that gave rise to the Boomers), where the father worked outside the home, the mother was a homemaker, and junior had two or more siblings to torment. It's worth keeping in mind that in the case of family, tradition depends on your frame of reference. At various points in recent history, families have looked very different from the Cunningham or the Cleaver families on television. Wars are notorious for producing single mothers and orphans, and both depressions and recessions have spawned more than their share of double-income families. In the late twentieth century, the traditional family is a moving target, and Nexus is taking careful aim.

Why Do Today What You Can Put Off
Until Tomorrow?

A more appropriate question for Nexus is not "What does family mean?" but "What *will* it mean?" This generation currently puts off the nuptial pact longer than past generations ever did. In 1970, the average age to marry was 22.7 for a Canadian woman and 25.1 for her male counterpart.[2] By 1995, those averages had risen to 27 and 29 years, respectively,[3] and a full 62 per cent of Canadians aged twenty to thirty had never been married or in any sort of common-law arrangement.[4]

What is Nexus waiting for? At first blush, the hesitancy might seem economic. Uncertainty about career and other economic prospects is forcing many in this generation back to school in their mid-twenties. The conventional wisdom, after all, is that you get an education, you get a job, and you get your own life together before you agree to share it with someone else. But this economic argument does not stand up to scrutiny. The trend towards marrying later began in the 1970s and was steady throughout the 1980s,[5] when economic times were relatively good for everyone. Further, as Alan Mirabelli of the Vanier Institute for the Family suggested in the *Globe and Mail* article cited earlier, long-term relationships can actually be "the one stable thing in life" when things are not going well. If economics were a key determinant in whether to marry, then there ought to have been a rash of Nexus weddings in the early nineties, with young people hooking up to find more stability, to share the costs of living, to share their pain. This was not the case.

Clearly there are other forces at work when it comes to Nexus and its attitude towards marriage. One to consider is the simple fear of divorce. In 1968, Canadian divorce laws were greatly relaxed (prior to that, proof of adultery was a necessary legal condition) and the overall number of divorces soared. The next round of legal liberalization in 1985 resulted in an even steeper climb in divorce numbers. The trend peaked in 1986, when in Canada one divorce occurred for every two marriages.[6] What did this mean to Nexus? By some estimates, close to two in five would have experienced their parents' divorce by the time they were twenty.[7] And if your parents stayed together, chances are the parents of your closest friends did not. While we won't attempt a full discourse on the effects of divorce on children and teenagers, there can be no doubt that this experience has shaped the generation's own expectations about the institution of marriage.

In the wake of divorce, new and unfamiliar family structures emerge. Nexus grew up in an era when single parents, stepfathers, and stepsiblings were commonplace. Many grandparents were called back into child-rearing duty, as Mom and Dad were too pre-occupied with their own problems to do the job. We also know that children frequently blame themselves for divorce, and that this often causes them to withdraw from family altogether. To the children of divorce, family is suddenly not the steady and reliable source of emotional (not to mention economic) stability it was supposed to be. Nexus has been something of a test generation when it comes to the institution of family. The results are just coming in.

The first result seems to be that Nexus is more comfortable with the notion of cohabitation than past generations. Today, 40 per cent of Canadians fifteen to twenty-nine who live as couples describe themselves as common-law. This "try before you buy" approach to long-term relationships has been around for a while, though in the past decade it experienced a shift in age. In 1981, common-law arrangements were most popular among people aged twenty to twenty-four. Since the mid-eighties, those twenty-five to twenty-nine have been the most likely to "shack up." The church's waning influence over Nexus (which we'll discuss later) makes common-law more of an option for Nexus; marriage as a rite of religion is not as relevant to it as to past generations. One thing is for sure: common-law marriage is a convenient way to avoid the inconvenience of divorce.

A second (and perhaps less intuitive) result is Nexus' optimistic outlook on its own prospects for long-term relationships. Given the generation's formative years, a healthy level of scepticism would seem justified. But our findings indicate that just the opposite is true. Nexus is a highly confident generation when it comes to its own expectations around marriage and/or relationships. Its members seem to want to get it right where their parents and the Boomers could not.

In the *Building Bridges* survey, conducted in 1997, we asked eighteen- to thirty-four-year-olds just what they thought about their prospects for finding a life-long partner; 64 per cent answered that it was very likely to happen. It is worth noting that when we asked the same group if they expected to marry, have two kids, and drive a mini-van (the stereotypical eighties definition of "the family"), less than half as many (31 per cent) thought that was very likely.[8] Nexus is attracted to the idea of long-term attachment, but its definition of success in a relationship may be different than for past generations.

Those from Nexus who *do* make the trip to the altar seem less likely than their parents or the Boomers to be destined for divorce court. Data from Statistics Canada's *General Social Survey* indicate that younger Canadians are likely to be more conservative when it comes to reasons for divorce.[9] Nexus agrees with other segments of society, for example, that abusive or adulterous behaviours are intolerable. In some cases, divorce *is* the best solution for all parties involved. But this generation is less inclined to view disagreements over finances, bad sex, or fertility issues as grounds for a divorce.[10] In commenting on the study, marriage historian Roderick Phillips implies that the naïveté gene is responsible for this conservatism, noting that youth's "optimism is often dulled by experience."[11]

We're not convinced this is entirely true. It isn't surprising, for example, that Nexus does not think financial insecurity is a good reason to terminate a marriage—financial insecurity has been its norm for several years. When we talk to members of our d~Code network, we find that several are making choices that almost defy financial security. Carla, a college professor, and her husband sold their townhouse in Vancouver to be at the mercy of the rental market. Freddy quit his job and went back to law school shortly after tying the knot. For Nexus, the burden of financial security is a shared responsibility between the man and the women. But the root of a stable marriage has little to do with money in the first place.

First Comes Baby

If you thought high divorce levels had diminished Nexus' zeal for having children, you'd be wrong there too. Just as its memory of divorce has not dulled its confidence in long-term relationships, it has not significantly affected its determination to have children either. Studies have shown that the "fertility intentions" of thirty-year-olds in Canada are independent of a childhood experience with divorce, while those of twenty-somethings seem to be affected only if the divorce happened after Nexus turned fifteen.[12] Very few from Nexus intend to be childless (only 4 per cent of men and 6 per cent of women[13]) and close to 30 per cent want three or more kids. Though "wishes" do not always amount to "horses," Nexus is currently quite optimistic about the prospects for building a family.

Nevertheless, this generation has delayed having its children. The average age of a first-time Nexus parent in Canada is twenty-nine,[14] and the number of births for mothers in their early to mid thirties is climbing rapidly. This child-bearing activity is closely tied to Nexus' marriage habits, since nearly two-thirds of all births in

Canada still occur in wedlock.[15] As common as the common-law arrangement has become, there is still some apprehension about adding kids to the mix.

Interestingly enough, one of the sub-segments of Nexus most "into" having children is educated males. Men between the ages of twenty and twenty-nine with university degrees want, on average, 2.5 children each, compared with 2.1 for those with less than a high-school education.[16] Women aged twenty to twenty-nine, on the other hand, indicate no differences based on education in their family intentions. And for women between thirty and thirty-nine, education actually dampens the enthusiasm for kids. Nexus women appear to be carefully weighing both the financial and the non-financial costs of raising a family—costs that are still most often borne by mothers. In the future, it seems likely that in some Nexus relationships, the men will be pushing to have children while the women hold back.

Overall, women from this generation seem to regard their family and career aspirations with a greater sense of realism than many Boomer women did. Having witnessed firsthand how difficult it is to have the dream marriage, the dream home, the dream family, and the dream career simultaneously, many Nexus women have come to view life as a series of events. They may still achieve some or much of what Boomer women strove for, but they're likely to be less keen on trying to do it all at once. As our chapter on Nexus the Employee will show, this generation of female workers is wary of the myth of the superwoman.

Empty Nest?

Another family-related phenomenon worth noting is the return—albeit in a different incarnation—of the extended family. Economic concerns have driven many from Nexus back into their parents' basements. Today, close to half of all parents in their forties and fifties live with at least one of their sixteen- to twenty-four-year-old kids, and one in ten puts up children over the age of twenty-five.[17]

What's also worth observing, however, is that the Nexus Generation appears prepared to return the favour. More than one in three expect their parents to live with them as they get older.[18] This trend is partly driven by the diverse make-up of this generation, and the traditions associated with immigrant families. A stronger factor is Nexus' reduced confidence in the state's ability to care for the elderly, particularly when the Baby Boomers burst onto the retirement scene. If the Boomers think they are the so-called Sandwich Generation—trying to juggle demanding children and needy parents—Nexus could become the Clubhouse Sandwich Generation—with multiple layers of responsibility (hold the mayo).

Apartment, Sweet Apartment

Traditionally, the home has been the centre of the family universe. Kitchen, dining room, two bathrooms, three bedrooms, and a backyard—what else could a typical family ask for? As it stands, Nexus is not asking for this—at least, not yet. Research shows that its members are predominantly renters rather than buyers. In the 1997 Angus Reid/Royal Bank *Housing Study*, 33 per cent of Nexus respondents were living in apartments, and only 8 per cent were saving specifically for a home purchase. Fifty-eight per cent of eighteen- to thirty-four-year-olds were renting their principal residence, compared with 29 per cent for thirty-five- to fifty-year-olds and 24 per cent for those over fifty-five. The average age of a first-time home buyer in Canada was thirty-nine in 1994.[19] A more informal poll of the d~Code office, with respondents ranging in age from twenty-two to thirty-two, shows the number of homeowners at zero and the number of renters at six. It seems that not much has changed.

The knee-jerk reaction to this point is, of course, that members of Nexus would buy if they could afford to. But considering that the cost of rent in urban centres is not vastly different from the cost of carrying a mortgage, Nexus is making the decision not to purchase based on other factors. For one, home ownership is not the status symbol it once was. As the definitions of family and career change, so too does Nexus' definition of "success." Second, postponing home ownership reflects this generation's hedge against the migratory qualities needed to survive in our economy. While parents may wring their hands, worried that their children are somehow unstable, members of this generation are looking for a new and different kind of stability—one that matches their need for freedom and mobility.

Extended Freedom Zone

At d~Code, we refer to these Nexus' "procrastinations" around family, children, and home buying as the *extended freedom zone*. Its roots are part economic and part personal choice, though in our experience Nexus finds the extended freedom zone fully liberating. For past generations, most of these major life-altering decisions were usually made by the age of twenty-five, but Nexus has the opportunity to take its time and to experiment. Increasingly, society has deemed it okay to be twenty-five and live with your parents, to be twenty-nine and not finished school, or to be thirty-five and start a family. As we will explore in subsequent chapters, the extended freedom zone has serious implications for Nexus as a consumer, an employee, and a citizen.

However, the extended freedom zone does not mean that Nexus members are an isolated lot, living in some kind of solitary confinement. In lieu of partners or families, Nexus seeks out alternative forms of support. Community, as we will see, is one such surrogate.

[Community Ties]

We once had a Boomer tell us that she had moved into a "better" community, because there were fewer renters living there. Renters, after all, are usually from somewhere else, have no money (otherwise they would do the right thing and buy), and are apt to suddenly pick up and move (often in the middle of the night), clearing the way for a new group of transients to take their place. Transients don't make for stable communities.

Nexus is a transient generation. Thanks to the extended freedom zone, it is able to pick up and move to where the opportunities are—whether those opportunities are educational, occupational, or experiential. Many d~Coders in our network have already lived in several major Canadian and American cities, not to mention more exotic international locales. As we touched on earlier, many from Nexus rent, not because they can't afford to buy, but because they recognize the benefits of being mortgage-free. In the Royal Bank's *Housing Study*, close to one-third of Nexus respondents indicated that they had been in their community three years or less, compared with one in ten Boomers. In the same study, nearly 40 per cent of Nexus stated that they did not know their neighbours by name, versus 13 per cent of Boomers.[20] For this generation, it seems that community is not quite as it was in the bar on "Cheers," where "everybody knows your name."

But if Nexus is being made to feel unwelcome in its communities, it doesn't show. Members of this age group are just as likely as other generations to agree with statements such as "people in my community like to get involved and help one another" and "it is easy to make friends in my community."[21] More generally, one in two from Nexus says that community is a very important facet of their lives.[22] While the larger community of Canada has had some heavy knocks from this generation, local communities are something they're more comfortable being a part of.

It's the time horizon of community membership, not community values, that's in question for this generation. Because of its need to be a "generation on the move," Nexus views its current place in the community with pragmatism. In the *Housing Study* we cited earlier, 60 per cent of Nexus-aged respondents indicated that they would leave a community where friends and family live for a better job, and close to 30 per cent of rural Nexus thought it likely that they would move to the city in the next five years. For this generation, in other words, migrating to attend school or to find work has become firmly rooted as a ritual of youth. It's not that Nexus is the first generation forced to move in search of opportunity; but it is being forced to move farther and farther away at an earlier age, and to keep moving on a regular basis. Nevertheless, almost two-thirds remain confident that they will eventually wind up in the community of *their* choice.[23]

A Social Call

It used to be that if you were new in town, you would join the local church congregation or a service club in order to make new acquaintances. Historically, however, established clubs have struggled to stay relevant to younger constituents. Consider, for example, that the Kinsmen Club was founded in 1920 by a twenty-one-year-old war veteran who had been denied membership at the local Rotary Club.[24] Today, in a similar spirit, Nexus is adapting and creating new social communities to meet its needs. The rules of these new communities are simple: they must enable meaningful relationships between people with common interests. These relationships need not be intimate or permanent. In fact, they don't even have to be *real*.

Toronto Bridge, a card and social club, is illustrative of a new Nexus twist on an old community theme. Its co-founder Grant Gordon, a thirty-four-year-old d~Coder, dreamed up the idea while living in Montreal because he loved bridge but found that few people his age played the game. He also, in his words, "found existing clubs, most often run out of basements by bridge 'know-it-alls,' to be not enormously welcoming." His goal in launching Toronto Bridge was to create a new culture around the game that would be less intimidating for beginners and novices but still satisfying for more serious players. The key is social interaction. "We play a variation called duplicate bridge, which means that you wind up playing a hand with pretty much everyone in the room," says Gordon. Younger people are there as much to play bridge as to meet people. One pleasant surprise has been the intergenerational bonding that goes on at the club. According to Gordon, there has been a "profound interaction between young and old, based on both a love and [a] respect for the game."

The bike-courier phenomenon might seem, at first, to be a good example of Nexus counter-culture. Couriers appear to be rather solitary creatures: each works alone and has a slightly different hair-style, colour of uniform, and brand of bicycle. You rarely see them interact on the street; they are in too much of a rush for small talk (they are, after all, independent businesspeople who are paid by the delivery). But bike-courier culture reflects, in many respects, what Nexus communities are all about. Bike couriers are transient by nature, often changing companies or adopting new cities without hesitation. Their community extends far beyond city, and even national, borders, and interaction within it is often infrequent or temporary. Each year, Toronto is host to an event called the Alley-

Cats Scramble, billed as a "family reunion" of bike couriers from around the world. They come together for two days of competition and fun, then it's back to work. The bike couriers are another example of a Nexus community where individuality is flourishing within the context of a larger tribe.

Virtual Communities

One of the more traumatic experiences of youth is having your best friend move away. We've seen this familiar plot acted out on countless sitcoms: Dad gets transferred and friend must break the news to friend that her family is leaving town. They promise to call, to write, even to visit one another. But the reality is that things will never be the same. There is just no technological substitute for hanging out at the mall or playing a game of pick-up ball on the vacant lot. Or is there? Technology is making physical proximity less and less important to meaningful interaction. Today, you *can* have a best friend in another city, province, or even country. Communication is now instant, global, and increasingly inexpensive. Emerging technologies are making remote interaction more realistic, more emotional, and more *human*. Beverly, a d~Coder from the West Coast, puts it this way: "The Internet could bring blessed relief for those small-town dwellers who crave more exposure to the outside world."

Thanks to technology, communities need no longer be bound by physical parameters. To a diverse and transient group such as Nexus, technological communities that are independent of geography have great appeal. Indeed, for a generation on the move, virtual communities are often the only stable ones. Reliable interaction is only a phone call or an Internet hook-up away. Willow, a member of our d~Code network, has consistently maintained her connection to us despite living in Newfoundland, New Brunswick, Toronto, and England (not to mention on a cruise ship), all in the last two years.

Virtual communities mean that people with even the most eclectic interests can find and "hang out" with like-minded people, wherever they happen to be. The Internet boasts some sixteen thousand newsgroups, essentially on-line special-interest communities that cover such diverse subjects as Winona Ryder and black widow spiders. Virtual communities also permit you to belong to several at the same time. If you happen to dig both Winona Ryder and black widows, no problem. In fact, virtual communities are most often free of the kinds of discrimination typical of more traditional communities. By design, they can't really discriminate on the basis of sex, race, religion, or age. By design, they are distributed, not hierarchical, meaning everyone gets an equal say.

On the Web, community-oriented domains are among the most active and successful. Aside from the search engines (which are really intermediary Web destinations anyway), community-based sites Geocities and Tripod are the most hit of any on the Net.[25] Geocities works by providing a free piece of "cyberspace" to some 1.5 million individuals (with eight thousand additions daily), who then build and manage Web sites around virtually any kind of content you can think of. After just ten minutes spent in the Geocities domain, we found five thousand homepages having something to do with tea and seven thousand related to China. The idea is that residents of this city will stroll around and look at what others have done (much like checking out your neighbour's flower garden), rather than venture out onto the Net at large. Geocities is also based very much on the traditional community tenet of "help thy neighbour." When it comes to building and maintaining a site, "homesteaders" (as individual webmasters are called) are encouraged to assist and guide one another whenever possible. Tripod is also based on the idea of providing free Web pages to individuals, but it tends to specialize in the eighteen- to thirty-year-old market. *Fortune* magazine heralded Tripod as one of America's twenty-five "coolest companies,"[26] and its twenty-five-year-old president describes it as "a community of a million voices all in chorus."[27] Lycos, a dominant search engine on the Internet, paid $58 million to acquire these voices in early 1998.

Not everyone shares the view that these technologies make us more social. In *Silicon Snake Oil*,[28] self-proclaimed Net addict and Net sceptic Clifford Stoll contends that computers and networks serve only to isolate people, and that virtual interactions most always "lack depth, commitment and ordinary etiquette."[29] He also hints at the more malevolent side of virtual interaction in suggesting that "anonymity and untraceability seem to bring out the worst in people."[30] The fact is, hate groups are also well served by technology and the Net, as are kids under eighteen who want to look at pornography. Still, we think the advantages of cyber-communities outweigh the risks.

First, if you treat virtual interaction as a complement to, rather than a replacement for, real interaction, then Stoll's isolation argument carries less weight. Just make sure you have both Net friends *and* real friends and you'll be okay.

The issues of thwarting hate-mongers and protecting minors on the Net are a lot more serious and difficult to attend to. While various forms of censorship are being proposed for the Net, they all share practical and philosophical limitations. How can we monitor content that is theoretically infinite? How can common guidelines for decency or tolerance be developed and enforced when the Net operates in every country in the world and is beyond the reach of any particular enforcing body? And to what extent will we pit censorship against freedom of speech? We think that the answers must lie both in educating users and in finding ways to flush out and punish the abusers. Don't penalize the Internet.

As a final word on virtual communities, we should mention that d~Code was "born" on the Internet, and that our d~Coder network continues to be a big part of who we are and how we operate. d~Code co-founder Robert Barnard says, "We didn't deliberately set out to build a community, we set out to build a business." But in the end, the virtual connections we have created among Nexus Generation Canadians have established a community that many in our network thrive in.

[Nexus and Religion]

In late 1997, the *New York Times Magazine* published a series of articles, under the banner "God Decentralized,"[31] chronicling the state of religion in America. The articles suggested that while Americans remain among the most religious people on earth, their faith is increasingly of the "do-it-yourself" variety. People are finding spiritual fulfilment not as devotees of traditional institutions, but instead as participants in smaller groups or as individuals. The power of God, distributed to the people.

We Canadians are less religious, in the traditional sense, than our American neighbours,[32] though we are perhaps no less spiritual. The challenges for our domestic religious institutions, however, are just the same: they are struggling to maintain more than a peripheral relevance to the lives of Canadians. In 1975, 31 per cent of all Canadians attended weekly religious services. By 1995, that figure had dropped to 25 per cent.[33]

Members of Nexus do not appear to be the harbingers of any religious revival. Many have picked up where the Boomers left off, joining what the *New York Times Magazine* says may be the biggest "church" of all—the unbelievers. In a 1996 survey of people's religious attitudes, only 12 per cent of Nexus respondents said they were weekly churchgoers, and nearly two in five had not been to a religious service in the past twelve months.[34] When we were conducting research for *Building Bridges*, 30 per cent of the eighteen-to thirty-five-year-olds we surveyed gave religion a one out of seven in terms of importance to their daily lives, and 60 per cent gave it a three or less. More than half of Nexus indicated that they have little or no confidence in the church or other religious institutions.[35]

While Nexus shares many of these attitudes towards organized religion with the Boomers, the causes underlying them may be different for each group. For many adolescent Boomers, skipping church was a relatively low-risk act of rebellion. Others simply drifted away from religion in the course of becoming adults. And while Vatican II brought a much-needed modernization to the Catholic Church, its continued hard line on birth control was a "deal-breaker" for many Boomers.

Nexus, on the other hand, grew up in an era when stories of church-related sexual abuse, such as the scandals at Mount Cashel and a number of Native residential schools, were rampant in the media. At the same time, religious conflict, in places like Ireland and the Middle East, dominated news headlines. And as we learned in Chapter 2, Nexus also had full access to the ridiculous and ongoing sagas of televangelists such as Jim Bakker and his wife, Tammy Faye, as well as the actions of suicidal cults like that at Jonestown and, more recently, California's Heaven's Gate. Thanks to the media, Nexus didn't need firsthand experience with organized religion to recognize that things can go seriously wrong.

Just because Nexus questions established religion does not mean, however, that it is without a soul. While it is more likely than any other generation to feel that the concept of God is an "old superstition no longer needed to explain things in these modern times,"[36] Nexus is also *more likely* to believe in life after death and the spirit world.[37] The immense popularity of television programs such as "The X-Files" indicates Nexus' profound interest in the supernatural and the quest for truth. Moreover, this generation's early exposure to New Age fads such as "pyramid-power" and "spiritual channelling" has left it more open to *new* New Age phenomena, such as holistic medicine and blockbuster books like *The Celestine Prophecy*. Although the credibility of established religion, and its ability to answer fundamental questions about "the meaning of life," has been undermined for Nexus by scandal and infighting, interesting secular alternatives have emerged. The generation has a genuine need for spiritual fulfilment, but traditional religious icons and traditions are not always able to deliver satisfaction.

Claire Heron, a past president of the Catholic Women's League of Canada, would agree. She notes that in most churches "the lights haven't gone on to spirituality." In other words, they do not recognize and adapt to the spiritual potential in younger members, who are more interested in individual faith journeys than rigid doctrine. Other interests, such as the pursuit of happiness, become their new religion. Similarly, the traditions of religion don't sit well with the new rituals of Nexus. Jean Beneteau, coordinator of the Catholic Youth Ministry in London, Ontario, finds that "the meaning of the Eucharistic symbols is empty to many young people, yet they can find spiritual community in a gathering over pizza and beer."

Nexus also finds some of the more traditional incentives of organized religion un-motivating. Though he wasn't referring specifically to religion, Michael Adams suggests that "more than any generation in history, young Canadians have abandoned fear, guilt and duty as major motivating factors."[38] Threats of eternal damnation and hell-fire just don't work with Nexus. And the hierarchy of the church is just as unappealing to Nexus as the heirarchy found anywhere else. François Brassard, representing an organization of married Catholic priests called Corpus, thinks that rigid hierarchies are a fundamental problem for the church, particularly when it comes to engaging young people. He sees "small-faith communities as the way of the future," with the days of the hierarchical parish numbered, because these smaller groups can recognize the individual and still provide support. This, he believes, will be a key to re-engaging Nexus.

Brassard also contends that young people today like to know the common "spiritual points" that relate one religion to another, something most religions have had difficulty with in the past. Essentially, "my God is better than your God" arguments don't fly with many from Nexus. For them, spirituality is about individual interpretation and expression, not unwavering devotion to a higher power. In many ways, this attitude parallels Nexus' acceptance of and curiosity towards diversity—things it learned growing up in a highly multicultural society and travelling to new parts of the globe. One Ottawa member of our network, who is Jewish, gladly accepts her friends' invitations to Ukrainian Orthodox Easter and Roman Catholic Christmas year after year because she finds the similarities between the faiths compelling. Trust Nexus to find ways to connect different faiths, rather than isolate them.

The Red Herring Cathedral in Winnipeg operates on this principle of commonality through spirituality. It's a drop-in centre for local youth whose patrons generally subscribe to some kind of faith or belief, though are not necessarily connected to any particular denomination. Some simply follow a personal moral code. Coffee, alternative music, and conversation on any number of issues mark most nights at the Red Herring, which boasts a modest number of Nexus regulars. Another "Nexus friendly" religious establishment is the Westside King's Church in Calgary. Run out of a converted curling rink, the Westside has fifteen hundred patrons whose average age is twenty-eight. Their secret? A modernization of the entire process of delivering the sermon, including the use of video clips and electric guitars. The Westside was founded on the very notion that attracting Nexus-aged individuals required bringing elements of *its* culture into the service.

Still, not all are convinced that these GenX Churches, as they are sometimes called, are the perfect solution to the woes of organized religion. Don Posterski, author of *Teen Trends*, suggests that we need both spiritual frameworks and individual spirituality to "nurture our values collectively as a society." Values, he suggests, must come from somewhere, and today they come from the individual or the family—not the institutions they once came from. Posterski is not convinced that these new churches are "operating with enough depth or substance"[39] to solve what he calls our crisis in values transmission.

Whatever the case, any religion that proves inflexible to changing times will find itself in trouble with Nexus and the generations to follow. As a final example, consider the case of d~Code's twenty-two-year-old co-op student, who is Muslim. His decision to "keep the faith" is very much tied to the fact that he is able to engage his religious elders in meaningful dialogue, even over more controversial matters such as sex, the consumption of alcohol, and smoking cigarettes. Because he is able to discuss these issues in a religious, intellectual, and adult context, his faith remains consistently relevant.

[The State of Affairs]

If there is one institution in Canada that could use a dose of youthful enthusiasm, it is the state. Governments at all levels are being openly questioned as to their capabilities, credibility, and relevance. Unfortunately, Nexus is not on the government's side either. The combination of the generation's formative experiences with government and more recent let-downs in dealing with youth issues has left Nexus a little bitter towards the state, if not detached from it entirely.

80

From the Welfare State to the
Competition State

In Nexus' early childhood, our welfare state was the stable provider for and protector of Canadians. As a protector, it inoculated Nexus kids against diseases like polio and strengthened our teeth with fluoride treatments. It also secured our borders with northern radar systems, and developed an impressive array of weapons and search-and-rescue hardware. As a provider, the welfare state tried to insulate Canadians from certain global economic forces by imposing foreign-investment reviews and offering subsidies to nurture home-grown industries. It also provided every Canadian with a health card and access to affordable education.

In the adult world of Nexus, it has been harder to recognize the state's protector role. First, this generation has seen a number of crushing blows dealt to the military establishment—most recently through the Somalia inquiry. Second, Nexus Canadians have been spooked by the spread of infectious diseases—whether it's mad-cow disease, the Ebola virus, or the Hong Kong chicken flu. Even the once-trusted Canadian blood supply has come into question (a scandal that Nexus could watch live on CBC). And third, Nexus has lived through a multitude of attacks on the Canadian dollar, evidently fuelled by New York bond traders, which state structures appear powerless to counter.

It would be equally easy for Nexus to conclude that the Canadian state has forfeited its claim to the provider role. Much of recent Nexus history has seen the government (both federal and provincial) clawing its way out of massive debt, leaving a trail of cut-backs in its wake. As a result, Nexus has lived without a range of services and redistributive arrangements enjoyed by its parents' generation and is considering private solutions to fill the gap. For many, the state has become invisible.

The realities of globalization mean that rather than focusing on insulation, Canada's "competition state"[40] is increasing Nexus' exposure to the global marketplace and pressuring the companies it works for to be more competitive internationally. In the process, the state has given up control over a range of crucial policy instruments. The 1997 election debate—the first for a large number of Nexus voters—saw Canada's prime minister claiming his "hands were tied" by the International Monetary Fund and international financial markets. It's a far cry from the days when governments actually built things, like railways, hospitals, schools, and roads.

The Decline of Confidence

As a consequence of these developments, Nexus is simply not impressed with government institutions. Sixty per cent say they have little or no confidence in structures such as our Parliament,[41] and only 18 per cent have faith in their provincial leadership.[42] Although the federal government recently returned its first balanced budget in three decades, close to 60 per cent of Nexus expect it to lapse into deficit spending again.[43]

But perhaps most disturbing is the number of young people who simply don't care. In *Reconnecting Government with Youth*,[44] the Angus Reid Group found the single largest segment of young people to be the "Ambivalents"—the 25 per cent who seem to have tuned out from government and the issues altogether. The next largest segment was the "Dissatisfied Independents," 21 per cent of the sample who feel that government is irrelevant to them, and that less of it is always better.

There has also been a significant shift in Nexus' expectations of what government will provide. Three decades ago, Canadians received a great deal from the state. For every dollar Nexus' parents gave to the government, they got back much more in services. In fact, members of the Nexus Generation benefited greatly from these goodies—such as family allowances—in their childhood years.

But in the 1990s, just as Nexus was entering the workforce, the returns on tax investment suddenly became less impressive. Slowly, our roads have become littered with pot-holes, our schools have fallen apart, and our emergency rooms have filled to capacity. It seems that everywhere you turn, government dollars are being removed from the places that need them most. For example, d~Coders we've talked to from coast to coast express serious concern about the quality of health care they can expect for their tax dollars. "Canada in 2005: The 1997 *Maclean's*/CBC National News Year-End Poll" revealed the same attitudes: younger Canadians both expect and accept a two-tiered health system. It's worth observing, however, that there is a split within Nexus. Because older members of the generation have stronger memories of the state as a stable provider, these twenty-five- to thirty-four-year-olds lament its passing. Those between eighteen and twenty-four, who were more influenced by the Thatcher-Reagan-Mulroney era, seem to have accepted the state's diminished role as a firm reality.

To combat these reduced expectations of government, Nexus has acquired a "do-it-yourself" outlook on the world. Members of this generation fundamentally believe they will have to finance their own futures and have started saving for it already. Only 8 per cent of Nexus respondents in a recent survey thought it likely that the public-pension system would be there when they need it.[45] As we will see later, this concern about living in a competition state is reflected in Nexus' investment and long-term savings habits—a concern that sometimes conflicts with the "live for today" impulses of youth.

If Nexus is questioning the services the state can provide, it is also exhibiting a greater scepticism about another pillar of Canadian society: state-funded post-secondary education. As we shall see, this generation has awoken to the fact that it is taking over some of the state's provider responsibilities, and it is demanding some payback.

[The Ivory Tower]

Don't be a fool—stay in school! Even coming from the mouth of the ridiculous Mr. T., this piece of advice was taken very seriously by Nexus. All indications point to it being the most educated generation in Canadian history. Yet for Nexus, the pay-offs of that education have been difficult, if not impossible, to realize. For many, attempts to graduate from school to the working world have been marked by delay, displacement, and disappointment. This generation is now beginning to rethink higher education as we know it.

Nexus has, in fact, been part of an overall Canadian trend towards more education. From 1976 to 1991, mean educational attainment in this country jumped from 11.3 to 12.5 years.[46] This increase was the result of both deliberate attempts by policy makers to better educate Canadians and the relative affluence of the post-war period. The sixties and seventies saw government build many more schools and hire many more teachers to accommodate the vast numbers of Boomers going through the system. High-school graduation rates soared and more and more people began to consider the option of higher education. Women, for the first time, were seriously encouraged to stay in school, and many did. Where once the norm was to "get out there and get a job as soon as you are able," the new norm became "stay in school."

Resources were simultaneously being poured into the university and college systems, creating more room for these prospective scholars. Meanwhile, the cost to the student remained relatively low, making post-secondary education in Canada a truly universal option. In the seventies and eighties, our schools pumped out

84

hordes of professionals—doctors, lawyers, nurses, accountants, and teachers—and our private and public sectors, still relatively flush, gobbled most of them up. Prior to 1990, the educational contract in Canada went something like this: get good grades and a university degree and you will be all set—the great job, the two-car garage, and the membership at the golf club. All this could be yours. Unfortunately, those at the front end of Nexus, who graduated in the early nineties, quickly learned that the contract had become null and void. To those who followed, and those still in school today, the validity of the contract remains in question. It's not that simple any more.

Nonetheless, Nexus did heed Mr. T's advice and stay in school. In 1994, 126,500 undergraduate degrees were granted in Canada, 35 per cent more than were granted ten years earlier.[47] More than 21,000 master's degrees were granted in 1994, close to 45 per cent more than a decade earlier.[48] And this despite there being a smaller number of people in the graduation window (i.e., their twenties). Canadian census data from 1996 shows that 51 per cent of women and 42 per cent of men in their twenties had received some form of post-secondary accreditation.[49]

While all this might seem like a good-news story, the reality is that the downsized private and public sectors have not been able to absorb these new graduates as they did in the seventies and eighties. We are all familiar with the youth-unemployment saga that has plagued Nexus since the end of the last decade. Though the exact numbers vary depending on who you ask, youth-unemployment levels haven't dipped below about 13 per cent in some time. As a result, the higher numbers of graduates reflect the "might as well stay in school, there's nothing else to do" attitude as much as anything else. Forty-two per cent of respondents in *Reconnecting Government with Youth* chose "no job" as a primary reason for continuing their education. This statistic drives the point home: the number of degrees granted per 100,000 twenty- to twenty-nine-year-olds rose an astonishing 25 per cent from 1990 to 1994 alone.[50]

Basic economics says that when there is an oversupply of labour, employers are in a position to offer lower wages for the same job. Alternatively, the same wage level can offered for better-qualified people. Such is the nature of the labour market facing Nexus. Opportunities have shrunk, and an older generation is ensconced in the workforce. Couple this with a glut of eager and educated young candidates, and the result is a phenomenon called educational inflation.[51] Highly educated people wind up having to take what is left over, usually positions that appear to require minimal training. Also, as maturing economies shift in focus from manufacturing to services, the bulk of entry-level opportunities tend to involve standing behind counters, working call-centre phones, or lording over change rooms at the Gap. Andrew, a thirty-year-old d~Coder from Lindsay, Ontario, reckons he was one of the "most educated bartenders in Canada" through much of the early part of this decade. He has since found a suitable application for both his educational training and his bar-room experience: the world of public relations.

Estimates are that this kind of underemployment in the Canadian workforce is shared by one-third of all college and university graduates. Educational inflation and underemployment often leave those lucky enough to have jobs chronically dissatisfied with their careers and always on the lookout for something better, and those who can't get jobs in the first place feeling bitter. Those with credentials ask, "What the hell did I waste five years for?" while those without either withdraw from the labour force altogether or go back to school to get the requisite degree. Though not entirely at fault, the post-secondary education system is turning out a significantly high number of dissatisfied customers, while at the same time attracting people for the wrong reasons entirely. Either way, the value of a university degree in today's workforce is diminishing.

Many people, like Hoops Harrison of the Canadian Alliance of Student Associations, feel that "a university degree is equal to a high-school diploma ten or fifteen years back."[52]

Wall of Debt

School in general has become progressively more expensive in Canada, with the cost of education per capita increasing some 67 per cent from 1983 to 1993.[53] What has been particularly tough on Nexus, though, is how these rising costs are being pushed down to the end-user. In 1980, when a mere 13 per cent of operating revenues were covered by tuition, the subsidization of Canadian universities reached its peak.[54] A decade and a half later, thanks to serious cut-backs in government support, universities were looking for students to cover almost a quarter of their costs. That's right, educational institutions are asking students to pay a whole quarter of what it costs to educate them. Complaints about having to pay such a small proportion might, at first, seem a little thin. But before passing judgement, consider the following: from 1990 to 1995, average tuition fees in Canada rose in real terms by 62 per cent.[55] We need not consult *any* statistics to state with confidence that the student summer or part-time job markets could not have made up the difference. The income of the average Canadian family has not kept pace with rising tuition either; it's tougher for Mom and Dad to help out. Even student-loan programs have significantly lagged behind tuition increases. The average Canada Student Loan rose by 55 per cent from 1984 to 1995, trailing increases in tuition fees over the same period by some 20 per cent.[56] With the Ontario government's announcement in the spring of 1998 that it would no longer regulate how much universities and colleges can charge for tuition in certain courses, students will likely carry an even greater share of educational costs in the future.

As a result, Nexus students have had little trouble piling on the debt. According to the department of Human Resources Development Canada, the average debt per graduate in 1998–99 will be around $25, 000—about as much as an entry-level salary. Of course, it takes the average graduate between six months and a year to find a job, and these levels are virtually impossible to service with a transitional or part-time positions. The federal government has acted, though. It announced in its fall 1997 Speech to the Throne the establishment of the Millennium Scholarship Endowment Fund, which is designed to help offset the costs of education. The trouble is, the scholarship won't start being awarded until the year 2000—too late for many Nexus students. But they haven't lost their sense of humour over the issue. In February 1998, Kraft sponsored an event called National Student Debt Day on the campus of the University of Western Ontario. The purpose of the event was to create awareness about the rising costs of education, as well as the mounting debt load that many young graduates face. Events included a cook-off and the building of a "wall of debt" made from Nexus' favourite budget food, Kraft Dinner.

One consequence of these funding changes and level of indebtedness is that members of Nexus approach their higher education like demanding consumers. And why not? They *are* paying for it, so they want to see the value. Where at one time students would have greeted a cancelled lecture with cheers, today they are more likely to grumble at the inconvenience *and* demand it be rescheduled. But as serious as Nexus is about school, it also asks to be entertained. Remember that, to pay for their education, many work during the day, meaning that social activities such as going to the movies or watching television often give way to the night class. Lectures delivered drily from behind lecterns or read from prefabricated notes just don't cut it any more. Nexus wants to be amused and entertained as well as educated.

The cutthroat world of education is producing some very savvy students as well. As David Kinahan and Harry Heft explain in their book *On Your Mark*,[57] students these days must be highly strategic in order to get the extra "few percentage points on their transcripts that can add up to the difference between full scholarships and the student loan repo-men."[58] Understanding the professor and the psychology that makes her tick is a first step, say the authors. Kinahan also finds Nexus students are fast becoming aware of the politics inherent in higher education, as well as the coping mechanisms to deal with them. "Some people find our take on the university cynical," says Kinahan, "but it is also pragmatic." No wonder Nexus is catching on.

Once considered a "ticket to ride," the post-secondary education has become a necessary, though often not sufficient, condition for obtaining meaningful employment. Those with a traditional education, on average, still fare better than those without, but many from Nexus are beginning to consider alternatives. In 1993, the growth rate for university enrolment in Canada was negative for the first time since 1978[59]—perhaps a sign that the ivory tower is losing its lustre as an institution. All this must be troubling news for alumni associations, who have long depended on nostalgic university graduates to maintain the glory of Canada's universities and colleges. Members of the Nexus Generation—who are likely to leave university breathing a sigh of relief for having "made it"— could be an awfully hard sell.

[Nexus and the Media]

Arguably, Canadian society is one of the most media literate in the world. Historically, we have been at the top of the list of modern nations in adopting media-related technologies such as telephones, televisions, VCRs, fax machines, personal computers, and now the Internet. But interestingly enough, Canadians appear unwilling to give up on the "old" in order to make room for the "new." Instead, the number of media conduits people regularly connect with has multiplied at an astonishing rate: telephones, fax machines, e-mail, pagers, newspapers, magazines, and television, to name but a few. Navigating through today's multimedia universe requires more than just literacy; it requires savvy.

Savvy, we believe, best describes Nexus' current relationship with the institution of media. This generation regularly consults a diverse range of media sources, and trusts its well-honed ability to assimilate them to get at the "truth." Nexus also possesses a robust immunity to media manipulation, often turning the equation around and manipulating the media itself. As the largest bulk consumer of media, Nexus demands interactivity, customization, and involvement. As some of the most innovative creators of media, many from this generation are rewriting the rules of what it looks, sounds, and *feels* like.

As institutions go, the media is a bit different from those we have looked at so far. Unlike the state and the ivory tower, the media has no elected president or board of directors to oversee operations (setting aside the issue of concentration of ownership for the moment). And while media can and does facilitate the exchange of ideas and the telling of stories, it falls short of providing nurturing and support the way a community can. Still, many post-McLuhanists believe in the increasing importance of media. Douglas Rushkoff, for one, says the media is "the only place left for our civilization to expand—our only real frontier" and that the "datasphere is the new territory for human interaction, economic expansion and especially social and political machination."[60] If Rushkoff is correct, and we think he is, then being media savvy is perhaps the most important skill for anyone to take into the next century. For the remainder of this chapter, we will touch briefly on Nexus' relationship with both established and emerging forms of communication that make up the institution of the media.

In Defense of Print

In the spring of 1998, media mogul Conrad Black announced his intention to launch a third national newspaper in Canada. Some observers were a bit puzzled by the move, given that the existing national had already staked claim to the ideological right, and that the new paper would be in competition with several of the metropolitan dailies already in Black's empire. As well, investments in paper media might seem a little passé, with the future of media seemingly tied more to virtual-delivery channels. Whatever Black's true intentions, he seems to understand Canada's love affair with print media, and is banking on its staying power. Print has become part of our national character, pulling people of this vast and thinly populated nation together in the spirit of the transnational railway and the CBC.

Nexus does not appear ready to terminate the Canadian infatuation with print. About 80 per cent of Nexus read a newspaper at least weekly,[61] and more than two-thirds indicate that the papers have a moderate to strong influence on their opinions on issues of the day.[62] This generation is sceptical of media manipulation, but compensates by consulting multiple sources. David, a Toronto d~Coder, reads both the *Globe and Mail* and the alternative paper *Now* every week. In his words, consulting both papers "provides [a] balance between liberal and conservative biases, as well as local versus national perspectives." In fact, Nexus generally favours local papers, often because they are much better sources of cultural and community information. *Now* and its national counterparts—such as *Georgia Strait* in Vancouver, the *Mirror* in Montreal, and the *Coast* in Halifax—target young people with a mix of arts, music, culture, and political commentary. Mainstream advertisers, such as Eaton's, Bell Mobility, and Volkswagen, are beginning to pop up in these alternative weeklies because of their considerable ability to reach the elusive Nexus market.

In delivering the news, papers face stiff competition from innovative new sources such as Pointcast, which "pushes" a customized assortment of headlines onto a computer desktop. The Elevator News Network is another innovator, pumping up-to-the-minute news, weather, and sports onto television screens mounted in elevators. At the moment, people still seem most enamoured of their own reflections while riding in elevators. But even if these new technologies do catch on, we believe they'll help the old ones, not obliterate them. We have Pointcast in our office, but our newest staffer, Natalie, claims that "Pointcast really only reminds me to read the paper; it doesn't replace it."

The magazine is another form of print media that is highly attractive to younger consumers, and Nexus is more likely than any other generation to say that magazines exert a strong influence on its opinions.[63] As evidence, consider the growing popularity of bookstore cafés and the continued appearance of specialized magazines on the racks. Specialty magazines are the only real growth segment in the domestic periodical industry, with a cumulative circulation growth of 35 per cent from 1990 to 1994.[64] Although the Web was supposed to be a death-knell for the glossy magazine, this format is holding its own.

One simple explanation for this is that pictures on the Internet still can't compare with those in magazines, and they take forever to download. Another is that the ritual of magazine buying—leafing casually through your favourites at the corner store and gradually making your way over to the counter—is just not an option with the Web. Nexus still wants to touch and feel something that is unique, something that is theirs. *Shift* magazine publisher Andrew Heintzman feels that young people "crave physical objects in a world where everything is losing substance." But he believes there are two other reasons why magazines are still popular with Nexus consumers. First, magazines merge together two important foundations of our culture: literacy and design. They are very visual and are multimedia-driven by nature, and therefore appeal to a group that has been raised on complex blends of type, colour, graphics, and written words. Nexus is the "font generation"[65] after all, the first to have type choices beyond Helvetica and Times New Roman. Second, more than any other media, magazines make a statement about a reader. They define what he is all about. Perhaps that's why, Heintzman argues, younger consumers "treat magazines with incredible reverence, displaying them proudly on their coffee tables or desks."

This is not to say that the Web has had no impact on the look and quality of magazines. According to Steve, a d~Coder who works with an interactive-media company, many current magazines have tried to meet the challenge of the Internet by improving on their basic materials. "*Wired* magazine uses some of the thickest stock and richest inks of any magazine I know. This is significant, in that it suggests where print is going in the future: there will be less of it, and the only way to justify it will be to make it almost like art." The average Web page has a long way to go before it can make the same claim.

Radio

Radio is the oft-forgotten medium when it comes to the Information Revolution, though if its relationship with Nexus is any indication, it too is on solid ground. Sixty per cent of the generation listen to radio daily,[66] while nearly one in three describes it as a highly influential media source.[67] The relationship between Nexus and radio is still largely predicated on music (Nexus drives that industry as well), though the more interactive "talk-radio" format is making a play for this generation's radio loyalty.

Radio is the quintessential media format for a generation on the move. The airwaves are wherever you are, and are easily scooped up with a Walkman (a technology Nexus has grown up with) or a car stereo. Radio is also well suited to a multi-tasking generation that grew up doing its homework in front of a television set. "When I was a kid, I'd have my radio on and my television blaring *while* talking on the phone to my friends," recalls Hollis from our office. Today Nexus listens to the radio while behind the wheel of a car, reading a newspaper, surfing the Web, or on the job. When it comes to media, Nexus is adept at walking and chewing gum at the same time.

Although the shape and content of radio will need to evolve to keep pace with the other forms of media, the immediate challenge for individual stations seems to be in holding Nexus' radio loyalties. As is the case with television, surfing the radio is rampant. According to Michele Erskine, research director for Toronto's alternative-rock station the Edge, the industry golden rule used to be that people listened to an average of 2.4 radio stations per week. Now, says Erskine, young people "know how to get around the dial and find a station to match their mood; it's a challenge for one station to meet all their needs."

Nevertheless, talk radio is beginning to appeal to significant numbers of Nexus listeners. In Montreal and Toronto, U.S.-based "shock-jock" Howard Stern arrived in late 1997 and promptly pulled many Nexus listeners away from local morning shows. While Stern's initial popularity may have been based more on hype and controversy (around, in particular, derogatory remarks he made about French Canadians) than good content, it hints at the fundamental appeal of talk radio to Nexus. First, it is intrinsically interactive, and we already know that Nexus does not enjoy passive consumption—it wants to be challenged and involved. As much as we too lament Peter Gzowski's retirement from CBC Radio in late 1997, it marked the end of the old paradigm of Canadian talk radio: the host and his guests do all the talking while those at home listen intently. The Nexus Generation came of age with the help of interactive programs like "Sex with Sue," a call-in radio show that has been fielding questions about sex from nervous teenagers in Southern Ontario for at least fifteen years. Members of Nexus aren't afraid to hear themselves on the radio. It seemed that even the immutable Howard Stern was a bit surprised at the number of confident young Canadians who called in to take him to task over his comments.

Ever since television burst onto the scene mid-century, radio has been fending off challenges from newer "gadgets" bent on taking away its listeners. Today, emerging technologies such as RealAudio Web-casting, digital radio, and customized CDs pose competitive challenges for contemporary radio. But given Nexus' tendency to take on more and more media without giving anything up, these technologies might just as easily make radio more popular.

Television

When it comes to media about media, television is frequently overlooked in favour of sexy and innovative newcomers like the Web. When television is in the news, the stories are usually about how bad or violent the programming has become, how many millions Fox paid to broadcast NFL football last year, and how much we all miss Seinfeld now that he is gone. The tube's own record when it comes to innovation has been relatively dismal of late—the only thing new about television in the last decade is that there is more of it. But to make these complaints is to forget what a powerful medium television still is. To all intents and purposes, television is in every single home, everywhere. Just about everyone watches the nightly news, and certain programs demand the attention of billions of people worldwide (raise your hand if you *didn't* watch the Academy Awards this year). If you really want to say something, say it on television.

There are signs that this may be changing, however. Don Tapscott tells us, for example, that his Net Generation already prefers surfing the Web or playing video games to watching television. Network and cable television beware, should these young net-junkies carry this trend into adulthood. And the Nexus Generation, though it has too long a history with TV to give it up overnight, is at least watching television differently.

Observers of the relationship between Nexus and television point out that the fact that we even have television about television speaks to how integral it has become to modern culture. Where the television that the Boomers grew up on was built on direct cultural references, Nexus television is just as likely to use media references instead. On "The Simpsons," as Douglas Rushkoff points out, the characters are watching television much of the time we are watching them, allowing this seemingly harmless cartoon to deliver its subtle and sarcastic media commentary. If this all seems a little confusing to you, it probably isn't to Nexus. As Rob Owen points out in *Gen X TV*,[68] people in their twenties and early thirties have a more "extensive knowledge of television than any previous generation," and they both draw from and react to a vast collection of references learned from years of studying the airwaves.

The upshot of all of this is that Nexus now demands the innovation, in both content and form, that television has lacked for some time. It is watching on its own terms, and on its own time. The average eighteen- to thirty-four-year-old Canadian watches nineteen hours of television per week,[69] but what the statistics don't tell us is *how* Nexus is watching.

Me and TV

Members of the Nexus Generation today tend to identify with programs, not networks or individual stations. They use peripheral technologies like the remote control and the VCR to help them navigate the expanding television universe and to customize their viewing experience based on their interests and their schedules. This style of viewing presents a significant challenge to the "big three" U.S. networks, as well as to our own CBC. Networks have typically preferred to choose programs for us, by building an entire evening line-up around one or two shows they know people like and crossing their fingers that their viewers won't "change that dial." This strategy presupposes, usually incorrectly, that viewers have committed a whole evening to the couch, or that they are even there, watching in person, in the first place.

In *Playing the Future*, Rushkoff calls this "the old style of television viewing,"[70] where programmers banked on commitment from those watching. He also points out that the networks didn't call what they were doing programming "for nothing."[71] But Nexus is much more immune to this practice than previous generations were. While NBC's successful and long-running Thursday night line-up (consisting of Nexus favourites like "Friends," "Seinfeld," and "E.R.") might have seemed like a triumph for old-style network programming, remember Nexus' proficiency with the VCR. A crop poll of our d~Code network suggests that half of all viewers don't watch these programs on Thursday nights at all, but tape them and watch later. They fast-forward through the commercials too.

Pop music icon Bruce Springsteen laments the fact that we have "57 channels and nothin' on." We're not sure what he watches, but the reality is that specialty channels have added breadth and scope to television. Rick Mercer from "This Hour Has 22 Minutes" articulates this point perfectly: "'Do we really need five hundred TV channels?' What a stupid question. Has anyone ever said, 'Do we really need five hundred books in the library?'"[72] If your particular interest happens to be outer space, golf, or food, you now have destinations on the television dial that will serve your needs twenty-four hours a day. Other channels, such as the Women's Television Network and YTV, program around the interests of a particular demographic. Would a Nexus Television Station work? The jury is still out on this one, although the majority in our network still think that mainstream television is primarily targeted at Boomers, making the notion of a Nexus station unique and attractive. But the rise of the specialty channel also helps Nexus customize its viewing experience, since it can explore even further to find programming to match its mood. In the end, more channels may mean less viewer loyalty.

The Plot Thickens?

A typical "Seinfeld" episode consists of three to four different plots running simultaneously. Sometimes there is a common theme, but more often than not, members of the ensemble cast go off on separate half-hour tangents that weave themselves together by the closing credits. Consider the following episode, entitled "The Bizarro Jerry":

> Elaine breaks up with Kevin but he still wants to hang out as friends. George leads Kramer to the "best" bathroom in town, which is in an investment office, and as he leaves the bathroom he is caught in a crowd of workers and accidentally attends a meeting in the conference room. Kramer continues to work at the investment office, working long hours, leaving Jerry feeling

very alone. Jerry goes out with Elaine's pretty friend Gillian and discovers she has huge "man hands." George shows a picture of Gillian to a beautiful receptionist, Amanda, and tells her that Gillian is his deceased fiancée. Gillian's beauty makes George more attractive to Amanda and she takes him out to a hot night spot full of beautiful models. Elaine meets Kevin's friends, Gene and Feldman, who are really nice, generous and love to read, the exact opposite of George and Kramer. Elaine has entered into the bizarro world of Jerry, George and Kramer.[73]

This might seem more like a frenetic collection of random occurrences than a linear or coherent television plotline, but Nexus is able to follow it without missing a beat. The show's multiple-access points hook different Nexus viewers in different ways. Although it was a "show about nothing," according to its creator, "Seinfeld" had something for everyone.

"The Simpsons" is another program that uses multiple-access points to engage Nexus, relying on depth, sophistication, and subtlety rather than several plots. On one level, it is a ridiculous-looking cartoon. But as Rushkoff observes, it is also a "platform for sophisticated social and media satire."[74] Although the show's main character, Bart Simpson, is a perennial ten-year-old, he should be considered an honorary member of the Nexus Generation. According to Rushkoff, Bart is "a media strategist—or at least an unconscious manipulator." Nexus watches and identifies with "The Simpsons" and "Seinfeld" because these programs are clever, ironic, simple, and absurd all at the same time.

No-Name Television

Remember those generic channels on your local cable system? Remember the scrolling text on a blue background, with the time and current temperature displayed in tiny letters in the bottom corner?

These channels were always a good source of local news and events, and Nexus skipped over them as fast as it could. But those channels have evolved into the latest trend in broadcasting. Pioneered by Bloomberg TV News in the United States, and more recently taken up by CityPulse 24 locally, these new television interfaces closely resemble framed Web sites. Typically, only a third of the screen is reserved for old-fashioned video, with the rest taken up by graphic weather reports, sports headlines, a stock ticker, and of course advertising. Other stations such as the Weather Channel and StarTV spend more and more time broadcasting text and other kinds of information, not just video images and sounds. These stations were designed with Nexus' multi-tasking abilities in mind. Even the stodgy old CBC has catered to its multi-tasking younger viewers on occasion; it sometimes splits the screen and shows parts of two important play-off hockey games at once.

Interactivity: I Want to Be on TV

Interactivity in media is fast becoming a Nexus norm, though mainstream television has been slow to catch on. But Toronto's Citytv and its national sister-station, MuchMusic, have long known the benefits of using interactivity to appeal to younger viewers. City's "Speakers Corner" is a popular, low-budget piece of programming featuring minute-long monologues submitted by ordinary people. Topics range from "I don't understand men" and "I don't understand women" to "I think politicians are idiots." With minimal production and zero planning, it captures the street mood of Toronto perhaps better than any other program in the city.

"Electric Circus" is another Citytv/MuchMusic programming innovation that features its viewers, not media icons. The program includes a mix of music, videos, interviews, and dancing. While the stylishly dressed dancers inside the studio are the focus of the show, the enthusiastic crowds pressed up against the glass are just as much of a draw. The program airs twice—live on Friday and taped on Sunday—so that the people who go down to the studio get a chance to see themselves on TV later.

The Internet

In marketing speak, the diffusion of a product into society is often described in terms of how far the product has "penetrated" various segments of that society. The so-called Innovators and Early Adopters, usually the younger, more educated, and more mobile members of society, are the first to play with the newest toys. Not surprisingly, members of Nexus are the Early Adopters of the Net.

Early Adopters have distinct advantages over other market segments. First, they are afforded opportunities to shape the product, as well as use it. On the Web, for example, Nexus helped to invent what is commonly called netiquette—the rules of conduct that have spontaneously emerged for doing business or socializing on the Web. These rules, which revolve around issues of freedom of speech and respect for others, are policed by ordinary users. The Nexus Generation also serves as a test-market for a broad range of Web applications, which may or may not reach a broader market, depending on how well they fare. Today the beta-testing of products and services is even moving beyond software to more tangible goods.

Perhaps more than anything, however, being an Early Adopter on the Net comes with the bragging rights of being first in. Nexus thinks of the Net as its turf, the claims of Tapscott's Net Generation notwithstanding. Nexus likes to and does play on the Net, but to paraphrase Denis Leary from his string of software commercials, Nexus actually "works" on the Web too. The emerging wave of Net entrepreneurs, those busy finding new and better applications of Web technologies, is increasingly made up of people under the age of thirty-five. Success in the Internet business seems to come from being comfortable not only with technology, but also with change and risk. Dave, a d~Coder from Silicon Valley and a Net entrepreneur himself, puts it this way: "What sets apart the under-35 CEO from older executives is a pre-conditioned mindset for innovation and the sense of urgency in leading and responding to market change." The business fundamentals still have to be there, but these can be learned. Risk taking, on the other hand, is more of an attitude that comes from *inside*.

Early Adopters are usually attracted to a product because of its intrinsic appeal or because it fills an explicit need—in other words, they are leading, not following, a trend. The Web has an intrinsic appeal for Nexus because it provides the user with immediate feedback. Requests for information are answered in seconds, as are calls for help and companionship. You can get what you need in a do-it-yourself way. In a recent study, 72 per cent of Nexus members who use the Net indicate that they use it for their studies.[75] As we discussed earlier in the chapter, the Web also represents a new way to socialize and a new way to build a community. Seventy-six per cent of Nexus members on the Net use it to keep in touch with friends.

The Net is also intrinsically democratic and non-hierarchical, and hence attractive to Nexus. Martin, a d~Coder from New York who works in educational software, thinks the Net "has shattered the old paradigm of organization, which really dates back to the days of running railroads or the military." In theory, the "little guy" has as good a chance to be recognized as the large corporation. Consider what it takes to launch a television station versus what it takes to build a Web page on the Net.

Last, but certainly not least, the Net is an intriguing new place to play. The Nexus Generation was brought up to expect constant improvements in the toys it plays with. It started with dedicated game machines like Pong, Atari, Intellivision, Nintendo, and Sega. But the personal computer and the Internet make a highly potent gaming combination. A user can play Doom against someone across town or across the country, and the latest scenarios can simply be downloaded from the Net. A game that is always changing never becomes boring. With the Net, Nexus need not wait for Christmas for the latest new toy—she can simply download it whenever she wants.

But the Net is not perfect from a Nexus point of view. As Early Adopters of this medium, Nexus users are starting to demand that issues such as speed, security, and lack of standards be addressed. As the Net becomes more and more cluttered, the generation has grown frustrated with dated and unreliable data and links that take you nowhere. In the same way that netiquette implicitly guides conduct on the Net, these issues are being tackled thanks to user feedback and innovation.

[Conclusion]

In fact, the concepts of feedback and innovation underlie Nexus' favourable relationship with media in general. It tends to view media, and particularly new media like the Internet, as being open to change and adaptable to the times. Nexus' media consumption habits, and most notably its reliance on multiple sources, force individual forms of media to compete with each other for Nexus' attention. Nexus demands relevance, authenticity, and innovation or it will simply tune out.

Nexus' chief complaint about all of the other institutions covered in this chapter would be that they have been too slow to adapt or are too closed to changes that would make them more relevant to a younger generation. Generally, this has made Nexus feel less attached to the traditional institutions—it is delaying marriage, creating new forms of community, opting out of religion, rethinking traditional education, and disengaging from the state. Of course, the news is not all bad; members of this generation can also be found within many of these institutions, pushing for change from the inside.

Our discussion of Nexus and traditional institutions, when combined with an understanding of the generation's formative experiences, completes the background you will need to best understand Nexus today in its roles as a consumer, a citizen, and an employee. These roles are the focus of Section II.

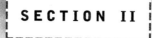

SECTION II

NEXUS THE CONSUMER

We e-mailed members of our d~Code network and asked them to tell us about their most exciting recent shopping experiences. We wanted to know not only what they bought, but also where they bought it and what prompted their purchase decision. Their answers revealed a great deal about the role of consumption in the life of Nexus, and about what drives its consumer behaviour. Here are a few of our favourites:

Laurie, twenty-nine-year-old marketing manager, Toronto

"I just bought a box of Bugs Bunny animal crackers in San Francisco. I bought them because I think animal crackers are awesome, and because it was an amazing example of a cool, licensed product. I just ate Porky Pig, Pepe Le Pew, and Bugs Bunny for breakfast."

Patrick, thirty-year-old intellectual-property lawyer, Montreal

"I recently bought a Marshall JCM-800 guitar amp at a music store on Mont-Royal/Papineau. I bought it because it rocks, it's loud, it frightens kids of all ages, and it has the world's evilest feedback."

Ryan, twenty-four-year-old lifeguard and editor, Vancouver

"I bought a Tintin watch while I was on vacation. I bought it because I collect watches and because, as a child, I read every Tintin book. I have such a strong attachment to the character . . . I somehow turn off my brain at the price. . . . I slapped down the credit card and bought it after thinking about it for two minutes. I've worn it every day since."

Leah, twenty-six-year-old multimedia artist, Toronto

"I recently bought a car, from the dealership (after much research in person and on-line). It's a 1998 Isuzu Rodeo. It was a combination of need and 'spoil me' attitude. . . . Okay—it's yuppieish to have a 4 x 4, but I feel like my large dog and occasional sculpture distances me somewhat from the 'status seekers.'"

Tanya, thirty-year-old non-profit director, Halifax

"I just bought 3 tubes of M A C lipstick (it doesn't take much to make me happy). I bought them because I like the quality of the product—lasts long—and they have funky colours with great names (Diva, Media, Verve). The MAC clerks are very helpful and you actually try on the colour before you buy it."

Denise, twenty-nine-year-old scholarship administrator, Ottawa

"Last week I bought a Bauhaus couch (sofa bed for all those coming to visit!). I got it from the ol' reliable Bay store (hey— it was on sale). I bought it to replace my smelly old futon. Futons are for poor students who drink beer. I wanted a couch for the professional woman who drinks Perrier. . . ."

Matt, thirty-year-old TV producer, Toronto

"I don't think the used dishwasher I bought will make it into the book. . . ."

The goal of this chapter is to show why Nexus consumers like these are a key engine of our economy, and also how marketers and retailers can learn to connect with them. To counter some of the biases about this generation's relevance as shoppers, we'll begin by demonstrating the purchasing potential of Nexus and its willingness to indulge in conspicuous consuming. We'll then discuss some of the buying patterns of this generation, the most important being its attraction to what we call "experiential consumption." Next, we'll consider some of the challenges associated with reaching Nexus the Consumer and suggest how to overcome them. Finally, we'll position Nexus as a potential guide to understanding the future of consumption: shopping trends, retail formats, and marketing strategies. In the ever-changing world of buying and selling, this generation can provide a link between the old Industrial Age shopper and the savvy, new Information Age consumer. The first step in planning for tomorrow is to understand the opportunities and challenges that Nexus the Consumer presents today.

[Show Me the Money]

Forget Nexus consumers. They're the poorest segment of the market. They have the misfortune of being born into the wrong demographic group. Even if they do like your clever advertising, they're not in a position to make any significant purchases.

That's the essence of the argument put forth by Klaus Rohrich, president of Toronto-based Maturity Marketing, in the January 1998 edition of *Marketing* magazine. Rohrich claims that advertisers need to stop "taking years off their image in an attempt to reach younger markets" and start focusing on the needs of the aging population. Agencies that fail to adjust, he contends, will "soon find themselves in the company of the dodo or the carrier pigeon."[1]

Many within the advertising and retail world have already taken Rohrich's advice to heart. Indeed, for the past several years, marketers have been on a quest to capture what David Foot positions as the real cherry in the consumption pie: the Baby Boomers. Whether it's through Bob Dylan background music or the prominent sponsorship role of Candice Bergen, advertisers appear bent on profiting from this famous generation as it moves through the key stages of life. In her book *Marketing to Generation X*, Karen Ritchie shows how the targeting of this wealthy demographic bulge has been reinforced by Boomers themselves, who have risen through the ranks to head up ad agencies or creative teams. In writing about her own experiences, Ritchie describes how the sheer weight of the Boomer cohort was often the deciding factor between a successful or unsuccessful marketing concept. "I, like many other marketers, had learned how to take a quick initial read on the potential of a new product, a new media opportunity, or a new campaign by asking one simple question: Will Boomers like it?"[2]

We believe the obsession with affluent thirty-five- to fifty-year-olds is too narrowly focused, and tends to downplay the consumer power of the cohort coming *after* the boom. Contrary to the stereotypes, younger consumers bring more to the table than debt and low salaries. Let's have a look at some of the opportunities the Nexus Generation offers for those in the business of selling or marketing.

The Power to Purchase

The first fact to re-emphasize is the sheer size of this generation. Within Canada, those born between the early sixties and late seventies number just under eight million. When you take these figures and combine them with average income, that translates into approximately $104 billion[3] in after-tax purchasing power per year.

And when you discount everyday living expenses, that leaves a fair amount of cash for conspicuous consumption.

Take Mr. N, an average twenty-seven-year-old single Canadian male with an income of $23,961. When you subtract the standard expenses for taxes, CPP/UI, housing, and food, Mr. N is left with a yearly disposable income of $13,473. Now let's take Mr. B, an average forty-four-year-old married Canadian male who has an income of $40,877. When you subtract his standard expenses (which include mortgage payments and child-rearing costs), Mr. B. is left with $17,478 in discretionary spending.[4] The relatively small gap between these figures suggests that marketers should be cautious about "adding years" to their advertising programs. Although the Nexus Generation is frequently left in the shadow of the larger Baby Boom segment, it is a significant source of spending dollars *in its own right*. More important, it is unlikely to be inspired by Maturity Marketing's campaigns for the "aging population."

The comparison between Mr. N and Mr. B also picks up on a notion we introduced for you in Chapter 3: this generation's extended freedom zone. Because young Canadians are marrying, having kids, and buying homes later than they did in the past, they have fewer financial commitments beyond "me, myself, and I." Even at their modest income levels—$20,023 on average for the age group as a whole—Nexus consumers often have more spending money at their fingertips. This is particularly true for younger women, who are less likely than their Boomer counterparts to have children and more likely to have high salaries. In fact, when you compare income figures between Nexus and Boomer women, the differences between generations starts to shrink: although the gap in average income between Mr. N and Mr. B is $16,916, it is only $6,232 for Ms. N and Ms. B.[5] In other words, the freedoms gained by women over the last thirty years are starting to pay off for female members of the Nexus Generation.

Living for Today and Saving for Tomorrow

Another characteristic worth noting about Nexus the Consumer is that he's constantly battling between the present and the future. While the conditioned voice is warning him to put money away for an uncertain tomorrow, the reckless voice of youth is encouraging him to indulge in today.

Nexus' generational conditioning shares some similarities with the group of Canadians that grew up during the Depression. Recession, debts, and deficits have been the order of the day for members of this generation, and their exposure to government cut-backs has made them more financially self-reliant. This concern for the future is reflected in the size of the Nexus RRSP contribution pool. In 1995, Nexus Canadians contributed $4.5 billion (or $730 per person), compared with $9 billion for the much wealthier Boomers (or $1487 per person).[6] And as shown in the following chart, RRSP investments top this generation's wish list of big-ticket spending items. One twenty-eight-year-old d~Coder from Calgary claims that RRSPs are becoming the new topic of party conversation for Nexus—particularly during the peak spring buying season: "When you're standing around the kitchen at a house party, it's as normal for someone to ask, 'Did you max out this year?' as it is to ask, 'Did you see the Blue Rodeo concert?'"

In the next year, are you planning to buy or spend money on any of the following?

	Percentage who said yes	
	18 to 34	35 to 54
Renovations to your home	31	44
A vacation	62	62
Furniture or appliances	47	39
A computer	35	31

Investment in RRSPS	64	71
Investments other than RRSPS	44	45
Home entertainment (stereo/TV)	37	25
Children's education	28	46
Personal education	62	41
Elder care	19	25
A car	36	23

Source: Canadian Big Ticket Purchase/Royal Bank, January 1998

It seems that Canadian financial institutions have yet to grasp the potential of this generation to contribute to their bottom line. The *Building Bridges* research showed that only 10 per cent of Nexus are satisfied with their level of long-term savings, and that most are keenly interested in planning for their financial futures.[7] Yet many within Nexus refuse to seek help from banks, complaining about a lack of respect and poor customer service. Chris, a thirty-year-old d~Coder from Ottawa, describes a common problem faced by members of this generation when trying to secure a line of credit. "The adviser turned me down, claiming that because I had moved and switched jobs three times I was somehow 'unstable.' He didn't seem to realize that in each case, I had made the change in order to increase my salary and enhance my skills. That is how most people my age think." Cheryl Stern, president of Stern Marketing, has discovered the same problems south of the border: "Banks have the view of Xers that they're still walking around with a tattoo and a nose ring and that they're only thinking about what movie they're going to rent that night. . . . They've got to wake up and get worried because they're not in touch with this emerging generation that holds their long-term future and viability."[8] Perhaps financial institutions should stop marketing their investment products only to the Boomers and think about a designing a Nexus-friendly mutual fund.

On the other hand, Nexus is heavily swayed by the recklessness gene, which urges it to "seize the moment." Remember Tanya's lipstick and Ryan's Tintin watch? Even though members of this generation are worried about ever having enough money to pay off debts or buy a house, they're still willing to shell out cash for the small luxuries of life: $2.50 for a morning latte or $5.00 a week for their favourite magazine. One of our authors—who will go un-named—likes to indulge in the occasional massage and sushi lunch at Holt Renfrew.

The love of small luxuries is true even for students, who, despite legendary stories of surviving on Kraft Dinner and peanut butter, engage in frequent acts of impulsive consumption. Eric Weil, publisher of a newsletter for advertisers interested in the university market, estimates that the typical monthly student budget can be broken down as follows: food (32 per cent), debt (18 per cent), car (13 per cent), clothing (8 per cent), telephone (6 per cent), and other (23 per cent).[9] Given the size of the "other" category, it's not surprising that universities themselves are trying to get in on the act. The University of Regina recently remodelled and expanded its campus bookstore and food hall to try to grab a piece of the student spending pie.

Research consistently provides evidence of the saving-spending tension running through Nexus. Refer back to the chart and you'll see that members of this generation frequently lump long- and short-term purchases together: investments, a vacation, new stereo equipment, a car. (It's also worth pointing out that in several categories, they have a greater intention to buy than their Boomer counterparts.) We think this tug of war within Nexus' wallet is good news for the consumer industry. Product developers and marketers should be on the lookout for a generation of consumers that is ready to spend—even if personal purse strings remain tight.

"You Can Never Run Out of Cash"

Before we leave the topic of money, it's worth touching on some of the factors that make spending easier for this generation. One innovation that is driving the volume and pace of Nexus consumer activity is the automated teller machine (the successor to that now-endangered species, the live bank person). For the parents of Nexus, consumption patterns were dictated to some degree by the amount of available cash they had; if they missed getting to the bank on payday or during business hours, or if they didn't have a spare hour on a Friday to wait in line, they often had to forgo some of life's pleasures. Nexus, on the other hand, has been raised on the "you can never run out of cash" mantra—all you need to do is get yourself to the nearest bank machine. With cash flow less of an issue, the opportunities for impulse buying multiply.

Another factor contributing to Nexus' spending habits is its more relaxed attitude to credit and debt. An obvious example of this, which we've discussed already, is the heavy debt load being carried by many members of Nexus from their post-secondary education. In 1998, the average student-loan debt on graduation was $25,000, five times what it was in 1982. And because of the tight job market that greeted Nexus when it left school, many of those who were unable to follow the Boomers into a secure career path are now facing personal bankruptcy. To quote West Coast journalist Jennifer Nicholson: "We are living in an age of credit. And where there is easy credit, debt will follow. We can vow never to buy anything or do anything . . . unless we have the cash in our pockets. Or we can transform debt into a manageable tool, one we use consciously, rather than letting it use us."[10]

Most within the generation have accepted the reality of debt and refuse to let it rule their universe of consumption. In the *Building Bridges* research, we found that two-thirds of respondents

115

agreed with the following statement: "While sometimes I am anxious and concerned about my financial situation, I still feel I have the freedom to do most of the things I want." Moreover, consumer research demonstrates that Nexus is less willing to postpone a purchase and more willing to use credit than older-age groups.[11] While low credit-card balances may have been conditioned into the parents of Nexus, members of this generation appear more comfortable living in the red.

A good example of a company that *has* grasped the spending potential of Nexus the Consumer is American Express. Its new Amex Blue Card, which is targeted at consumers between twenty-five and thirty-five, is designed to make spending easy and help those who "want more out of life." In the words of Susan Austin, director of advertising for Amex Bank of Canada: "This generation thinks our traditional charge card is just for their father." They are looking for a product that is fun and upbeat.[12] With the blue card, Amex has managed to excel in both product and delivery. The card offers no annual fees, low introduction rates, and Front-of-the-Line privileges for Nexus members. In addition, the approach to marketing is fresh and unique. It delivers a typically downbeat message—how to manage money—in an innovative and positive way.

Companies like Amex recognize that locking in Nexus today could pay off in the future as younger consumers begin to deepen their pockets. This gamble is particularly common in the world of student marketing, where companies believe that if a consumer chooses their brand for some of his first big purchases—an airline ticket, a mattress, a car, a credit card, or a long-distance service—there's a chance that he'll stay with them for life. As pointed out in an *American Demographics* article on the student market, companies like Toyota, Sony, and AT&T aren't making "just a first date come-on"; they're offering the full marriage proposal.[13]

Making these strategies even more compelling are other demographic and social trends that could favourably impact on the income of Nexus in the decades ahead. First, as shown in a recent Royal Bank study, Nexus is likely to benefit from an "inheritance windfall," whereby parents leave bags of investment savings to their children. The older members of Nexus will start to cash in around 2008, while those under thirty will start to ride their inheritance wave around 2022. And because families have become smaller, the new generation of inheritors will be splitting this larger pie in fewer pieces. The second projected benefit for Nexus surrounds the much-anticipated years of government surpluses. Members of this generation could stand to gain from a return to balanced budgets, either through tax cuts or through programs designed to improve their economic fortunes.[14] In sum, while unemployment is still hitting part of this demographic hard today, Nexus is well positioned to benefit from a wealth transfer in the future.

[Experiential Consumers]

If Nexus is willing and able to play the consumption game, what items is she looking for? Our own d~Coders helped provide the answer. Whether it's cars, couches, or animal crackers, Nexus consumers are looking for more than just "stuff." They're looking for an *experience*.

The Intangibles: Work Hard—Play Harder

Some of the products most likely to attract Nexus the Consumer today are the "little things" in life: soft drinks, fast food, cigarettes, alcohol, music, and movies. For example, consumer data reveal that Nexus is well above average in its purchase of cassette tapes and compact discs (65 per cent of eighteen- to thirty-four-year-olds bought these items in the last twelve months) and its rental of videotapes (64 per cent of Nexus Canadians rented a movie in the last thirty days).[15]

Figures like these suggest that one key feature of Nexus consumers is a thirst for the intangibles: leisure and entertainment. While the credo of the workaholic eighties was "live to work," many within this generation "work to live." An analysis of the *Building Bridges* survey showed that the "amount of money I have available to spend on leisure and entertainment" related most strongly to Nexus respondents' quality of life, ahead of other contributors such as "my relationship with my family" or "my career choice."[16] Perhaps that's why in Canada members of Nexus are emerging as the primary creators and consumers of media and entertainment, and the major consumers of sports and leisure clothing (ahead of the Boomers).[17]

Given their youthful generational genes, it should come as no surprise that Nexus consumers are more interested than the average Canadian in leisure spots such as cinemas and amusement parks, and more likely to engage in physical activities like in-line skating, canoeing, ice hockey, and skiing.[18] It is interesting to note, however, that there is some backlash against the 1980s glitzy health-club scene and a desire to find a no-nonsense approach to physical activity. "The problem with the Boomers," according to a twenty-nine-year-old d~Coder from Vancouver, "is that they made physical fitness too much like *work*. We all thought we had to run from our offices to the gym to get in those forty minutes of 'cardio,' or to take three months of lessons to become the ultimate skier. My generation approaches this whole scene differently—it is much less regimented." In fact, when it comes to sport, we think the two distinguishing features of this generation are chaos and camaraderie. Nexus is much less interested in pure physical fitness, and more concerned with fulfilling its thirst for experience. Let's consider an "extreme" example.

Members of Nexus have eagerly embraced the new movement of so-called extreme sports, which are defined by Peter Beyak, executive producer of Extreme IMAX films, as "sports which by their very nature present ever-increasing challenges to go further." Nexus has jumped into activities such as skateboarding, rock climbing, snowboarding, and downhill mountain biking, often with little or no formal training. The key benefits, according to Beyak, are a connection with nature, a sense of independence, and personal accomplishment. "Everyone has their own idea of what 'extreme' can be for them."

In his book *Playing the Future*, Douglas Rushkoff aptly captures the chaotic thinking that dominates these kinds of physical activities: "Think of the way a trained, adult skier tackles a slope. With nimble finesse, he avoids obstacles in order to glide smoothly down the hill. . . . The techniques involve steering and, when necessary, slowing down. A snowboarder, in contrast, thrashes his way down the slope [and] intentionally seeks out the most dangerous nooks and crannies. No poles; just raw balance. Rough spots are his dominion."[19] What's also interesting about skateboarding, mountain biking, and snowboarding is that while they allow expressions of individuality—in everything from clothing to stickers—they are also highly communal sports. The participant loses himself in the camaraderie of the pack. This same Nexus desire "to be part of something" applies to professional sports; younger Canadians are the most likely age cohort to be spectators at sporting events, despite the significant rise in ticket prices.[20]

But the Nexus Generation's quest for experience is perhaps best reflected in its insatiable appetite for travel. In our earlier discussion of globalization, we observed that Nexus Canadians are the most well-travelled young generation to date, and that they are keen followers of global fashion and music trends. Whether it's through vacations to far-flung places or long stints of living and working abroad, young Canadians are taking advantage of a world where there are fewer and fewer restrictions on freedom of movement.

What's critical to underline is that Nexus has taken its travel aspirations one step beyond that of the Boomers. Members of this generation seek out *meaningful* journeys that will change their attitudes as well as their surroundings. According to Chris Frey, publisher of the Canadian magazine *Outpost,* "Travel for this generation is a part of life, not a vacation from life. It's all about immersing yourself in a global environment." Despite being raised on TV shows like "The Love Boat," Nexus seems to be steering clear of cruises and package tours in favour of do-it-yourself adventures that offer exposure to different ways of living and working. Furthermore, the rise of global media has made it easier for today's traveller to participate—in real time—in social and political change. Members of Nexus are on the lookout for experiences like the fall of the Berlin Wall or the end of white rule in South Africa, which provide them with a chance to be a part of history in the making.

Another of the hot new travel magazines, *Blue,* picks up on the Nexus desire for chaos and camaraderie. In the words of founder Amy Schrier, "At *Blue* we have attracted people who share values and interests revolving around global travel, environmental consciousness and action sports."[21] The magazine describes exotic destinations that go well beyond the preferred Boomer hang-outs of the Caribbean, Florida, or Europe to the true "hot spots" of the world: Burma, Bhutan, and Kazakhstan, for example. *Blue* also features a travel-gear section (which focuses on snowboards and wet suits), as well as a world-music review from countries like Angola and Senegal.

Another travel-and-adventure phenomenon that has captivated members of Nexus is the Eco Challenge, a wilderness competition that brings together co-ed teams from around the world for a three-hundred-mile journey using mountain bikes, white-water rafts, canoes, horses, and climbing ropes. First run in 1995, the Eco Challenge has been held in back-country lands across the globe, including British Columbia. The aim is to combine adventure sports with teamwork and an environmental message. During the 1996 challenge in B.C., competitors joined with local residents to clean up a polluted salmon-spawning sanctuary. Eco Challenge has recently opened up to non-racers, offering them a self-guided experience using the same locations, facilities, and sports activities as regular competitors. For those in search of chaos and camaraderie, this is the ultimate in adventure travel.

Beyond the leisure outlets of sports and travel, Nexus has patented one final form of experiential consumption: clubbing or bar-hopping. In his study of nightclub life, academic Ben Malbon describes how clubs offer young people a space in which to express themselves and forge a temporary connection with others.[22] The bar scene is in many ways a reaction to the impact that modern city life has had on Nexus' sense of identity and belonging. Many within this generation have had to relocate to where the jobs are, and are faced with a cold, fast-paced environment in their daily work lives. The social spaces they encounter in urban settings—subway platforms, traffic lights, underground malls—are what Malbon rightly calls "more fleeting spaces than meeting places."[23] While bars and nightclubs offer a venue in which to interact with others socially, they don't require membership commitments or stringent rules of behaviour. In addition, many clubs pride themselves on providing a hybrid of music to appeal to a wide range of tastes. One thirty-two-year-old member of our network, Roger, describes the experience this way: "The communal ethic is the best part of the club scene. You feel part of something, but it isn't based on conformity. You can be an individual without feeling lonely."

Clubbing also offers Nexus a total experience, an encounter of mind and body. This kind of emotional and sensual release can help members of the generation overcome feelings of isolation and give them a break from the pressures that dominate their daylight hours. In other words, it's really the *atmosphere* that Nexus is consuming: the music, the people, the physical activity, and the social interaction. As Malbon puts it, the bar crowd contains "both the producers and the consumers of the experience."[24] And the evidence shows that they are willing to pay big bucks for it (the average price of a cocktail in a club is six dollars, not to mention the cover charge that often accompanies entry). It's no wonder that other kinds of retail establishments, such as coffee shops, are also trying to leverage this craving for atmosphere. Check out the comfy couches in Second Cup.

The Tangibles: Material Boys and Girls

Lest you think Nexus consumption is all about doing things or going places, it's worth pointing out that members of this generation are adults. Remember Leah's car and Denise's couch? At some point, the stability gene kicks in, driving them to the same big-ticket items as any other adult. But even in this realm, the experiential nature of Nexus consumers shines through.

First, let's look at some of the traditional consumption items for homes and apartments. Consumer data shows that eighteen- to thirty-four-year-olds are just as likely as Boomers to have purchased household appliances in the last twelve months. The most popular items are fairly predictable: washing machines and dryers, fridges, water filters, and—yes, Matt—dishwashers. Nexus Canadians are also heavy consumers of smaller electrical appliances such as irons, toasters, coffee-makers, and blenders; almost half (44 per cent) of eighteen- to thirty-four-year-olds purchased these items in the last twelve months. Given their craving for music and videos, it's no surprise that Nexus Canadians are more likely, on average, to have bought audio/visual equipment such as stereos, CD players, video machines, or televisions in the last year.[25]

For some within this generation, preoccupation with the home goes well beyond basic fixings into the realm of the artistic. Even if Nexus can't afford to buy the big house with the three-car garage, what she puts in her rented apartment has to provide an "experience." *Wallpaper**, a new magazine sensation started by Winnipeg-born Tyler Brûlé, plays on the disposable income of this generation and its desire to embellish its comfort zone. According to Brûlé, the vision was to create a publication that could redefine "what it means to live in a city . . . about great food, interiors, seeing the world, mixed seamlessly with fashion and everything."[26] The magazine's slogan is "The stuff that surrounds you," and it features an eclectic collection of objects and artifacts—all arranged with perfect precision by the best photographers. Some professionals in the magazine industry criticize *Wallpaper** for lacking substance and focus, but the appeal for this generation can't be denied: Douglas Coupland recently contributed an article, and copies of *Wallpaper** now conspicuously grace the cash-register counters at stores like Banana Republic. The magazine was recently acquired by Time Warner and is now sold in more than fifty countries.

Let's consider another highly traditional "adult" product: the engagement or wedding ring. Despite the extended freedom zone of Nexus, the buying of rings is a traditional ritual that is poised to survive generational differences. As we saw in the previous chapter, members of this generation place a heavy premium on commitment and believe they will have longer-lasting relationships than their parents did. Nevertheless, there are two factors that differentiate this generation of jewellery buyers: who is doing the buying and what the rings actually look like.

In the past, the male partner would usually shop for the engagement ring on his own, and would choose from what was available in the store. But according to Brent Trepel, president and CEO of Winnipeg-based Ben Moss Jewelers, the trend today is for couples to share in this important buying experience. And rather than buying from existing inventory, they tend to mix and match from available designs or to fully customize their rings. Even those who do opt for an official engagement ring often choose a contemporary dinner ring or band of diamonds, rather than the traditional solitaire. In order to meet the changing preferences of younger consumers, jewellers like Ben Moss have had to adopt a much more customer-driven process.

Another interesting trend is for the two partners to exchange the same band, often in a simple unisex design that they have created. Two of our d~Coders, Grant and Gill, bought their silver bands on a trip to the West Coast and chose two Native Canadian engravings, the Raven and the Killer Whale, to symbolize their personalities. "We knew instinctively that we didn't want any diamonds or gems. . . . Rather than following the traditions or rules set before us by our parents or much of our culture, we tried to find ways to express what coming together meant to us as two individuals."

Finally, it's important to remember that Nexus the Consumer can be a lucrative target for the major car companies. Here, too, the need to experience as well as consume is a key characteristic of Nexus shoppers. To date, however, there have been only a few designs and models on the market that speak to that desire. The Pontiac Sunfire offers younger consumers access to a sports-car experience at an entry-level price. The Chrysler Neon is a quality-made but inexpensive car for young drivers that comes in vibrant colours and with an environmentally friendly design. And the Volkswagen Jetta gives Nexus buyers a link to their favourite leisure pursuits, through alliances with Trek mountain bikes and K2 skis and snowboards. By joining forces with two sports-equipment leaders, Volkswagen has been able to broaden and deepen the experience of owning a Jetta.

One more intriguing car to consider is the new Volkswagen Beetle, a product that seems to have caused attitudinal genes to cross over the standard age divide. Dubbed the ultimate Boomermobile by the mainstream media, the Beetle offers a compelling consumer experience for Nexus as well: quirkiness, a sense of rebellion, and emotional appeal. Steve Wilhite, senior marketing executive for Volkswagen, explains the phenomenon in this way: "Consider a fifty-year-old investment banker walking down the sidewalk, and an eighteen-year-old with multiple body piercings walking towards him. Now, these people would probably avoid each other, or even cross the street to get away from each other, and you would expect them to have nothing in common. However, they do share a common reaction to the Beetle. The banker might remember the first time he had sex in the back of an old Beetle or some cross-country adventure. The eighteen-year-old has no memory of the sixties but thinks the car is cool and different." For VW, there is no generational targeting going on. It would appear that the experience of owning a Beetle speaks for itself.

[It's a Tough Crowd]

To sum up so far, members of the Nexus Generation constitute a powerful source of spending in today's economy. They are also highly experiential consumers who identify themselves and their values through their purchases. But retailers and marketers beware: Before you declare victory for a glorious future of consumption, there are some challenging features of Nexus consumers that make them hard to hold on to. Three in particular are worth singling out: experimentation, sophistication, and fragmentation.

Experimentation

Though there may be a large Nexus market to attract, establishing long-term loyalty is the real challenge. Think back to the hair-trigger thumb of Nexus. This is an experience-seeking and channel-surfing generation that embraces change effortlessly and bores easily. It is also a generation that has been inundated with "new and improved" versions of products. For some of those, like Tide and Coke, Nexus can't really see the difference. But for others, like software upgrades, the new version *is* the real thing.

As a result of their experimental nature, Nexus consumers tend to describe themselves as less brand loyal. They readily admit that in sectors like grocery and retail, they are open to change if the price, value, and image are right. Asked in consumer research about their brand loyalty, Nexus consumers turned out to be less likely than older Canadians to agree with the statement "Once I find a brand I like, I stick with it," and more likely to admit that "I tend to pass up my favourite brand if something else is on sale."[27]

Innovators like Vancouver-based Urban Juice and Soda have accepted Nexus' experimental nature and even tried to leverage it. "In connecting with younger consumers," says thirty-four-year-old company president Peter Van Stolk, "the first thing you have to do is accept that you are playing a new generational game. The old rules don't apply." Rather than banking on long-term loyalty, he advises, let brands die when their time is up and be ready with the next fresh one. Van Stolk's core product, Jones Soda, is interactive and ever-changing. "You can't make a single claim about your product," he argues. "The consumer has to do that in his own mind." That experimental philosophy has led Van Stolk to place Jones where other sodas aren't—in record stores and tattoo parlours. Customers are asked to send in photos they took themselves, and Jones grafts these on to the soda bottles, a campaign that has generated more than five hundred different versions of Jones Soda. This approach has also given the product a real "soul" or personality—something that can't be fabricated in an office tower.

Still, despite the challenges of experimentation, loyalty isn't impossible to achieve. There's no doubt, for instance, that in some key image-making categories—jeans, running shoes, or cigarettes—Nexus consumers define themselves through core brands. Why is it that younger consumers will shell out $150 for a pair of Diesel jeans? What explains the current surge in demand for tattoos, an image cemented for a lifetime? Drew, a twenty-eight-year-old TV producer who is part of our network, describes it best: "Nexus consumers are looking for *some* measure of stability and consistency in their lives. A brand can become an anchor in a sea of change." If a product can offer a compelling philosophy—like Diesel's hard-core approach to "Successful Living" or Calvin Klein's "Just Be"—Nexus is likely to take it on board.

One thing is clear: given the channel-surfing tendencies of Nexus consumers, companies can no longer rest on their laurels with one product or slogan. Brands that try to say in a definitive way "We stand for Z" are less likely to resonate with the Nexus Generation. Instead, the companies that have succeeded with this age group have developed a strong core identity that ties into a lifestyle or a philosophy, but also allows for multiple individual expressions. Volkswagen's "Drivers Wanted," Molson's "I Am Canadian," and Nike's original "Just Do It" campaigns are great examples. In all three cases, the basic brand has a personality, which is multidimensional and flexible and indicates that the company has moved beyond treating consumers like marketing statistics.

For Volkswagen, the success of the campaign lies in its engaging and unpretentious message: "On the road of life, there are passengers and there are drivers. Drivers wanted." According to Wilhite, this statement is genuine, straightforward, and inspirational. "It appeals to those who seek to be in charge, in control, and seek new experiences. This attitude can manifest itself in many ways, and we see it in people who demonstrate independence and a real zest for life." For Volkswagen, the product is about experimentation, and the customer can give it any individual meaning she wants.

Molson's "I Am Canadian" campaign was another interesting illustration of how to promote a state of mind, rather than a static brand image. This campaign helped to break the mould of the "stupid beer commercial" by offering a powerful but subtle core philosophy and a constantly changing application. Whether its focus was a backpacker returning from a trip to Europe or Paul Henderson's 1972 goal against the Russians, "I Am Canadian" was the first beer marketing initiative to connect with young Canadians' sense of pride in their country and themselves. It was able to portray Canada in a contemporary way, with all of its diversity and complexity.

Nike's approach, meanwhile, draws on the wisdom of psychologist Abraham Maslow's hierarchy of needs[28]: recognize that all humans have basic requirements around self-esteem and a sense of belonging, and ensure that your communications address those needs. The original "Just Do It" campaign touched these emotional triggers by inspiring Nike buyers to experiment and define themselves in whatever way they saw fit. Its new series, "I Can," appears to be following the same strategy.

The recent changes in Nike's advertising raise a final point: no matter how flexible a campaign or brand, even the great ones have a shelf life. As Nike's "Just Do It" campaign proliferated across continents and on sporting-goods products, it became harder and harder to convince consumers that they could give it their own unique spin. Marketing guru Jean-Marie Dru insists that the best strategy for keeping pace in a world of constant change and experimental consumers is to embrace the tool of "disruption": continuously look for ways to create new phases in the life of a brand. Dru believes this is the only way to speak to a generation that "hates being labelled" and quickly tires of the "image advertisers try to project of them."[29]

Sophistication

The second complicating feature of Nexus the Consumer is her high level of knowledge about buying and selling. Consumer sophistication began with the Boomers, but has intensified among today's cohort of young Canadians.

One driver of Nexus consumer savvy was the "latch-key" experience of its formative years. Many within this generation were exposed to consumption early on in life—through buying groceries after school or dealing with the plumber who came over to fix a leaky faucet. Those who did go shopping with Mom and Dad might remember playing "The Price Is Right" at the cash register, trying to guess the bill total before the store clerk rang it in. This shopping apprenticeship period prepared Nexus well for later life, when it became the primary consumer voice for key household items like the microwave, the VCR, or the computer. Kevin, a thirty-year-old d~Coder from Vancouver, recalls his experience with the family microwave: "Given that I was going to be the dominant user—warming up pizza after school—I was the one to choose all the cool features. I was also the only one in the family who had any clue how to program it and use it."

The next key contributor to consumer sophistication is that members of this generation don't see business—or profit—as mysterious. Part of this knowledge came through the media, where

Nexus consumers have learned about issues ranging from the fluctuating value of the Canadian dollar to the uncovering of consumer scams. Most, however, developed their business savvy firsthand. By the time they reached the age of eighteen, Nexus men *and* women were likely to have had at least four or five part-time jobs, most often in the retail or service sector. In fact, Strauss and Howe report that they constitute "the biggest child labor generation since the days of turn-of-the-century newsboys and garment girls."[30] These early McJobs (as Coupland might have called them) gave members of Nexus a chance to be on the other side of the cash register, learning about things like mark-ups and discounts. But it also gave them spending money to engage in their own bouts of consumption.

The final contributing factor to the sophistication of Nexus the Consumer is access to information. By using the media skills we discussed in the last chapter, Nexus gathers its own inside intelligence on every consumer good imaginable, from the price of discount flights to Florida to the memory capacity of a Dell computer. Members of this generation have become confident in their ability to mine the marketplace and gather the information they need to make the right purchasing decision. As a result of this self-directed research, Nexus frequently believes (rightly or wrongly) it has got the best bang for its buck. It is interesting to observe, for example, that when asked to characterize themselves, 28 per cent of Nexus respondents agreed with statement "I consider myself to be sophisticated," while only 19 per cent of fifty- to sixty-four-year-olds did so.[31]

The effects of Nexus consumer sophistication can be seen in its interactions with store clerks and customer-service staff, as it questions quality or bargains over price. But it is also manifest in the disdain many Nexus consumers have for in-your-face service cultures. Whether it's senior-citizen greeters at Wal-Mart, chatty cappuccino chefs at Starbucks, stiff hellos at Blockbuster, or smiling doormen at Holt Renfrew, sales and service staff are falling all over themselves to make up for years of indifference to customers. Most Nexus consumers we've talked to perceive this touchy-feely stuff as not only invasive, but also lacking in sincerity. It also tends to remind them of the days (not so long ago) when store clerks followed them around as suspected shoplifters. This is a generation that would rather do it alone. If it needs help, it will ask. And when it asks, you'd better be there.

The problem in trying to go head to head with the sophisticated Nexus consumer is that he often won't tell you what you're doing wrong. He'll simply go somewhere else—leaving you wondering whether the problem was the quality of your sales staff, the ingredients in your products, or the location of your factories. This act of "protesting with their feet" is something we'll come back to later in our discussions of Nexus the Employee and Nexus the Citizen. For now, suffice it to say that the best means of addressing the challenge of savvy-ness is to be better, faster, and smarter at developing and communicating your stuff.

Fragmentation

The third challenge facing those trying to connect with Nexus consumers is fragmentation. As we pointed out in the Introduction, this generation is highly diverse and increasingly difficult to segment into clear-cut categories. Age, income level, gender, ethnicity, geographic location, travel experience, exposure to technology, and educational background all have an impact on quality of life, societal attitudes, and consumption patterns. The segmentation challenges that we've experienced at d~Code have been encountered by others as well. Do you recall Michael Adams's division of so-called Generation X into five different "tribes," ranging from Aimless Dependents to Thrill-Seeking Materialists? This contrasts with the four segments of Boomers (a larger demographic) and the three segments Adams used to divide the over-fifty-five age group.

In addition, while the media tends to depict "youth" as a particular community, with shared interests and attributes, young people themselves are resisting these stereotypes and carving out their own unique communities. In contrast to the membership-driven groups their parents belong to—the Optimist Club or the golf club—Nexus communities are continually forming and re-forming to match the nomadic lifestyle of this generation. In their book *Cool Places: Geographies of Youth Cultures*, geographers Tracey Skelton and Gill Valentine chronicle the experiences of Nexus in some of these fluid communities: bars, raves, hostels, coffee shops, and public spaces in major urban centres. No matter how brief the encounter, coming together in these spaces gives Nexus a sense of rootedness in a world that always seems to be changing and moving.[32]

This fragmenting of Nexus into smaller tribes that are bound together by a narrow set of interests means that a product or brand needs to speak to a wide variety of styles and situations. In order to take off, it will need to offer consumers more than one "way in." As we'll see a bit later on, that means using a broad cast of people, messages, and media.

Fragmentation also makes the traditional focus group a much less reliable way to understand the needs and preferences of Nexus consumers. Indeed, while focus groups are often trumpeted as a quick way to get feedback from the "general population," it's next to impossible to find a truly representative sample.[33] During a recent episode of CBC's "Venture," retailer Harry Rosen demonstrated the limitations of this tool when he rejected the creative campaigns generated from focus groups in favour of his own intuition about what works with consumers. Nike also believes its knowledge and deep intuition are superior to what it could get from qualitative research. Rather than endlessly testing slogans in focus groups, it trusts its ability to provoke just the right response in younger consumers.

So how do you develop this deep intuition about Nexus consumers? One of the most effective methods is to understand their daily, weekly, and yearly habits. The Folgers coffee slogan—"The best part of waking up"—is an example of a brand that made itself part of one of the most basic human activities. The same approach can be taken with the rituals that help members of Nexus define themselves and find commonality with others. A few examples from our d~Coders include cramming for exams at university, stopping for coffee on the way to work, collecting money to buy beer, playing Ultimate Frisbee, long weekends, watching the Oscars, spring break, tree-planting, or backpacking abroad. Discovering the rituals of Nexus the Consumer offers a powerful means of communicating to this generation.

Mike Rapino, director of marketing for Labatt's, describes how his organization has tried to put this philosophy into practice. The marketing team at Labatt's regularly goes on outings to Nexus hang-outs and clothing stores to understand what the generation is doing, thinking, and feeling. By keenly observing the rituals of its target consumers, Labatt's believes it is better able to evolve to meet their needs. One of the TV spots in the 1998 "Out of the Blue" campaign, which featured a group of young people racing shopping carts down a busy street, is one product of this methodology. Unfortunately, the ad was pulled after several people complained that it promoted "reckless" behaviour in young people.

A more calculated way to develop deep intuition about Nexus consumers is to adopt some of the techniques of database marketing. Database marketers rely on key life-stage events or "moments of truth" that serve as triggers for consumption. In financial services, these might include getting married, buying a house, or sending a kid off to college. The challenge with Nexus, of course, is that its members are experiencing these things later in life—or in a different order. Nevertheless, they do face intense transitional periods that are no less monumental: leaving home, sexual exploration, buying a car, paying off a student loan, changing jobs. Recognizing these "moments of truth"—which are often accompanied by great anticipation and release—may decrease the distance between marketers and a fragmented mass of Nexus consumers.

Once you've managed to make contact with Nexus consumers, the best way of forming a lasting connection with them is to treat each one as a unique individual, not as part of a segment. Ultimately, they're looking for a dialogue, not a monologue. This message of listening to customers and tailoring your product or service is delivered by Don Peppers and Martha Rogers in their book about building customer relationships.[34] But it is also the underlying philosophy behind one of the emerging trends in database marketing: remote dialogue. This technique leverages the Internet's capacity for two-way information-sharing in order to learn what individual customers like and dislike about a product or sales approach. Through ongoing dialogue, companies are able to tailor not just *how* they sell, but *what* they sell. Netscape experimented with a variation on this theme by having its customers participate in the evolution of its software packages. As keen users of Internet technology, Nexus consumers will increasingly be on the lookout for companies that can speak to them as individuals through this medium.

A final aspect of fragmentation refers back to something we highlighted in Chapter 3: the media saturation of Nexus. Because this generation has been bombarded with media from such a young age, its members have developed complex coping strategies for making sense of information. For most, that involves pulling information from multiple sources, rather than trusting any single source as definitive. When asked in the *Building Bridges* survey which sources strongly influenced their opinion on issues of the day, Nexus responses were well distributed: 39 per cent for television, 33 per cent for newspapers, 30 per cent for radio, 28 per cent for word of mouth, 16 per cent for magazines, and 12 per cent for the Internet.[35] This result should make marketers think twice about relying on one communication vehicle, or about sending inconsistent messages through different channels. Nexus is covering all the bases to assemble its version of the truth; you're only as good as the weakest link in your communications chain.

[The Future World of Buying and Selling]

As we move into the twenty-first century, a myriad of consumption scenarios seems possible. Will we live in a world where individuals (and societies) continue to lead indulgent lifestyles, or will more puritanical values take hold? Who will be accountable for providing key collective goods like education, health care, and clean air—the individual or society at large? Will tax relief give people more disposable income to spend on recreation and luxury goods? Will segments become meaningless and give way to one-on-one marketing? What will happen to the "green revolution"? What effect will the Internet have on commerce?

To help guide you through this uncertainty, we'd like to survey three important aspects of buying and selling that are already being influenced by the Nexus Generation: consumer trends, retail formats, and advertising.

Trends to Watch

First, let's look at some key consumption trends that Nexus is driving today and that could significantly impact the retail world of tomorrow.

Enviromentalism

Those born during the sixties and seventies were the first generation to grow up with recycling and conservation as second-nature activities. In the present day, that has translated into a keen Nexus interest in urban gardening, river clean-ups, and environmental businesses. It has also led to what d~Coder Jennifer Corson, who runs a used-building-supply store in Halifax, calls "reverse environmental mentoring": young people teaching their elders about the basics of green etiquette.

At the consumption level, however, the jury is still out. Some marketers seem bent on appealing to the green conscience of the Nexus Generation. Perhaps that's why rockers like the Tragically Hip use recycled-paper casings for their compact discs or why the Body Stop emphasizes its environmental standards. Yet it seems clear that this generation's sympathy with the environment is not borne out at the cash register. When asked whether they would be willing to pay a "reasonable extra price" for environmentally friendly products, only 39 per cent of Nexus respondents said yes— the lowest result for any age group.[36]

These numbers may be driven by the fact that many environmentally friendly products are expensive and hard to find. As a result, members of this generation are not likely to go out of their way to be on the side of the angels. Nexus consumers want green products only as long as they are equal in every other respect; they expect companies to be environmentally conscious without passing the cost on to them.

But there is also a deeper issue here: one of scepticism. As Karen Ritchie points out, this generation makes a big distinction between the act of recycling—something tangible an individual can do—and the purchase of recycled products. In the latter case, there is a middle person intervening who may or may not be green to the core. As Ritchie asks: "How do you know that an advertiser who claims his products are safer is not concealing something or ignorant of an element that will ultimately turn out to be worse than what we have now?"[37] Members of this generation are reluctant to take a marketing label about environmental safety at its word. Ultimately, Nexus is seeking a product where environmentalism is not hyped up as the key benefit, but is part and parcel of the whole.

Finally, as we'll see later, Nexus is a lot less likely to believe in grandiose solutions to social problems and more likely to focus on smaller, personal contributions like recycling. While individual actions can make a difference, this generation appears less optimistic than the Boomers about the ability to have large-scale impact through their choices and actions.

Do-It-Yourselfism

Another Nexus trend to watch is its love affair with customized products. This is a do-it-yourself generation that has taken control over its own destiny. Whether it be personally blended fragrances from the Body Shop or build-your-own furniture from IKEA, Nexus is demanding the tools to create its own unique solutions.

Many of our d~Coders believe do-it-yourselfism reflects a deeper Nexus desire to be unique and strike back against globalizing consumer fads. After all, just how many Benetton stores can you handle in one downtown core? Juggy, a twenty-four-year-old member of our network from British Columbia, argues that "Nexus rebels if what it thought was 'alternative' suddenly becomes marketed as mainstream. We are on a constant search for the *real* thing." The fall from grace of Molson's Red Dog beer is a case in point. Originally, Nexus consumers flocked to the product because they thought it was something new and unique; when they found out that it was just another big-brewery beer, sales began to plummet.

What is still uncertain, however, is whether this quest for individuality and customization is a generational attribute that will recede as Nexus grows older and becomes more "time poor." Do-it-yourselfism is extremely labour intensive, and may not survive higher incomes or the pressures of work and family. Nexus could just as easily follow the Boomers into the new cottage industry of personal services—from interior decorating to grocery-buying to dog-walking.

Multiculturalism

The third Nexus consumption pattern to watch is the propensity to "go global." As outlined in Chapter 2, this age group saw a multi-cultural explosion in its formative years owing to the impact of globalization. Nexus adults have built on that foundation through their frequent globe-trotting. The result is a generation accustomed to goods and services from around the world.

Here, foreign foods are an illuminating example. While Nexus might have spent his early childhood eating roast beef and seasonal vegetables, he is now likely to view Italian pasta and spicy foods as a regular part of Canadian food fare. Thanks to President's Choice and late-night take-out joints, foreign cuisine is no longer the prerogative of the rich and famous.

It's still unclear whether there will be a backlash against the globalization of consumption. Alongside the promises of the business community about the virtues of free trade, Nexus has heard the voices of those who encourage them to "buy Canadian." Given their attachment to local communities, Nexus Canadians may be fertile soil for these nationalistic messages. So far, however, the evidence is weak.

Retro-ism

Finally, it appears that Nexus consumption trends are closely mir-roring the retro lead of the fashion industry. Fashion has consis-tently borrowed from the past to create the future—be it bell-bottoms, wedge heels, or polyester shirts. But over the past decade, retro-ism has branched out into other areas, including architecture (three-storey brownstones), furniture (vinyl chairs and couches), home appliances (bread-makers), cars (the Beetle), candy (Pez and Gummy Bears), leisure pursuits (cigar and martini bars), reunion-concert tours (KISS and the Eagles)—even politics (conservative "family values").

In their book *Retro Hell: Life in the '70s and '80s,* the editors of *Ben Is Dead* magazine describe the "retro-ideal" as a new fact of life in the late twentieth century. Although the Industrial Age was all about progress, the Information Age has seen a backlash against this kind of linear thinking.[38] In the mid seventies and early eighties— the height of economic and political gloom—North American so-ciety began to reminisce fondly about the world of *American Graffiti* and *Grease,* allowing nostalgia to triumph over history. We haven't looked ahead since.

Today, younger consumers also look to a rose-coloured past to find familiarity in a world of constant change. The summer of 1989, for example, was rife with sixties memorabilia such as pot, the Doors, and tie-dye.[39] In recent years, there's been a similar revival of bubble chairs, disco music, satin shirts, tube tops, and down vests from that oh-so-unfashionable decade, the seventies. What better proof than the remarkable come-back of actor John Travolta, who has "morphed" from Vinnie Barbarino into Bill Clinton?

Now, we're sorry to say, the big nightclub fad is eighties retro. A recent comedy out on the cinema circuit, *The Wedding Singer,* features songs from eighties icons like Boy George and Duran

Duran, and a cameo appearance by Billy Idol. Will big hair, surfer wear, and shoulder pads come back too, or will Nexus stop this retro madness and forge some new styles for the future? It's still too soon to tell.

Retail Formats

As we look to the future, *where* Nexus buys will become as important as *what* Nexus buys. Innovations in formats are fundamentally changing the economics of retailing, as companies try to keep pace with the preferences and behaviours of a new breed of shopper. McKinsey and Company's Kathleen McLaughlin, who specializes in retail, estimates the average shelf life of a retail concept today is just four to five years—a third of what it was in the 1960s. "That means that retailers must repeatedly renew their formats to survive; in fact, the best retailers renew their formats continually."

Let's start by considering Nexus' relationship to traditional formats, and then move on to discuss the newest player on the scene: electronic commerce.

Bricks and Mortar

Currently, two "bricks and mortar" formats are fighting for survival in the marketplace. On the one hand, warehouses like IKEA and Home Depot and large discounters like Price Club and Zellers are meeting younger consumers' demands for reliable and cheap household goods. On the other hand, Nexus shoppers are turning to smaller, specialty-store formats for key items like music, audio/video equipment, computers, make-up, prescription drugs, and clothing—even when prices are higher.

So what does the future hold for all the formats in between these two extremes? Retail stars like the Gap have developed a winning compromise by providing a compelling retail concept that

140

grabs the attention of the Nexus Generation. Others, like the traditional department stores, seem to be struggling to find their place. To attract Nexus, retailers will need to provide a distinct experience. They can't be caught in the middle.

If we go back to the example of compact discs and cassettes, consumer data show that the specialty stores like HMV and Sam the Record Man are the top two choices for young buyers of music in Canada, despite the fact that prices are often cheaper at larger discount stores like Zellers.[40] The same preference for niche retailers can be seen in the cosmetics/beauty industry, where 73 per cent of eighteen- to twenty-four-year-olds chose specialty stores (like Jean Coutu or the Body Shop) and only 19 per cent chose traditional department stores.[41] Finally, it's worth noting that Nexus women are more likely than Boomers to choose specialty stores over department stores for their clothing and lingerie. This consumption behaviour helps account for the fact that while younger women buy clothes less frequently than Boomers, their average yearly expenditure ($529 a year for eighteen- to twenty-four-year-olds) is higher.[42]

There are two factors pushing Nexus consumers to more niche-oriented formats for their favourite consumption items. The first, touched on earlier, is that Nexus is as interested in consuming atmosphere as it is products. The bookstore chain Chapters has clearly recognized this desire and is offering its shoppers a chance to turn consumption into a two-hour leisure activity: stop in for a coffee, sit on the couch, read some magazines, and buy a few books.

To understand this phenomenon, recall that many in this generation were raised in the shadows of that big retail format innovation: the shopping mall. As the authors of *Retro Hell* describe it, the mall was "a vast, timeless void at the navel of soulless Suburbia. It sheltered us, provided for us, and eventually employed us." It was the place where Nexus went to hang out with friends, to find protection from the cold, or simply to "be seen." But as members of this generation grew older, and "money came to matter more than mis-chief," they began to see malls "for the empty shells they were."[43]

Today, the smaller niche stores—found on Robson St. in Van-couver, Queen St. in Toronto, and rue St. Denis in Montreal—are pulling younger consumers away from the malls and meeting their need for uniqueness and a "real" shopping experience.

The second critical piece of the puzzle is that Nexus the Con-sumer is faced with a tyranny of choice. No doubt about it. There is simply more stuff on the market today than there was two decades ago. If you want taco chips, you can choose from twenty different varieties—some baked, some fried, some with cheese, some with salsa. If you want jeans, there are literally hundreds of brands and styles to choose from. And if you want CDs . . . well, you get the picture.

Any format innovation that can educate young consumers and help them work their way through the maze will likely be a big hit with this generation. According to Mike Arseneault, national ad-vertising manager for HMV Canada, young music consumers who choose to buy through a physical store—as opposed to the Inter-net—expect an exciting and user-friendly environment. HMV meets this demand by offering new technologies like the multi-unit CD listening stations, some of which offer a hundred CDs for pre-listening. "With respect to service," says Arseneault, "we train store staff to ensure they are accessible and approachable to people of all ages. Our staff bring the knowledge to help customers in the buying decision." Other retailers, like Mountain Equipment Co-op, have provided their customers with climbing walls to test their climbing boots and education and reading booths to help them choose their gear. American-based Recreational Equipment Inc. (REI) has taken this "try before you buy" philosophy to the ex-treme. REI's flagship store in Seattle, which covers a whole city block, contains a biking trail for those who want to test-drive their mountain bikes and a "rain room" for those who want to check the efficiency of their waterproof outerwear.

E-Commerce

Perhaps the greatest wild card in thinking about the future of retail formats is the Internet. Depending on whom you talk to, the World Wide Web is heralded as the most significant change in retailing since the invention of the cash register, or the most overrated tool since the Thigh-Master (sorry, Chrissy).

As usual, the truth lies somewhere in between. A recent Angus Reid Group survey, *Canadians and the Internet*, demonstrates that less than one-third of Web users (22 per cent) currently carry out business transactions on-line.[44] Similarly, in July 1997, the *Globe and Mail* reported that 80 per cent of Canadian businesses neither buy nor sell products and services over the Internet.[45] Yet if you take a broader definition of e-commerce, it is clear that the World Wide Web is supporting a large chunk of business in today's economy. Consumers are using the Net as a key tool in gathering information (largely through corporate Web sites) to support the purchases they will ultimately make through traditional channels. Once they leave the house, they already know which store to go to, what they want to buy, and how much it is going to cost. More significantly, the number of consumers turning to the Internet as a shopping channel appears to be growing, despite concerns about the security and reliability of this medium. While 22 per cent seems like a small number, it's important to remember that it was close to zero per cent only five years ago.

Nexus consumers have been on the leading edge of e-commerce, taking advantage of the timeliness and immediacy of this retail format. But to understand Nexus' attraction to this medium, you need to get beyond the obvious benefit of customer convenience. Indeed, consumer research shows that younger Canadians are not always convenience-driven shoppers, and are less likely to pay more to save time shopping.[46] For Nexus—and perhaps for other future Web shoppers—the real value is about something more.

So what are some of the other key consumption advantages of the Internet? Our d~Coders, who populate the Early Adopters segment of e-commerce, insist that the virtues of the Web as a consumption tool go much further than convenience. Not surprisingly, the benefits they talk about match many of the key attributes of Nexus the Consumer.

To start with, our d~Coders believe Web browsing has contributed to their consumer sophistication by putting them in a state of "perfect information." Shopping on the Web increases the likelihood of making the best choice and getting the best deal because consumers can quickly check out all competitors for price and value. To quote Esther, a d~Coder who lives and works in California, "The Internet grants me the illusion of making up my own mind about a product." Canadian Tire's e-flyer speaks to this desire by sending its customers up-to-date information on the items they have expressed an interest in buying. Another spin on this theme is the growing popularity of on-line auctions, which create a close-to-perfect market for consumers: infinite buyers and sellers and transparent pricing. Internet Liquidators, the first on-line auction company to be listed on the Toronto Stock Exchange, is currently focused on creating a market for computer-related hardware and software. But as Nexus experiences this fun new way to buy, auction items will likely spill over into new consumer categories.

The second related benefit of e-commerce is that it provides Nexus with the ultimate expression of do-it-yourselfism. On the Internet, the user drives the shopping experience and is an active, rather than passive, audience. In addition, the Web provides Nexus consumers with an opportunity to skip over the "let's get to know each other" phase of shopping, thereby avoiding salespeople who know little more than the consumer does about the product. Sabaa, a graphic designer from our network, uses an interesting metaphor to characterize this consumer benefit: "Imagine that. You get your fix straight from the source; no distasteful crackhouses or middlemen in between." Air Canada's Web Saver allows customers direct access by sending out a weekly e-mail about discount items like plane tickets, hotel rooms, and car rentals.

Finally, and perhaps most important, the Internet offers Nexus consumers a new interactive avenue for customization. By answering a few simple questions, they can tailor the buying process to their own needs and develop the exact item they want. A personal favourite of several of our d~Coders are the "compilation Web sites" that allow consumers to create their own custom-made compact discs. One of the newest Internet companies on the scene, Custom Revolutions, has access to over a hundred thousand songs of every music type, including rock, blues, jazz, rap, classical, and meditational. According to the company's president, Canadian entrepreneur Nick Darveau-Garneau, the driving force behind Custom Revolutions was a nostalgia for the days when he made party tapes for his friends. "We thought, 'If you could bottle that feeling and sell it, get people to make their own CDs at their own convenience, that would be a fantastic idea.'"[47] Because the ultimate product can't be found in any record store, young consumers are willing to pay a premium over the cost of a regular CD.

One area where all three of these benefits converge is financial services, an industry where Nexus can be a dream customer. As the first generation to embrace low-cost channels like the automated bank machine, Nexus consumers have an inherent level of trust when it comes to "machines and their money." The Web supplies mobile Nexus consumers with yet another point of access to their funds, giving them increased flexibility and convenience. Furthermore, Internet banking meets their needs for information, self-direction, and customization. On-line accounts provide banking customers with instant profiles of their financial health, as well as up-to-date information on rates that will help them make decisions about loans and investments. Innovations like the Bank of Montreal's Mutual Funds Self-Test help consumers determine their investment-risk profile without the help of an intermediary. And most PC-banking packages include features that allow younger investors to create scenarios for future growth so that they can choose the right financial solutions to meet their goals.

If banking is any indication of future trends, e-commerce will be the consumption story of the next century and Nexus will have a large part to play. Barring a crisis of technology or confidence, we think the Internet will see increased usage as a format not only for information gathering, but also for real transactions and customer interactions. The challenge for retailers is to ensure that they can deliver the same quality of customer service through this channel as they do through any other.

The more interesting problem for Nexus consumers is whether their adoption of e-commerce will lead to a decline in retail employment, a sector that currently employs 35 per cent of the generation. To put it another way, is Nexus going to "e-shop" its way out of a job?

Our d~Coders tend to split on whether the salesman is dead. For some, the Net has displaced the sales agent by allowing customers to take control over the buying process. For others, time is a valuable asset, and they are willing to pay for the services of a professional. Still others lament the replacement of humans with technology. Beverly, one of our network members from British Columbia, believes that "when computers become more and more the norm, we will long for a certain 'human-ness' to our consumer experiences."

Perhaps a better question to ask is how the role of the salesperson will change as a result of e-commerce. According to Roberta, a d~Coder who works on Internet strategy in New York, "It won't be about 'Will the salesperson disappear?' but rather 'What will the salesperson of the future look like?'" Over time, the Internet could become a key selling tool, with the well-trained salesperson using it to demonstrate knowledge of her industry, generate options for the consumer, and provide an easy means of follow-up and communication. Technology will free her from routine tasks and questions (which a Web site can now handle) and allow her to focus on the real value-added tasks that service excellence comprises.

The Future Art of Persuasion

The future world of advertising and promotions must also revolutionize to attract and retain the loyalty of Nexus the Consumer. Members of this generation may be more likely than older age groups to use advertising as an information source,[48] but they are extremely demanding about its form and substance. The Boomers were raised to believe that "you shouldn't trust anyone over thirty," but Nexus has adopted the "you shouldn't trust anyone trying to sell you something" philosophy.

For those in the business of speaking to Nexus through marketing, we'd like to conclude with the following "codes of conduct" to help guide you in the evolving art of persuasion.

Code #1: Strive for Invisible Cool

First, recognize that Nexus consumers are searching for something we call Invisible Cool. Although they are as trend-conscious as any other generation of young people, they do not want to be *seen* as trendy or conformist. That's why companies like the Gap and Doc Martens have been so successful: they provide Nexus consumers with simple, up-to-date apparel that can enhance their look, but they avoid "in your face" brand association. Nexus shoppers want

147

to think of their buying decision as an act of rugged individualism—one based on their specific needs and views of the world. In the words of d~Coder Ryan Bigge, the managing editor of *Adbusters* magazine: "Too often we turn to consumer durables to reflect or underscore our moods and personalities." Some members of Nexus even like to indulge in "trend-busting." When someone or something gets too popular, they'll turn on a dime. After months of watching the black-and-white placards of Bank of Montreal's "Can a bank change?" TV campaign, many were relieved when "This Hour Has 22 Minutes" finally stepped in.

For advertisers, this search for Invisible Cool means avoiding the temptation to throw the latest cool word into a campaign. Superficial attempts to be trendy will be viewed as condescending and the impact will last only as long as the fad stays alive. Instead, advertisers should look for ways to leverage humour and subtlety. As evidenced by the huge success of the TV show "The Simpsons," irony and intelligent comedy are two of the defining features of cool for today's younger generation. In fact, marketers may want to use the trick of having their product displayed on one of these cool television programs. Think back to the classic "Seinfeld" episodes that featured Jerry and Kramer eating Junior Mints in the operating-room gallery and George eating a Mars bar with a knife and fork.

In the end, Invisible Cool may require you to avoid high-profile promotions, for fear of making your product *too* mainstream. A couple of years ago, Adidas noticed that the sales of one of its sports shoes had suddenly sky-rocketed in some of the major cities of North America. But instead of creating a flashy new campaign to capitalize on this, Adidas sat back and let Invisible Cool take over.

Code #2: Be Real

Second, recognize that Nexus has a highly developed "bull-shit detector." As the first generation to be targeted as consumers in its childhood years, Nexus is ingrained with scepticism about flashy marketing campaigns. It isn't advertising *per se* that members of Nexus dislike; it's overkill, hype, and attempts to slot them in. According to Van Stolk of Jones Soda, "You have to start by grounding a product—building it from the ground up. Don't start with a marketing wall; people will just bounce off."

The way to deal with the bull-shit detector is to strive for what is known in the business as "authenticity." In other words, *be real.* To quote Volkswagen's Steve Wilhite: "You should try not to tailor what you think these people need to hear. Be honest. State who you are, what you stand for, and then invite people to participate." Authenticity—which is ultimately about you, not about them—will go a long way in engaging this generation. If you build it properly, they will come.

One good example of authenticity in the Canadian marketplace is Sleeman's beer. One of its radio commercials features company president John Sleeman and members of his organization discussing which brews they like and why. Rather than moving in for the hard sell, the advertisement ends with a simple, inviting statement from Sleeman: "We brew good beer—we hope you like it."

In other cases, authenticity means telling the truth and having the courage to fight against hype. Just ask the advertising team of Lorraine Tao and Elspeth Lynn, who created the now-famous "Look good on your own terms" Special K commercials for younger women. According to Tao, the purpose of the commercials was to "encourage women to reject unrealistic stereotypes about body image, thinness and beauty." The response was overwhelming: bags of positive letters from watchers who thanked Kellogg's for listening to their fears and offering them an alternative "truth."

Companies like Kellogg's, who dare to demonstrate leadership, are likely to win over the wallets of Nexus consumers. They acknowledge that marketing is moving away from the classic features/benefits model towards an emotional model that reaches into the value systems of potential customers. To gain the loyalty of Nexus, a product needs to build up qualities that earn respect.

Code #3: "Read Me" into the Script

Sociology 101 tells us that people aren't afraid of dying, they're afraid of not being remembered. In the past, a belief in the after-life and children used to provide the mechanisms for living on into the future. But for many within Nexus, these things are being rejected or postponed. It's also worth pointing out that the very act of re-membering has become less fulfilling for members of this genera-tion. They lack the big heroes and historical events that marked the generation before them. Boomers may remember where they were when John F. Kennedy was assassinated, but Nexus has the unfortu-nate task of trying to erase the moment of Ben Johnson's gold-medal victory.

We think this generation is carving out a new approach to remembering, one that involves taking part in something in "real time." As we saw earlier in the chapter, Nexus' travel experiences take them to many of the world's trouble or transition zones, where they have an opportunity to take part in an unfolding story. Street murals, which change daily, are a particularly attractive medium because they enable members of the generation to be involved in the evolution of "art." The same desire to make their mark can be seen in their openness to interactive media.

In order to meet this Nexus craving to be a part of something, marketers should find ways to "read Nexus" into the script. They need to get them involved. In some cases, like the Saturn cam-paign, this is as simple as featuring customer stories during an advertisement. A more powerful approach, however, is to create opportunities for real interactivity—much like "Speakers Corner." So far, only a few companies have strayed into this territory. A few years back, Neilsen candy bars launched a cross-country competition to find the next Crispy Crunch couple. Couples auditioned in portable TV booths by teasing each other about who would get the last bite. Another example was the Labatt's "X vs. Y" campaign, which invited consumers to vote on which brewing formula they liked the best. While that particular campaign suffered from poor execution, the spirit behind the initiative was dead on: entice Nexus to participate in the product and the story. Members of this generation are dying to make their own memories.

The Internet is another tool for achieving interactivity with Nexus, through things like games and quizzes. This ability to entertain as well as inform offers a new and more playful way to connect with Nexus consumers, one that may leave them feeling more positive about a company's brand or image. New York–based Yoyodyne Entertainment has already tried to leverage this potential by building marketing campaigns around game shows and contests. Consumers give the sponsoring company permission to send them e-mail messages about their product or service in return for the opportunity to win prizes. In an interview in *Fast Company*, Yoyodyne's president, Seth Godin, describes how this interactive process is transforming mass-market advertising from something that interrupts consumers into something that persuades them to *volunteer* their attention.[49] For a generation raised on computer games like Nintendo and TV shows like "Jeopardy," the Internet's entertainment capabilities may be the best strategy yet for making Nexus part of the script.

Code #4: Establish Multiple-Access Points

Finally, keep in mind the fragmentation of this generation: its members are highly diverse and confident in their ability to assimilate information from a variety of sources. This reality means you need to give Nexus multiple-access points for your product. As you'll see below, these "ways in" can be physical, in the form of media channels, as well emotional, in the form of story-tellers.

On one level, multiple-access points mean experimenting with different types of media. In the past, marketers had to worry about only three TV networks and a few major magazines or newspapers. Today's strategists need to consider a host of traditional and non-traditional channels: cable television, radio and RealAudio, weekly and monthly magazines, local and national papers, billboards, guerrilla-marketing techniques like construction sites and chalk drawings, New Ad Media postcards, community-relations initiatives, the Elevator News Network, pagers and Vista phones, Web advertising—the list goes on.

Given this plethora of possibilities, how do you decide where to spend your marketing dollars? We believe the answer lies not in maximum coverage or volume of viewers/listeners, but in integration. (In fact, if technological convergence happens as expected, we will no longer think of media conduits as distinct things, since the same technology may be delivering all of them.) The marketers who are most successful with Nexus analyze each potential channel to determine if it connects with the audience, and then bring them all together to build a coherent message. No matter what "door" Nexus chooses to open, she should discover the same underlying philosophy.

One company that has successfully targeted Nexus through multiple media channels is Clearnet, the newest entrant into the fiercely competitive mobile-telecommunications market, which expects close to 70 per cent of its growth to come from eighteen- to thirty-four-year-olds. Clearnet recognized that Nexus consumers were continually on the move, with very little time to stop and read advertising tag lines. Consequently, they began with a simple but powerful outdoor advertising campaign (including billboards and subway posters) that featured bright, primary colours and large, vivid images from the natural world: roses, fish, leaves. The accompanying television spots played on this nature theme by showing an ant getting a dung ball stuck on a thorn. The subtle humour of the commercial was reinforced by a voice-over familiar to Nexus: former "Saturday Night Live" weekend update host, Norm MacDonald. Clearnet extended the campaign into its collateral materials by creating catalogues, manuals, and T-shirts with nature-based imagery. The crowning touch was a series of Clearnet retail outlets with the same simple and crisp feel.

Other companies have been more adventurous in their access points, by experimenting with promotions and community relations. Ralph Lauren, for example, has broadened his advertising strategy by sponsoring a series of parties in the hip bars of London and New York. In a similar way, Molson's has tapped into the Nexus concert-going ritual through its "Blind Date" promotion, which features famous bands showing up unannounced in small bars across Canada. A final case of a company successfully finding new access points is the community-relations strategy of Jones Soda. Under Van Stolk's leadership, Jones was one of the first retailers to support "LifeBeat," an AIDS benefit in Vancouver that now attracts large numbers of Nexus members. "Now Coke and Pepsi are all over it with big money," Van Stolk explains. "I guess you have to dupe them into doing the right thing."

There is also a deeper and more emotional meaning to multiple-access points: the idea of multiple story-tellers. Why is it that Nike had at least five different TV spots for its "Just Do It" campaign—a girls' basketball team, a goaltender, a skateboarder, a golfer, and Michael Jordan? Why is it that "Seinfeld" episodes always have four plotlines (one each for Jerry, Kramer, George, and Elaine)? Why did Quentin Tarantino develop a series of vignettes, in a non-linear order, to create the cinema sensation *Pulp Fiction*? All of these examples speak to the need to offer this new generation of consumer different characters and stories to identify with. One hero or one plotline won't do it any more.

[Conclusion]

In this chapter, we've demonstrated both the opportunities and the challenges confronting those trying to connect with Nexus the Consumer. While members of this generation may not share the wealth of their Boomer counterparts, they are both ready and able to spend money on a whole range of tangibles and intangibles. More important, as our d~Coders illustrate, buying is *fun* for this generation. These are experiential consumers who seek out ways to be part of something through their purchases.

In trying to leverage this purchasing potential, retailers and marketers need to overcome the barriers of experimentation, sophistication, and fragmentation that are the hallmarks of Nexus the Consumer. They also need to adapt to the new consumption trends and changes in retail formats that Nexus is helping to spearhead. This involves recognizing the areas where this generation's values and needs are just like yours, but also accepting the ways in which they are truly different. Above all, today's marketing strategists need to fine-tune the art of persuasion to meet Nexus' desire for Invisible Cool, authenticity, interactivity, and multiple-access points. Be where they are. Think as they think. And look for ways to make them part of the story.

Some of the key themes we've highlighted here—experimentation, customization, interactivity—cross over from the world of buying and selling into the world of work. Nexus is driving our economy not only through its purchasing power, but also through its skills and ideas in the workplace. Attracting and retaining Nexus the Employee is the topic of our next chapter.

NEXUS THE EMPLOYEE

If you could work for any company in the world, what would it be? That's a question we put to our d~Code network, and here are some of the answers they gave us:

Jon, twenty-five-year-old working for an interactive media company, Toronto

"I would like to work for NinjaTune Records or any other company that believes that a job worth doing is worth doing yourself."

Elise, twenty-three-year-old marketing manager, Montreal

"My actual company. I wouldn't change my job for anything in the world. Not because of the paycheque, but just because I think our team is the greatest."

Fred, thirty-five-year-old investment analyst, Calgary

"Fredco, wholly owned and benevolently guided by me, because I find hierarchies frustrating."

Drew, twenty-eight-year-old freelance writer and producer, Toronto

"Atlantis Films—the brainchild of three university grads, which has grown into a multi-faceted, fully integrated film company. They tell Canadian stories, using Canuck crews and talent. By integrated, I mean they develop, finance, produce, market, distribute, broadcast . . . the whole enchilada."

Dave, twenty-nine-year-old Internet entrepreneur, San Francisco

"I would say *Wired* magazine. I was fortunate enough to meet some of the folks and get a tour of their facilities. What struck me above all was the buzz and energy in that place. No kidding, they truly BELIEVED they were part of a revolution— and more importantly, among the few insiders who were translating the revolution to the masses."

Cindy, twenty-five-year-old student, Victoria

"This question presumes I would actually like to work for a company, and I wouldn't. The only company I could ever see myself working for would be my own. A cozy bookstore on a small Gulf Island or in the Kootenays."

Jared, thirty-year-old displaced Edmontonian

"For me, the ideal company was Apple in the eighties. It had a vision: to put a computer on every desktop. It was the underdog. And it was a pioneer of the now established Silicon Valley culture."

The core themes running across these responses—freedom, control, task variety, vision, and a sense of community—are some of the attributes of work that are enticing new Information Age Nexus employees. This chapter will probe into these attitudes and expectations and suggest what they mean for you as employers or co-workers of the Nexus Generation. We'll begin by looking at the potential contribution of Nexus the Employee to our changing world of work. Next, we'll discuss where Nexus workers are located in today's economy and where they see themselves moving in the future. We'll then move on to consider the challenges facing larger employers who are trying to connect with Nexus the Employee, and offer advice on how to attract and retain them. To conclude, we'll reflect on the evolution of the workplace and how Nexus may shape its culture in the decades to come.

[Human Assets vs. Human Costs]

The first half of the 1990s saw an explosion in books and articles raising alarm bells about the changing nature of work in industrialized societies. William Bridge's *Job Shift*, written in 1994, studied the fallout from the management fads of the late eighties—outsourcing, re-engineering, and job re-location—and provided tips on how to survive in the new "workplace without jobs."[1] In a feature article in the *Utne Reader*, "After Work,"[2] Jeremy Rifkin echoed these themes by analyzing the impact of automation and the phasing out of whole categories of employment, such as secretarial and retail. The shift from "mass labour" to "elite labour," he argued, would be accompanied by riots and massive social upheaval unless societies adapted with creative solutions like job sharing, shorter work weeks, and alternative employment schemes. Management guru Peter Drucker added his voice to the melody in this same article, claiming that "the disappearance of labor as a key factor of production is going to emerge as the critical unfinished business of capitalist society."

By contrast, the latter part of this decade has seen renewed optimism about the "people side" of the work equation. The premiere issue of *Fast Company* argued that information technology was not a self-standing virtue, and that it would be useful *only* if it helped human beings do their work better and differently.[3] It also discussed why re-engineering had foundered on the rock of people and how companies were now looking for new ways to rebuild the social fabric of their organizations. In other words, employees are becoming the human assets of production, not just the human costs.

What business observers like *Fast Company* highlight is the critical role played by employees in helping organizations cope with a changing and increasingly competitive economy. Some corporate leaders, like Toronto Dominion's president and CEO Charles Baillie, are starting to listen. "Both as a banker and a citizen," he recently said in a speech to the Canadian Club, "I believe we must treat our human resources with the same attention and concern we devote to the traditional economic fundamentals of interest rates, inflation and the state of our public finances. The nature of work is changing—and we'd better get the better of it before it gets the better of us."[4] We believe Nexus will be a particularly critical resource for organizations as they try to adapt to this upheaval in the nature of work.

Travelling at the Speed of Change

Change, of course, has been the dominant theme of all of these commentators. And we're not talking incremental change. We're talking about revolutionary change—change akin to the move from the farm to the factory that occurred during the late eighteenth and early nineteenth centuries. Change that you literally can't keep up with.

Nexus is an age cohort that has known nothing but change. Chapter 2 illustrated that while members of this generation have not lived through a textbook revolution, they have adapted to a series of significant economic, political, and social upheavals. Their comfort with change has carried over into the world of work, where many within Nexus appear confident about their ability to navigate through these turbulent waters. In a May 1997 Royal Bank survey, entitled *State of Employment*, only 19 per cent of eighteen- to thirty-four-year-olds agreed with the statement "The workplace is changing so quickly, it is difficult to keep up"—compared with 40 per cent for those forty-five or older.[5] This ability to roll with the punches will make Nexus an important source of business leadership as we complete the transition from the Industrial Age to the Information Age.

Ideas Don't Diminish

There's a standard graph in all introductory economics textbooks that illustrates the law of diminishing returns. Essentially, the law tells us that economic growth is limited by fixed inputs and scarce resources. World-renowned economist Paul Romer has challenged that theological doctrine with the new law of the Information Age: innovation. For the bulk of history, Romer explains, we've lived in a world of scarce raw materials (land, water, oil) that have limited our prospects for growth. But with the advent of new technology, there are no longer any limits on how much we can create. As he stated in a 1998 interview in *Maclean's* magazine: "The fact is that new ideas and innovations arise daily, and keep building on each other, and simply aren't governed by such old rules as the law of diminishing returns."[6]

Romer and other proponents of the so-called New Growth Theory, like *Fortune* magazine's Thomas Stewart, argue that we now live in an ideas-based economy, where knowledge and insight are the greatest sources of wealth creation. As a consequence, says Stewart, "Managing intellectual assets has become the single most important task of business."[7] In other words, the most critical skills for human-resource professionals are finding and retaining *idea generators*. And to ensure relevance and originality, those on the look-out for ideas need to draw on multiple generations.

Nexus is an especially fruitful source of ideas for today's builders of intellectual capital. Members of this generation bring not only the open-mindedness and enthusiasm associated with their naïveté gene, but also important new competencies developed during their formative years. Nexus was raised in an education system that favoured critical reasoning and problem solving over rote learning. The name of the game was to dissect and reassemble concepts, not just memorize them. In addition, this generation has become extremely adept with the technological tools used to access, analyze, and disseminate the ideas of the Information Age. In the words of Jay Conger, a former McGill business professor and the current executive director of the Leadership Institute in California, "A suitable analogy is that older generations are using hammers to crack open sources of information while this generation is using pneumatic drills." According to Conger, the ease with which Nexus uses these information tools will give it a greater measure of power inside organizations, something older generations may find threatening. The key for successful organizations, he contends, "is to harness the knowledge and facility of Generation X, not to restrain it."[8] Today, the techno-savvy members of this generation find themselves in an unprecedented situation: they know more about the future of work than their bosses.

Re-reading the Résumé: What's Experience?

The power of ideas leads us to a third aspect of the new workplace: the changing nature of experience. While the old "wisdom through experience" adage may still apply, the speed of change today means

160

that wisdom can quickly and dangerously grow obsolete. More-over, the equation of wisdom with age or tenure is less compelling. Ron Close, president of Netcom Canada, aptly sums up the need to think differently about the age-equals-wisdom paradigm: "Given constant shifts in the external environment, senior people find it difficult to stay informed and can no longer claim to hold a definitive interpretation of what's going on outside."

Today's companies require employees with a broader set of conditioning experiences who can decipher changes in the external world and help organizations adapt to them. In some cases, that experience may be highly technical, such as the ability to write computer code; in others, it may involve an ability to assimilate information, analyze the implications, lead a team through a prob-lem-solving exercise, listen to and understand customer needs, or simply maintain grace under pressure. Keith Kocho, president and CEO of Toronto-based Digital Renaissance, has brought together a multidisciplinary group of twenty-somethings to serve as the cre-ative juice for his growing high-tech company. "What I'm looking for is life experience—not necessarily degrees. What's important to me is level-headedness during crises and the ability to handle ebbs and flows. They need enough experience to know the difference between 'a bad day' and 'the end of the world.'"

Given their formative years, Nexus employees already have many of these skills—whether fully developed or latent. First, be-cause of its early entry into the workforce, the Nexus Generation has accumulated real-life experience in a myriad of roles and work-ing environments. A brief survey of d~Code's six staffers speaks to the range of work stints Nexus members might have enjoyed during their high-school years: delivering newspapers, scooping ice cream, selling cameras, teaching piano lessons, stringing tennis rac-quets, making popcorn for a street stand, pitching seaweed out of a lake, delivering false teeth, loading people onto a ski lift, shredding cabbage at a restaurant, collecting used bicycles for recycling, taking the Companions Wanted ads for the local newspaper, watching gravel go through sifters, and delivering pizza (in thirty minutes or less, of course). Second, members of Nexus are likely to have engaged in a host of extra-curricular activities while at school. As a result, they often come to the workplace with a sophisticated ability to manage time and multi-task. Finally, Nexus' travel experiences or participation in work-abroad schemes like SWAP have helped them to adapt to diverse cultures and develop a greater sense of confidence and independence.

Some human-resource professionals have begun to look at résumés differently to take account of these life experiences. As Royal Bank's manager of recruitment strategy Mike Kavanagh explains: "In the past, the desired path seemed simple: you left high school, went straight to university and then worked in a company for four years. Any other stuff on the résumé made you appear unfocused. Now, we *look* for the extra-curricular and travel experiences as evidence that a candidate can cope with change and ambiguity." The multidimensional résumé of Nexus the Employee is custom-made for the Information Age.

A Mosaic of Perspectives

Another force driving change in the world of work is the increased diversity within our society. Companies experience a mosaic of cultures and belief systems not only in the global marketplace—where customer needs can vary substantially—but also within their own corporate backyards. Differences in ethnicity and gender have added not only richness, but also complexity to today's organizations. Effectively managing this complexity, both at home and abroad, requires opening up corporate culture to a wider array of perspectives.

Once again, Nexus the Employee will be a key participant in the further diversification of the workplace. Members of this generation grew up with their mothers working, and therefore expect their own workplaces to have a gender mix. Indeed, because they were raised in a context where programs to achieve employment equity were already in place, many of them take the underlying principles for granted. Moreover, we already know that Nexus is the most diverse of any generation in Canadian history, having had early exposure to different ethnic groups and religious beliefs during their school-age years and having absorbed global cultures through travel and media. Finally, a number of young Canadians have acquired a second language, whether it be through formal education, self-study, or the influence of immigrant parents. In many cases, that second tongue is English.

Some organizations have already seized upon Nexus' diversity as a competitive asset. Sue Halpin, director of North American resourcing for Northern Telecom (Nortel), claims that her company "craves the global perspective that members of this generation possess." Organizations like Nortel have wagered that a company that is multicultural on the inside will be better at understanding a more diverse world outside. At d~Code, we share that philosophy, which is reflected not just in our national network of d~Coders, but also in our own core group of staff. Our current employee base of six reflects ten different ethnic backgrounds, and five of Canada's ten provinces.

The "Free Agent" Phenomenon

A final trend that is dominating the new world of work is one *Fast Company* refers to as the "free agent" phenomenon: people who work on their own, moving from project to project, sometimes for weeks or months at a time, sometimes for longer. *Fast Company* editor Bill Taylor estimates that close to twenty-five million Americans (16 per cent of the working population) are "declaring their independence" from the corporate world—as freelancers, contract workers, temps, or small-business owners—to discover new ways of living and working.[9] In Canada, the movement is becoming just as strong. Increasingly, skilled employees are following the lead of film character Jerry Maguire (who moved from being the typical company man to being his own boss) rather than staying within the confines of one company or one job description. For free agents, *freedom is security.*

As an illustration, consider that some of the busiest members of our d~Code network don't actually have "real jobs." Rather, they have a "portfolio of things they do" and an uncanny ability to do them all at the same time. One of our favourites is Jay, who currently resides in Ontario (we think) and juggles several free-agent initiatives: heading up an environmental organization, fulfilling a contract with the Canadian government to serve at-risk youth, managing a project in Madagascar, documenting ideas on sustainable development, and acting as an intermediary on a high-speed boat connection between Mauritius and mainland Africa. He really *does* all this!

The resilient attitudes of the Nexus Generation make it well positioned to leverage this new free-agent status. In the 1997 *State of Employment* survey, only 15 per cent of eighteen- to thirty-four-year-old respondents agreed with the statement "I am concerned about losing my job"[10]—despite the reasonably high unemployment stats for young Canadians. This capacity to cope with ambiguity also makes members of this generation prime candidates for starting their own businesses, like thirty-year-old Haligonian Jennifer Corson did. Corson was trained as an architect, but now runs her own company, the Renovators ReSource. "Part of me was looking for the 'traditional' architecture role," she explains, "but another part of me wanted to pursue my environmental interests. In the end the recession of the early nineties made my decision. I chose my own path." We believe others in this generation will follow the same road. The survival skills and do-it-yourselfism of Nexus workers—a product of their generational conditioning—is giving many of them greater confidence about their ability to thrive in a labour force where many of the old rules have been washed away.

[Facts and Figures about Nexus the Employee]

Now that we've seen the potential contribution of this generation to the burgeoning Information Age, let's take a closer look at where Nexus the Employee currently resides in our economy.

Joblessness

We begin at the point where most observers of this generation usually start: youth unemployment. In 1997, the unemployment rate was 11 per cent for eighteen- to thirty-four-year-olds (15 per cent for eighteen- to twenty-four-year-olds, and 9 per cent for twenty-five- to thirty-four-year-olds), compared with the national average of 9.2 per cent.[11] Provincial and federal governments have been turning up the heat on youth joblessness, however. The optimistic view is that they acknowledge the waste of this critical national resource; the more jaded view is that they see the need to secure young Canadians' contributions to old-age pension schemes.

Whatever the case, we support the energy and attention being directed at the jobless issue. There's no question: youth unemployment is a big deal. Just as we'd be wary of wasting traditional assets like timber, we should be worried about wasting precious human ones. As we've suggested, members of the Nexus Generation possess precious skills and competencies that can help organizations compete in the Information Age. In addition, it's crucial to remember that being unemployed in today's "competition state" is a different situation than it was in the past: not only are skills losing their relevance more quickly, but government services to support the needy are declining and families are likely unable to pick up the slack. Nevertheless, we'd like to add a couple of points to the debate on what should be done to address the Nexus unemployment issue.

First, although the media rightly draws our attention to the tragedy of joblessness for Canada's youth—particularly for those under twenty-five—the story is actually more complex. As David Foot contends, we need to put employment stats in perspective and not instantly assume that current levels are unprecedented. Foot usefully recounts how the youth-unemployment rate historically has averaged about twice the national rate—largely because of the length of time it takes young people to gain work experience. He also shows that while fifteen years ago 48 per cent of unemployed people were under twenty-five, that number today has dropped to 27 per cent, owing to a marked increase in older Canadians without work. Furthermore, Foot encourages us to broaden our gaze beyond Canadian teens and young adults to consider the real losers in the recession fallout of the 1980s and 1990s: those born in the first half of the 1960s, his definition of Generation X.[12]

Second, while intervention is clearly required, the tone and the philosophy need to change. For the last several years, the media has painted the world of work as one of the most depressing places to be in our society. On page A1 of the paper, we read about unemployment statistics; on page A11 (if we get that far), we read stories about job hiring. What we *rarely* read about are the exciting possibilities that exist for the future working world, or ideas to help members of Nexus connect to it.

It's time to move away from treating unemployed youth as charity cases. The reality is that we cannot spend our way out of this issue. Hand-outs and government-sponsored make-work projects are only Band-Aid solutions.

Instead, we need to go much deeper and much broader to leverage the do-it-yourselfism of young employees. We should prepare them much earlier (during high school), by introducing them to the skills they will need to find their place in a new economy, by identifying mentors who can help them with career development, and by raising their excitement about the future of work. Career Edge, a national business internship program, has all the right intentions, but to date it has been able to reach fewer than one thousand young Canadians.

Where They Are Today

In sum, there is no doubt that a segment of Nexus is unemployed or underemployed. But where is the bulk of the generation? The *State of Employment* survey shows that of those eighteen- to thirty-four-year-olds who are working, 64 per cent are full-time employees. Twenty-five per cent are working part time—twice the level of those over forty-five—and the majority (55 per cent) earn an hourly wage. This large segment of part-time workers helps to explain the polarization of income within this age group: 62 per cent report a personal income of less than $30,000, while only 2 per cent report an income of $70,000 or more.

Despite the perception that this is a generation of "slackers," Nexus the Employee works roughly the same number of hours per week as the national average (38.6) and the same level of overtime (8.6 hours) as older age groups. Nexus is also spending most of its time within the four walls of the company: while 60 per cent of eighteen- to thirty-four-year-olds report having access to some kind of flexible work arrangement (flextime, job sharing, modified work week, etc.), this demographic is the least likely to work out of the home. Nexus reports 9.7 hours of work per week at home, compared with 18.3 hours for those over forty-five.

Ninety per cent of eighteen- to thirty-four-year-olds report being very satisfied with their jobs, roughly the same result as for older demographic groups. However, it is important to note that 53 per cent of this generation have been with their current employer less than two years, and 33 per cent expect to be where they are for less than two years. Nexus employees appear to have taken the Information Age philosophy of mobility and free agency to heart.

As shown in the chart that follows, Nexus employees work for a variety of company sizes: 23 per cent are working in a huge company (defined as one thousand or more employees) and 16 per cent in organizations with fewer than five employees.

In what size of company do you currently work?

Huge company	23%
Large company	18%
Medium company	21%
Small company	22%
Very small company	16%

Source: State of Employment, May 1997

The vast majority of Nexus members characterize themselves as being in a junior position (40 per cent) or a middle-management position (34 per cent); 13 per cent describe themselves as senior managers. At present, only 11 per cent of this age group is self-employed.

Last, it's instructive to look at where Nexus the Employee is concentrated in terms of the economic sector. Currently, 39 per cent of this generation describe themselves as working in clerical, service, or retail occupations—the highest percentage of any age group in Canada. These are followed by blue collar/skilled occupations (11 per cent), business-management positions (9 per cent), professional (doctor, lawyer, teacher, etc.) occupations (8 per cent), and technical jobs (7 per cent).[13]

These figures paint a picture of a generation that is hard at work and very much centred on the physical workplace. Although Nexus employees are working in companies ranging from the very large to the very small, they tend to be concentrated in the clerical or retail sectors. And despite the fact that most in this age group report a high level of job satisfaction, we suspect many are already looking ahead to a "better position."

Where They Want to Be

If this is the working reality of Nexus the Employee today, where does she see herself in the future? The *Building Bridges* report suggests a shift in younger Canadians' expectations about where they will work and what they expect to gain from work—a reflection of many of the new demands of the Information Age.

The first thing to highlight is the entrepreneurial spirit that runs through this generation. Research demonstrates that almost one-third (29 per cent) of Nexus expects to be self-employed five years into the future (this despite the low number who are currently entrepreneurs) and 13 per cent believe they will work for a small company of under thirty employees. Only 10 per cent of Nexus report wanting to work in a huge company in five years' time.[14]

As shown in the chart, the desire to be a part of certain professions also appears to be changing. The occupations thought to be most desirable by the Nexus Generation are entrepreneur and artist/filmmaker/musician, followed by company executive. Traditional careers in medicine or finance fall further down the list, as does the role of commissioned salesperson—a job that many in the generation currently find themselves in. And remember what we said in Chapter 3 about the general scepticism that Nexus seems to have for the institution of government? Check out the rank of politician.

Most Desirable *Profession*	Percentage who said strongly desirable
Entrepreneur	32
Filmmaker, artist, musician	28
Executive in a large company	27
Teacher	26
Lawyer	23
Doctor	20
Director of a not-for-profit	18
Stockbroker	8
Politician	6
Commissioned salesperson	5

Source: Building Bridges, June 1997

These results suggest that while members of this generation are justifiably concerned with job security, many no longer associate that security with a career in a larger organization—unless, of course, they can be the top dog. Memories of parents being displaced by downsizing, the increased scrutiny of large corporations, and the desire for greater flexibility in their working lives have led Nexus employees to look to other career options. Ironically, self-employment and entrepreneurship appear to offer more stability because they give Nexus a sense of meaning and control over her own destiny. Jon and Fred, whom we profiled at the beginning of this chapter, capture it best.

This desire for freedom and flexibility also appears to be driving Nexus employees towards the careers of filmmaker, artist, and musician. In fact, members of this generation are already visible in these industries today. The rise of new media is likely to make them even more prominent tomorrow, as they become the force behind design, animation, and creative content. Given that the media represents the one institution Nexus embraces, it seems likely that it will become a major forum for this generation's energy and creativity.

[The Challenges]

While Nexus' spirit of entrepreneurship may be positive for the Canadian economy as a whole, it hints at a deeper set of expectations about what the generation hopes to gain from its working life—expectations that pose serious challenges for today's employer.

Work as the Hub of Community

One of the greatest challenges lies in the prominent role that work and the workplace play in the life of Nexus. In *Building Bridges,* the item most often cited by Nexus members as likely to improve their quality of life was "better job/better career" (39 per cent), followed by "more income/big raise" (13 per cent). This underscores the importance that young people place on work and career, but implies that it is not solely a means to make money. In fact, when presented with the statement "I am only working for the money, I don't care about career," 66 per cent of full-time workers and 58 per cent of part-time workers strongly disagreed. Similarly, when asked to rate the importance of a variety of structures to their daily life, 56 per cent ranked the company they work for first—far ahead of community, religious organizations, and the policies of federal or provincial governments. This ranking of the company over other entities echoes the general decline in confidence that young people have in many traditional institutions, and their search for more meaningful surrogates.[15]

It's interesting that the *State of Employment* research reveals that Nexus is more likely than other generations to say that the aspects it likes best about a job are *social*, such as "the people I work with" or "meeting people." Furthermore, it rated these work features more highly than financial compensation. Because of Nexus' extended freedom zone, many in the generation are looking to the workplace as a centre-piece of their social life—a reality many managers we've worked with have trouble adjusting to. Perhaps you even share their belief that Nexus employees can at times be a little *too* social.

For Nexus, then, work has taken on a larger significance. While some members of this generation are looking to their jobs just for subsistence, and still others simply for spending money, we believe the majority are looking for something more. Employers need to figure out early on what type of animal they are dealing with, and find ways of responding to those who view the workplace as a critical focal point of social interaction and communal support.

Loyalty to People Rather Than Places

The second frequently cited challenge employers face with Nexus is its new approach to loyalty. Most human-resource professionals we've talked to say that this is the number-one issue they grapple with. Remember that the majority of Nexus members believe they will be with their current organization less than two years. We also know that among the more highly educated, job switching is actively encouraged. A 1996 article in *The Economist* showed that the average M.B.A. changes employers between three and four times in the ten years after graduation. In fact, executive recruiters tell budding managers that spending more than five years with the same firm could prevent them from getting to the top.[16] The perception is that better opportunities will come not by staying but by moving on.

The management practices of the last decade that Bridges and Rifkin talk about—downsizing and re-engineering—have also weakened traditional notions of loyalty. Although companies have started to realize just how important *employee* loyalty is to securing *customer* loyalty, they still have a long way to go to restore confidence. The conditioning experiences of Nexus—and the strong media images that accompanied recessions—have lead this generation to believe that even if you give your heart and soul to an organization, you can be phased out as fast as you can say "pink slip." Even in Japan, the former bastion of lifetime employment, the idea of a truly permanent job has evaporated.

To put it simply, the elements of the old employee/workplace contract are fading away. As Jay Conger explains: "For this new generation, work is more than ever before a transaction."[17] As for loyalty, it has taken on a new meaning, and members of this generation tend to attach it to things other than companies—their teams, their projects, or their workplace friends. Refer back to Natalie's comments at the start of the chapter. To her, team loyalty is everything.

Employability vs. Employment

Another set of challenges for employers surround this generation's opinions about the importance of particular job features. The chart below shows that after job security, the most desirable attributes involve challenging work opportunities and task variety, not the more traditional opportunities for advancement or promotion.

Which of the following is most important to you in a job?

	Percentage who said most important
Job security	30
Challenging responsibilities	24
Task variety	20
Direct responsibility over tasks	9
Opportunities for promotion	8

Source: Building Bridges, June 1997

We also find it illuminating that when d~Coders tell us about their job changes or career moves, they usually tend to gloss over the job title and focus more on the activity. Carla, a Vancouver member of our network, contends that "the days of identifying yourself by your job title have become stale toast. This generation is more interested in who you *are*, and what you *do*." Many members of Nexus show a high level of impatience with hierarchy, not only because it slows down decision-making (the standard reason), but also because it can stand in the way of task variety and skill development. Nexus employees quickly grow anxious if they feel they are marking time in their job; they want the chance to work on a diversity of projects.

Increasingly, Nexus is placing less emphasis on lifetime employment with one company and more on long-term employability in a variety of organizations and roles. Indeed, over a third (36 per cent) of Nexus respondents (and a higher percentage of those with a university education) expect to have multiple careers over their lifespan. As a result, their priority is to gain maximum exposure to the skills, competencies, and experiences they'll need for their *next* job. The data below illustrate that the opportunity for paid training and the chance to use up-to-date technology were rated highly among the desirable workplace benefits for this generation, well ahead of more traditional perks like "casual dress."[18] Both training and technology are seen as critical building blocks for Nexus' strategy of long-term employability and are likely to be the among the hottest topics of conversation at your company's recruitment booth.

Workplace Benefits

	Percentage who said strongly desirable
Basic dental/medical benefits	74
Extended leaves	55
Paid training	51
Flexible work hours	48
Up-to-date technology	40
Casual dress	23

Source: Building Bridges, June 1997

All Work and No Play?

This chart uncovers another challenge that Nexus is mounting in the workplace: a quest for a better work/life balance. Fifty-five per cent of eighteen- to thirty-four- year-olds identified the freedom to take extended leaves or sabbaticals as a key workplace benefit. The option of flexible hours was not far behind. Indeed, organizations we have worked with tell us that when given the choice of more money or days off, many of their Nexus employees opt for the time off. Some managers like to use this as evidence of the "slacker" stereotype of Generation X. We think it is about something deeper.

So does Demos, a British public-policy think-tank. It released a report in 1995 entitled *Generation X and the New Work Ethic* that highlighted the different approaches to work and life that exist between the generations. One of its core findings was that having control over one's time has become a critical goal of younger workers—just behind making money and using their brains. The "time bravado" work culture of the 1980s tended to trivialize leisure hours as wasted or effortless time, but members of Nexus are seeking a more "life-friendly" culture that allows them opportunities to fulfill their leisure and entertainment desires.[19] Consequently, Nexus employees are often critical of the Boomers' failure to use time efficiently—despite all their talk about teamwork and time management. Lisa, a thirty-year-old lobbyist and consultant, describes the resentment many younger employees feel when they are trapped inside an eighties-style work environment: "The senior consultants here don't get it. The only legitimate excuse for leaving before 8 p.m. is to spend time with your kids; they don't seem to realize that just because I don't have a family doesn't mean I don't need my leisure time. My needs are just as legitimate." Young lawyers from our network have expressed the same concerns about the out-dated approaches to work and time management that pervade their profession today. The culture of "presenteeism"—you're always at your desk no matter how little you accomplish—often stands in the way of meeting their work/lifestyle goals.

The Demos report also points to a trend we've been following at d~Code: increasing numbers of younger workers are leaving traditional workplaces, impatient with companies who have not been able to change their work environments fast enough. Martin, a Montrealer from our d~Code network, left the world of management consultancy to start his own bio-tech business largely because he felt he was being prevented from reaching his lifestyle objectives: "It's funny. In a way my decision to 'opt out' was very much in line with where my retiring parents are. It's those who are ten years older than me who are perpetuating this whirlwind of the eighty-hour week. I want to be there for my children and see them grow up."

Many Nexus women share Martin's philosophy. The question now is whether they too will opt out of the workplace, or whether they will be the generation that pushes the corporate world to provide more solutions to reconcile career and family ambitions. One thing does appear to be true: the choices that were made by senior women in corporate Canada are not always perceived as attractive—or possible—for the new career woman. Research conducted in 1997 by Catalyst and the Conference Board of Canada on approximately four hundred women in the senior ranks of companies revealed that 61 per cent had advanced only by putting their career ahead of their family life. Furthermore, those who had succeeded had done so by curtailing their fitness, hobbies, personal interests, and involvement in the community, and by conceding to expensive solutions like in-home childcare.[20] The latter is an answer that few Nexus women are in a position to afford, while the former are sacrifices that most feel they shouldn't have to make.

Amy, a twenty-three-year-old d~Coder and fresh university graduate, accurately summarizes the dilemma: "A lot of women my age have trouble identifying with older women: working women in their fifties are seen as alien because they had to become men; women in their forties still try to insist you can 'do it all' and are blowing their brains out trying."

It isn't that Nexus doesn't want to work hard; it's just that many in the generation have seen what too much hard work can do to families and relationships. Members of Nexus want their work to be judged not on inputs like time, but on outputs like quality and creativity. Thirty-year-old Mike Rapino, a director at Labatt's Breweries, claims that his company's new philosophy—"Do the big things that matter and get home earlier"—has resulted in a higher quality of work and a reduction in employee hours. It has also changed Labatt's attitude towards promotion: it's no longer about the time put in. "I tell my team that if they are here stressed out until 10 p.m. every night, then they are not ready for more responsibility. Quality work in a balanced life *equals* promotion." Mike's management style is also in tune with Nexus' renewed focus on the notion of personal rhythm, something the Industrial Age attacked and tried to destroy. At d~Code, we like to refer to this quest for balance as a preference for European values over North American ones. As we saw in Chapter 4, this generation likes to indulge in life's pleasures. It works to live rather than lives to work.

One final note of caution: While survey data show that over half (54 per cent) of Nexus respondents expect to be able to achieve this work/life balance in their lifetime,[21] this may be unrealistic for some. Many educated and highly skilled members of this generation have chosen to work in growing industries like high tech and find themselves in incredibly competitive and fast-paced environments. Despite the good intentions, it's all too easy to think of the body, in the words of Douglas Coupland, as "a station-wagon in which [to] drive [your] brain around."[22] Nevertheless, Digital Renaissance's Keith Kocho agrees that even the most driven of Nexus employees don't want to do what the Boomers are doing (i.e., put off finding this balance until retirement). Kocho's own solution is to break down the divisions between work and play, and ensure that the workplace offers opportunities to have fun, be casual, and find your personal "zen." In other words, redefine balance altogether. "When I think of it that way, university was my employment period. It was drudgery. Work has become my retirement—now I'm really living."

The Savvy Employee

Another challenge posed by Nexus the Employee mirrors a feature of Nexus the Consumer: savvy. This new generation of employee uses multiple sources of information (the Internet, peer networks, word of mouth, school associations, and mainstream media) to learn what companies have to offer. In addition, it is able to compare the offerings of different organizations with great ease and at lightning speed. And as any human-resource manager will attest, the rumour mill is fast and unforgiving. Few members of this generation will read an annual report; instead, they're on the lookout for the "real scoop" and will update it faster than any company's public-affairs machine.

Members of the Nexus Generation are also likely to scrutinize the behaviour of larger companies. Karen Walsh, general manager of human resources for Placer Dome, believes today's university students are more environmentally and socially aware than their predecessors. Consequently, they quiz representatives from mining and resource companies like Placer Dome about their business practices, both at home and abroad. "Students come much more prepared to our 'bear pit' sessions on campus, and ask us questions ranging from the impact of Bre-X to the intricacies of our environmental policies. They want to know what our values, policies and vision are."

In short, be aware that Nexus can and does compare you with your competitors on multiple dimensions.

Protesting with Their Feet

The final hurdle for potential or existing employers of Nexus is to understand how members of this generation express their dissatisfaction with their jobs. Our experience is that they're less likely to push for reform from within a company and more likely to leave, or "protest with their feet." Given the extended freedom zone, members of the Nexus Generation will less often feel compelled to stay with an organization just to cover the mortgage or pay for their kids' braces. In the words of Pam Withers, president of Publisher's Edge Consulting: "That's why they'll walk from an unrewarding job even in a bleak job climate, a trait Boomer bosses in 'old economy' companies find difficult to comprehend."[23] If the reality doesn't match her expectations, Nexus will take the chance that she can find the things that she wants from work—community, skills development, challenge, and balance—somewhere else. It takes more energy to stay put and lobby for change than it does to make a move.

This "protest with your feet" mentality raises interesting questions about the relationship between unions and Nexus employees. Despite some actions by young workers to unionize (the West Coast Starbucks case is the most prominent example), only 24 per cent of this generation are in unions today, considerably less than the national average of 35 per cent.[24] On a more fundamental level, the structure and philosophy behind unions pose difficulties for Nexus' work aspirations. For one thing, unions are wedded to a traditional view of experience, and are interested largely in protecting long-term employment and tenure. But as we have seen, the definition of experience is beginning to change in our economy and now includes a variety of perspectives and backgrounds. Second, unions presume an imbalance of power between worker and management that Nexus does not necessarily buy into. While some members of this generation are "kept in their place" by more senior managers, many Nexus employees are questioning authority and asserting their desire to contribute in more meaningful ways. Third, many unions operate in a hierarchical fashion, with a senior spokesperson negotiating on behalf of a large body of workers.

Most in this do-it-yourself generation feel uncomfortable entrusting a union leader with power over their livelihood, especially if they are not expecting to be in their jobs for very long. Finally, unions were created at a time when protesting with their feet was not an option open to most employees (old or young). Today, as we have argued, many members of the Nexus Generation are taking a chance that they can find a better opportunity—in good or bad economic times.

[Attracting and Retaining Nexus the Employee]

Let's take stock of where we are so far. As an employee, Nexus brings a variety of skills and attributes critical to succeeding in today's economy: high levels of education, comfort and agility with technology, experience with diversity, and an acceptance of mobility and change. However, Nexus is also less likely to buy into traditional notions of company loyalty, craves a better work-life balance, is impatient with hierarchy, and seeks out organizations that offer skills development, challenges, and opportunities to make an impact. This generation of employee is more informed about its options and is more likely to leave a place it is unhappy with.

So what can companies do to attract Nexus employees? Though the early 1990s saw many in this generation begging for jobs, the latter part of this decade has been marked by greater economic growth and an opening-up of opportunities—particularly for those with sought-after skills, such as computer programmers, accountants, and financial analysts. The cover story of the November 1997 issue of *Canadian Business* argued that recruiters are working overtime and companies are fiercely competing for this country's best and brightest with goodies like signing bonuses, stock options, flex-time, and high-profile assignments. "Companies now think nothing of spending thousands to woo and impress crucial hires, while salaries zip upward like mercury in an overheated thermometer."[25] Halifax-based FastLane Technologies (an affiliate of Newbridge) recently resorted to offering a thousand-dollar bounty for potential employees. The prize was promised to anyone in the community who could refer a successful candidate to fill jobs in software development and technical writing.[26]

If you think the competition for talent is occurring only in the information-technology sector, however, think again. After years of retrenchment, organizations in a variety of sectors are faced with a shortage of skilled people to participate in the next phase of growth. Even in Nexus' traditional stomping grounds, the retail and service sectors, we've heard the same complaint: it's getting tougher and tougher to find good people.

To assist in this challenge, we've provided the following codes of conduct to guide those in the business of attracting and retaining Nexus the Employee. At first glance, our words may appear more relevant for those seemingly disadvantaged "companies of size" (i.e., the large or huge company), but we think they ring true for organizations of all shapes and sizes.

Attraction Strategies

Code #1: Be Transparent about Who You Are

One of the greatest frustrations today's recruiters face is the tendency for prospective employees to pad their résumés with questionable achievements and embellished experiences. But those wanting Nexus to be up front about his strengths and weaknesses should apply the same philosophy to their own organizations. In short, don't lie on your corporate résumé. If greater loyalty is what you're after, then what employees are likely to experience "on the inside" needs to be carefully managed. We believe the best strategy is to borrow from the rules of marketing: strive for authenticity. Don't oversell, even if fierce competition tempts you to. Nexus has seen it all in terms of advertising, and she has also seen it all in terms of clever recruitment brochures and videos.

Microsoft strikes a healthy balance in approaching its potential Nexus employees, whether they be rising stars from U.S. campuses or our own Canadian grads from the University of Waterloo. Recruiters are clear about what a young person is likely to get at Microsoft: an unparalleled opportunity to work in what Bill Gates calls a "company of super-smart people." But they are also honest about the commitment required: it's not a summer camp. Rumour has it that Gates himself calls prospective employees to present this even-handed message.

Another approach is to be aware of the relative merits of the different sizes of companies, and to talk openly and honestly with Nexus about their pros and cons. In the mid-nineties, Placer Dome faced stiff competition for engineers and geologists from smaller mining companies who offered big salaries, stock options, and a lot of management responsibility. According to Karen Walsh, Placer Dome's strategy was not to try to become something it could never be—a mining start-up—but instead to talk about the things it could offer as a large established company: career planning, access to state-of-the-art technology, and broad-based training opportunities. Their core message, says Walsh, was straight to the point: "We are about more than engineers; we're willing to invest in you."

If you're a smaller organization, like Digital Renaissance, you can attract members of this generation with the chance to be part of a growing business. DR competes for recruits with the likes of IBM and Andersen Consulting, yet Keith Kocho claims that most of his employees have proactively sought out his company. "They come because of the openness and the opportunity to be in on the ground floor, driving the direction of the company." Companies like DR can be open about the risks and downsides of "going small," but still lure Nexus in with the possibility of building something better together.

Code #2: Leverage Your Greatest Strength—
Your Own People

A good way to talk about who you are is to hand the microphone over to your own employees. It's more authentic if it comes directly from them. Placer Dome uses an Ambassador Program, whereby alumni go back to their campuses to talk about their international work experiences, their career paths, and their overall impressions of what it is like to work in the company. Other organizations, like large law and consulting firms, make their young professionals available to meet personally with prospective candidates and even allow applicants to "job shadow" for a day.

Two years ago, when the Bank of Montreal embarked on a hiring blitz to strengthen its Operations Group, the recruiting team recognized the need to adopt a more relaxed, student-centric approach for connecting with this new generation of employee. According to Chris Chapman, a twenty-seven-year-old human-resource specialist who helped develop BMO's more casual on-campus presence, "The students needed the chance to interview us." This led to the decision to use peers and members of the senior management team to staff the recruitment booth. "When I was looking for a job twenty years ago," explains vice-president Mary Lou Hukezalie, "I was looking for those in the booth to be older and wiser. Today, these students want to hear from peers."

Nortel's Sue Halpin shares a belief in this approach. "Because candidates are now looking for a place they can have 'a say,' rather than just a job to build their résumé, they want more time to see what a company is all about. It's more about personal fit and individual identity than it is about corporate reputation." That's why Nortel has become such a big believer in its co-op programs, which placed twenty-five hundred students in Canada alone last year. Only by spending time with Nortel employees, Halpin argues, can young people work their way through the different career possibilities at Nortel and develop a clear mental model of how they can evolve with the company. Mike, a twenty-year-old University of Toronto student who started his co-op relationship with Nortel while he was still in high school, agrees: "My summer experiences gave me a sense of all the different businesses here and how I can fit in. They also allowed me to determine for myself the good and bad about this place. If I were to go somewhere else, that bad side would still be a big unknown." As a testament to his positive experience, he signed up last year to become an ambassador for Nortel on campus.

Code #3: Differentiate Yourself

Given the intensifying competition for talent, as well as Nexus' scepticism about certain aspects of the corporate world, companies need to adopt a more aggressive recruiting style. In fact, d~Code's experience with company recruiters draws on many of the marketing concepts we discussed with regard to Nexus the Consumer. If you want your voice to be heard above the noise, understand the elements Nexus is seeking from prospective employers and "brand" the ones you believe you can best provide.

The Operations Group at the Bank of Montreal adopted this approach when it appeared on campus under the name of Emphisys. The goal of the new brand—which opted for flashy red rather than BMO's characteristic blue—was to make the technology department of the bank seem more accessible and cutting-edge. Recruiters supported the brand by talking to students about the up-to-date technology the company had available. They also emphasized (pun fully intended) the new workplace culture that the Operations Group was trying to build: one based on self-direction, mobility, project teams, and task variety.

Nortel, which plans to hire five thousand young people over the next four years from the fiercely competitive high-tech pool, also revamped its approach to on-campus recruiting in 1997. The goal of Nortel's recruiting strategy was to differentiate the company on the basis of its corporate culture, and to showcase for students all of the ways in which Nortel could help them "live, work, and play." The result—the "Living in 3D" recruitment campaign—transformed each of the live, work, and play elements into a three-dimensional experience, complete with a redesigned recruitment booth, 3D glasses, video-release parties, and a CD-ROM of company testimonials. The campaign not only increased the number of Nortel offers of employment, but also generated a great deal of publicity for the company. Five university newspapers featured articles on Nortel's recruitment effort, and many students going to engineering class the next day were seen sporting 3D glasses.

Before leaving the subject of branding, a cautionary word about consistency. Remember that Nexus is not just an employee, she is also a customer and a citizen. If you are sending out any marketing or public-relations messages, she is likely to come across them while browsing on the Net or listening to the radio in her car. In fact, given that most public-affairs and marketing departments have larger budgets than human-resource departments, their voices are likely to be louder. If Nexus finds that the messages of the different departments conflict, that may be enough to turn her off. Take the example of the Royal Bank Financial Group, whose student-recruitment campaign a few years ago was nearly derailed by a series of stereotypical GenX radio ads from another department in the bank. Our advice is to bring the different departments together to collaborate on message development, ensure that they are consistently displayed on new and existing media, and get a bigger bang for your buck.

Code #4: Create a Memorable Experience

What the Royal Bank did recognize, however, was the need to give today's Nexus job-seekers something memorable to take away with them. Differentiation isn't just about creating an image or a fancy brochure. It's ultimately about creating an experience.

During its recruitment drive in Ontario and Quebec in 1997, the Royal Bank invited groups of fifteen students for a day of team-building and adventure-learning, rappelling down the Elora Gorge. The strategy was to use the event to grab the attention of prospective employees, then hold that attention talking about the kinds of skills the bank hoped its employees would develop. Rob Johnston, the human-resource manager who directed the event, sums up the philosophy behind it: "It wasn't a hard sell, but we knew we needed to differentiate ourselves and overcome the image of us as one big blue suit."

Memorable experiences like these, which aren't associated with skills evaluation or résumé collection, enable young people to learn something new about themselves and about an organization they might have written off as "unhip." This approach also extends the recruitment period beyond the standard two- to three-month window, thereby taking the pressure off both company and candidate. Members of Nexus want time to experiment and are looking for opportunities to learn about organizations at their leisure. The Internet is a tool well-suited to that experimental desire. Ottawa-based ObjecTime, a high-tech company that provides visual-development tools and support services, introduces young people to its organization through an interactive pool table on their company Web site. Tactics such as these acknowledge that recruitment is like dating. You don't necessarily propose on the first night.

Code #5: Diversify Your Pool through Diverse Channels

Even if you apply the codes we describe above, you still may find that you haven't created a large enough base of prospective Nexus employees from which to choose. We believe many companies—particularly those that are large and well-established—are too narrow in their perceptions about the ideal employee and are too quick to write off those who haven't jumped through the right hoops. Bankers tend to hire only bankers, consultants hire only consultants, and so on. Such practices do not permit you to introduce new genetic material to your organism. Over time, you become less able to adapt to changes in your environment.

To get around this obstacle, companies should consider making two adjustments. First, they should broaden the definition of the ideal candidate to take in a more diverse group of Nexus applicants. Many of the typical behaviour-based competencies used by human-resource professionals stress words like *achievement, motivation, initiative, proactivity*, or *team leadership*. Yet their screening processes associate those things with a particular program at college or university (e.g., a Bachelor of Commerce) or a well-known set of extracurricular activities (e.g., editor of the school paper). Recruiters need to start "re-reading" résumés to look for alternative ways that these competencies could be built. Furthermore, they should amend their list to include words like *innovative, adaptable, globally aware*, and *committed to learning*. These are the attributes needed for the Information Age. You can then train employees in the particular skills they need to do the job.

To find those innovative Nexus candidates who are committed to learning, recruiters should also diversify the channels of their recruitment drive. This may mean looking for employees in alternative programs like music, fine arts, social work, anthropology, or history, who have demonstrated an interest in business and in gaining practical experience. But it may also mean finding the new off-campus gathering places for Nexus: bookstores, movie theatres, volunteer organizations, cafés, temp agencies, or student travel agencies. One of our d~Coders recently left his job in a bakery to become the executive assistant to the head of a prominent foundation. He landed the position after several interactions with the foundation's president, who came in the store to buy pies and loaves of bread.

Diversifying your channels may also require experimentation with new media sources. School placement departments, newspapers, and the standard employment publications reel in the same kinds of fish. Instead, consider newer media such as Internet newsgroups or virtual communities, Nexus-targeted magazines, bus shelters, subway posters, even posters on bathroom walls. The same channels we discussed in relation to Nexus the Consumer can be applied (with the right tweaking) to Nexus the Employee as well. In each case, think about how you can surprise members of this generation and get them to think differently about your organization. You want a potential candidate to think, The last place I thought I'd ever want work is a bank. But maybe I do. . . .

There are, of course, risks to this diversification strategy. A new breed of Nexus employee might require *you* to change as well. It's much safer to stick to the traditional watering-holes, where you're likely to find members of this generation who will fit into your existing culture and refrain from rocking the boat. Unfortunately, the pool of conformist young employees—who require stable and trusted structures, who expect lifetime employment, and who are reluctant to embrace change—is getting smaller. If you want the best and the brightest from this generation, you're going to need to expand your horizons.

Retention Strategies

For today's employers, retaining the Nexus Generation is an even greater challenge than trying to attract it in the first place. It used to be that once you finally got the fresh new talent in the door, you could breathe a sigh of relief. Not so today.

We believe that despite Nexus' changing view of loyalty, employers still have a number of tools of the trade at their disposal to leverage the ideas and the commitment of this generation. But before we dive into our recommendations, two introductory points are worth making. First, be advised that the groundwork for retention is laid during the attraction and orientation phases. If you don't establish realistic expectations, or if you don't set the right initial mood, you're likely to be paddling upstream from there. In other words, if Nexus the Employee doesn't have a phone or a computer on her desk on day one, she's unlikely to make it past day 365. If she doesn't, you'll not only lose a valuable piece of your culture and intellectual capital, but also fail to recover many of the costs associated with recruiting, training, and mentoring new employees. Depending on the job, it may be two years before you reach what we call the magic employee break-even point.

Second, it's crucial to understand that the new employee contract involves a total package: rarely will Nexus leave a company because of a single factor, such as compensation. The *State of Employment* survey demonstrated that job satisfaction for eighteen- to thirty-four-year-olds is influenced more by quality of work and work environment than by salary, and that the top reason for leaving a company is a better opportunity (26 per cent), not better pay (16 per cent).[27] The decision to seek that elusive better opportunity is often made because of a variety of tangibles and intangibles. Indeed, many within this generation conduct a quarterly—or even monthly—check-in on the key factors of their working experience:

compensation and benefits; opportunities for mobility, learning, and skills development; regularity of feedback; peer and management support; and the meaningfulness of the work.

To help employers ensure that the Nexus balancing act will produce favourable results for them, we've provided the following codes of conduct.

Code #1: Create a Context of Continuous Learning

One of the major changes brought by the Information Age is a new, continuous approach to learning. Though high-school and post-secondary education are critical periods of growth for Nexus, they are no substitute for the constant learning that needs to take place within the workplace. The engine of innovation that drives our idea-based economy requires frequent upgrades of knowledge and skill. Furthermore, while initial orientation may expose employees to some essential competencies and working norms, it cannot and should not represent the bulk of an organization's commitment to educating its people.

Nexus is already attuned to the Information Age theme of continuous learning and expects its potential employers to march to the same beat. Recent research by the Canada Information Office shows that one in four members of this generation strongly agrees with the statement "My skills and knowledge could grow obsolete in five years."[28] A culture of continuous learning needs to keep in mind the following four success factors.

To start with, companies need to think more broadly about the types of learning that Nexus employees require, and then decide on the best vehicles for delivering them. In addition to developing the skills that are needed to get the job done, Nexus employees seek two other kinds of learning: organizational knowledge and personal self-awareness. The desire for organizational knowledge—which includes things like values, structures, and working norms—reflects Nexus' craving to see the "bigger picture" and the ways in which his work can have impact. Personal self-awareness involves an understanding of how effective he is in professional settings, how well he works in a team, and what kind of leadership style he should adopt. This kind of development can come only through honest feedback from others, time for introspection, and opportunities to engage in outside training, self-study, or extracurricular activities.

Organizational knowledge and personal self-awareness involve a different learning rhythm than other types of employee development. More important, they require a different kind of mentorship. The manager who teaches Nexus how to write code or manipulate a spreadsheet may not be the best person to talk to her about the basic life skills needed to survive in a company or how she should handle a difficult ethical decision in the workplace. Indeed, with so many within this generation experiencing divorce or living away from their families, those trying to coach them in the workplace may feel as though they are straying into the realm of parental guidance. This level of advice requires interaction with co-workers in other areas of the company who have experienced the same challenges, or senior managers who are not necessarily part of the employee's formal performance evaluation.

Alberta-based Nova Corporation recently sponsored a mentoring pilot program for its female employees that strove to give them access to different leadership styles and increase the number of cross-company relationships. According to Leah Lawrence, one of the pilot team members, "We intentionally matched mentors with apprentices that were *not* in a direct reporting relationship in order to provide for a more risk-free environment." At the conclusion of the pilot, there was a strong indication that apprentices had improved on their leadership skills and confidence level, as well as their business acumen and general understanding of Nova's operations. Interestingly, the consensus of the apprentices was that the impartiality of their mentor was a significant benefit, and that they felt more comfortable discussing career and organization-wide issues with them than with their own managers. One of the real proofs of success is that the overwhelming majority of the mentoring pairs will be continuing their relationship in an informal way, even though the pilot program has officially ended.

Second, successful learning programs need to take into account Nexus' habituation to frequent feedback. Members of this generation received measurable feedback at regular intervals while at school: when they did an assignment, they were given a mark (good or bad). Since many of them are arriving on the scene with a recent university or college degree—and bad memories of demanding professors—they're even more likely to be obsessed with how they are doing. In a similar way, Nexus' early use of technology exposed him to one of the most instant forms of feedback: the beep on a computer. When was the last time you saw a young person actually read the manual for a new software package? Most jump right in and wait for the computer to show them when they are doing something wrong.

Compare this kind of frequent feedback with the situation in most companies today. When members of this generation get to their first job, it sometimes takes close to a year before they receive any useful indication about their progress. In the meantime, they're kept guessing. We had a chance to see the dangerous effects of delayed feedback in our work with a large group of new high-tech employees. Two members of their "rookie class" had been let go from the company for reasons that, while perfectly legitimate, were not articulated to the other young employees in the group. Yet because their performance reviews were still months away, those that remained grew increasingly insecure about their own positions. Regular check-ins with new employees to discuss their progress and development goals is a crucial piece of the learning puzzle.

Third, pay attention to that dreaded "two-year rule." After twenty-four months with a company, Nexus will start to get itchy feet and will scout around for new job opportunities. For some, it is simply a case of the honeymoon being over. Much of the attrition data we've looked at for our clients show a significant satisfaction gap between new hires and those who have been around for two to three years. Clearly this is a point in Nexus' work life that requires some heavy intervention, particularly if you have your eye on the employee break-even point.

To deal with this inevitable flattening of the learning curve, companies should explore ways to reorient Nexus employees through exposure to new people and a new set of skills. If you're a large company, you may want to bring groups of two-year employees together from different cities or countries and present them with a business problem that the company needs help on. Alternatively, you may want to support the development of their broader professional skills, such as oral presentation or meeting facilitation. In the end, the best reorientation may come in the form of a sabbatical from the company to pursue a burning interest or to travel abroad. Whatever path you choose, leverage this opportunity to re-engage your Nexus employee in the values and direction of the company. Otherwise, he may become another subject for an exit interview.

Finally, continuous-learning programs within companies should experiment with multiple speeds and multiple media. The ol' cookie cutter just won't do. An uncharitable view of this generation claims that its members are suffering from attention-deficit disorder, and that they are too quick to tire of the typical company training materials. The more accurate interpretation is that Nexus has developed a new style of processing information, which affects how it learns and solves problems. In an article entitled "Twitch Speed," Marc Prensky, founder of Corporate Gameware at Bankers

Trust in New York, argues that this generation's exposure to technology "has emphasized and reinforced certain cognitive aspects and de-emphasized others. . . ."[29] The most notable of these new phenomena are *parallel processing*, which enables Nexus to engage in different tasks at the same time; *random access*, which allows Nexus to "click around" for the right answer, rather than move through a linear train of thought; *data visualization*, whereby Nexus consumes large amounts of information in the form of graphic images, rather than lengthy text; and *asynchronous communication* (e.g., e-mail, bulletin boards), whereby Nexus converses with people in different locations at whatever time of day or night she chooses.

All of these examples have profound implications for how learning materials are displayed and transmitted to this generation. As Prensky explains, "If I need a question answered I'll call the three or four people I think might know. It might take me time to get to them, and take them a while to get back to me. When my 22-year-old programmer wants to know something, he immediately posts his question to a bulletin board, where three or four *thousand* people might see it, and he'll probably have a richer answer more quickly."[30] In some cases, face-to-face learning experiences will still be the most appropriate; but in others, experimentation with new media like corporate Intranets will be a more fruitful way to connect with Nexus employees. In some cases, teaching Nexus a new skill will still require a gradual unfolding of concepts; but in others, giving her all the numbers and concepts at once—and letting her assemble the answer on her own—will be a faster and more effective method. In some cases, the corporate broadcast may still be a useful way of announcing something new; but in others, designing a new video game to explain a company policy may have more impact.

Prensky also alludes to another key learning impulse of Nexus: its craving to have fun with technology. While many older employees still view the computer as a necessary evil, this Nintendo generation is continually on the lookout for new ways to be entertained on the PC. One organization we worked with recently initiated a mini game show on its company Intranet to explain its new benefits package. We believe companies can leverage this playful, interactive side of its Nexus employees to develop individual skills and organizational knowledge.

Code #2: It's Not All about Money

As we hinted earlier, though salary is a key factor for some in this generation, it is not a dominating issue for the majority of them. In his book on compensation, *Punished by Rewards*, Alfie Kohn offers a simple but powerful philosophy about the money issue: "Less of it may hurt, but that doesn't mean more of it will help."[31] If a company's goal is quality or commitment, Kohn argues, behaviouralist tactics like incentive pay or bonuses can never match the power of raw, intrinsic motivation. Furthermore, if you make an activity (in this case, work) a prerequisite for getting something else (a bonus), then the activity itself becomes less desirable for its own sake.

There are two reasons why Kohn's warnings about "pop behaviouralism" are particularly appropriate for the Nexus Generation. First, because Nexus the Employee is savvy and sceptical, he is unlikely to be fooled by clever incentive schemes. This generation loves to trick the system, and will divert its precious curiosity and energy towards finding the ambiguities in your incentive plan. In addition, members of this generation are by their very nature looking for intrinsic motivation. They want you to provide the compelling reason to give their heart and soul to the job—otherwise they will start looking for that better opportunity. The best solution is to focus your energies on the reward that really matters to Nexus—the job itself—and on providing her with the freedom, tools, and supportive environment to help her get it done. That's what the new employee contract is all about. Once that foundation has been laid, there are a few rewards-success factors to keep in mind.

First, strive for fairness and openness in how you compensate Nexus employees. If companies set in place a salary and benefits structure that is seen as equitable, and are committed to keeping it up to date, they'll no longer have to worry if Nexus members check to see how their peers are doing. If they don't get the compensation right, nothing else they do will matter. We witnessed this dynamic last year when we were asked to conduct a series of workshops with a group of employees on a new rewards package. Most of our time was spent letting young employees vent about the discrepancies in pay between the company and its competitor, and between offices in different regions of the country.

For the do-it-yourself Nexus Generation, getting it right means providing a competitive suite of benefits. In the *Building Bridges* research, we found that this generation's uncertainty about state-funded pensions and health care led its members to rank basic dental and medical benefits the highest in terms of desirable job features.[32] For Nexus, the two adjectives that matter most in the area of benefits are "portable" and "customized." Nexus the Employee wants the freedom to take her retirement savings with her if she decides to move on; she also wants the ability to pick the benefits that match her lifestyle preferences.

The next key rewards-success factor is to go small, not just big. Thinking about a reward system as a support structure rather than an "if . . . then" proposition should open up the creative possibilities for spontaneous recognition. Traditional rewards like cruises, trips to Hawaii, or fat bonuses are scarce: because you can give out only so many, competition among employees frequently ensues. Good ideas, by contrast, are limitless.

One example of the spontaneous rewards that larger companies are experimenting with is the so-called corporate concierge, a Santa

Claus figure who gives out vouchers to hard-working employees to recognize their commitment. The vouchers might be exchanged for a hair-cut, a day at the spa, a new CD, a trip to the cinema, or a free house-cleaning service. The key element, however, is the unexpected nature of the reward.

The corporate-concierge idea suggests a third tip for structuring rewards: wherever possible, personalize them. If "getting to know the customer" is the new mantra of marketing, why not apply the same philosophy to employee recognition? Peers and managers should take the time to learn about a Nexus employee's hobbies, interests, and favourite luxuries so that the acts of recognition are tailored and therefore more meaningful. Companies may even want to let employees choose how to reward themselves. We recently heard Jim Treliving and George Melville, the senior team of Boston Pizza, describe their employee-recognition campaign, which involved awarding a cash prize to the Boston Pizza franchise that excelled in providing customer service. The winners were given free rein to throw the party of their choice, and Jim Treliving and George Melville were invited out to share in the festivities.

At d~Code, we applied the same philosophy to last year's Christmas celebration. In recognition of our company's achievements, each member of the team was given an allowance and was driven to his or her favourite store to spend it. For several weeks prior to the outing, secret e-mails were sent around the office speculating on where each of us should be taken to redeem our gifts. On the actual day, we spent the afternoon shopping together at a series of locations around the city: a trendy dress shop for a velvet New Year's Eve gown, a music store for a new electric-guitar pedal, a home-decorating shop for silver candle holders and a salad bowl, a CD store for the newest in acid jazz, and a men's shop for a groom's tuxedo shirt (one of us just "shrunk" the freedom zone).

Ultimately, the best reward for Nexus employees is what they want most from work: challenge, collaboration, task variety, and greater impact. While keeping compensation current and competitive is part of the equation, employers should spend equal time thinking about how they might recognize Nexus with the next project or opportunity.

Lest you think our advice works only in high-tech or new-industry companies, consider the example of Petro Canada's Guest Service Attendants (GSAs). Michael Ough, Petro Canada's service and training leader, points to a number of insights about recognition and rewards that the company has gained by listening to their operators across the country. "Because our retailers are constrained in the amount they can pay their employees, a GSA could take that attitude that minimum pay equals minimum work. But we want and expect more. And we can't solve this problem with money." One of the key strengths retailers have, according to Ough, is their ability to solve the "experience paradox": to get a better job, Nexus needs experience; but to get experience, Nexus needs a better job. "Petro Canada says, 'We'll help you solve the problem.' But we will trade the solution for better work from you." Once they're in the door, says Ough, young Nexus employees can learn important new skills in customer service and problem-solving from franchisees, which will help them move up. Eventually, if they've demonstrated the capacity to learn, they'll be rewarded with a new set of even more marketable skills: learning how to operate a small business.

Code #3: Community Is Relationships

Chapter 3 argued that one of the distinguishing features of the Nexus Generation is its new definition of community. The weakening of traditional community structures has led Nexus to search for new ways to belong. And the workplace is quickly filling the gap as the focal point of this generation's communal aspirations. As

Jay Conger suggests, "Workplaces that are able to create a true sense of community become the preferred work environment for this generation."[33] Many companies would argue that they already accommodate this need by having particular community events, such as the yearly staff picnic or golf day. For this generation, however, community is a much more demanding concept. It's not about one-off interactions. It's about ongoing relationships.

To meet Nexus' aspirations, think about the following three dimensions of community.

First, communities flourish when there is a sufficient *quantity* of interactions. Only then can true relationships be forged. In the workplace, that means increasing the opportunities for employees of all levels to interact, both intellectually and socially.

Some companies use sports to foster community ties. Nortel, for example, tries to enhance the quantity of interactions through its intramural softball league—the largest in the world. Mountain Equipment Co-op arranges field days for its employees to try out climbing, canoeing, and cycling gear. Another option is to look to the area of philanthropy or corporate citizenship. Karyo Communications, a Vancouver company that is part of our d~Code network, plans regular outings to non-profit organizations that are of particular interest or concern to employees. Recently, the entire office spent a Friday evening taking tickets and operating the concession stand at a fringe theatre company where one of Karyo's staff sits as a volunteer board member. Other organizations consciously create opportunities for employees to work together on business problems—be it a new orientation program for first-year employees or research in a field critical to the organization's future success. Electronics and technology giant Siemens AG recently established a Futurescape Team of young employees to collaborate with senior managers on strategic issues such as breakthrough technologies, demographic trends, and the competitive forces likely to affect

Siemens until the year 2005. Our own suggestion for community-building is to establish interest-based seminars led by employees and managers of all levels. Topics could range from photography to extreme sports to wine-making—or a combination of all three. This collaborative approach to learning, which eliminates functional and hierarchical barriers, is what community-building is all about.

The look and feel of a company's workspace can also do a great deal to increase the quantity of interactions and meet Nexus' communal aspirations. Ten years ago, the head office for Labatt's marketing division was in an ultra-corporate thirty-second-floor space. In the words of Mike Rapino, "It was white-shirt-and-tie territory, with lots of hierarchy and a long narrow hallway to the president's office." Today, Labatt House is on the second floor, connected to the street, and is outfitted with a neighbourhood-style pub as its main meeting space. Mike believes the team he leads—who are all between the ages of twenty-five and thirty—functions much more cohesively in this new environment, largely because its members have been able to equip it with their definition of comfort and creativity.

The recent redesign of McKinsey and Company's Toronto office is another case in point. Four years ago, senior management recognized that the layout of the office didn't allow for the kind of cross-tenure interaction the company needed to solve problems. "The old architecture was in conflict with what we wanted to be," says Mehrdad Baghai, a thirty-three-year-old McKinsey partner who was a main instigator behind the change. The town-hall design of the new office, winner of *Canadian Architect* magazine's merit award, uses a campus model to bring people together around a number of different kinds of spaces: brainstorming dens, video-conferencing rooms, informal client meeting areas, and team problem-solving spaces. At the centre of it all is a three-storey atrium, or "hive," where the office gathers for social events and key announcements. McKinsey also chose a very non-corporate location for its new three-storey building: the eastern edge of Victoria College at the University of Toronto.

Second, successful workplace communities require *quality* interactions between Nexus and a company's leadership team. All too often, managers and executives limit their contact with younger people to key company announcements or to the doling-out of year-end bonuses. Instead, employers should think about ways to make those rare encounters between senior and junior employees really count.

Let's go back to the example of Petro Canada's Guest Service Attendants. The standard half-hour interaction between a young GSA and his boss, the retailer, is extremely functional: the operator checks in to make sure the young employee has shown up for work, has kept the place clean, and the inventory is accounted for. But according to Petro Canada's Michael Ough, some franchise operators have recognized the potential to build a stronger relationship with GSAs by spending their half-hour differently: by taking the time, for example, to teach GSAs about accounting and inventory management, or by using a more positive approach to feedback. In Ough's words, "If I were a retailer away from the store for an afternoon, I could ask upon my return, 'How did things go?' and leave it at that. Or I could say, 'Tell me one thing you did that was exceptional that I don't know about.'" That establishes a new kind of relationship and positions the GSA to behave differently when left at a site by himself. One franchisee we talked to learned that his young GSA was hosting a late-night radio show in his spare time and decided to tune in one night to listen— at 2 a.m. "When I came in the next day and told the GSA that I had listened to his show," recounts the retailer, "he couldn't believe it. It gave us something new to talk about."

In larger organizations, company presidents have begun to create opportunities for more casual interactions with their employees. At

Urban Juice and Soda, CEO Peter Van Stolk schedules individual performance reviews and has established an open forum every couple
of months to allow people to discuss issues outside the immediate
scope of their jobs. In keeping with the theme of its Web site, ObjecTime's president, Jim McGee, has set up Pool with the President
on Friday afternoons so he can interact informally with his younger
Nexus staff around the billiard table. From virtuality to reality.

In huge companies, it may seem as though "quality time" with
senior executives is impossible to make happen. In the fall of 1997,
however, the Bank of Montreal brought together at its Institute for
Learning a group of new hires from the Operations Group and a
number of the bank's executives, including President Tony Comper. The evening gave the younger Nexus employees a chance to
listen to Comper speak about his career in a more relaxed "fireside
chat" setting. But it also gave senior executives the opportunity to
hear from the new hires about their experiences at the bank. One
member of the senior team we talked to believed the evening gave
her a window into a new generation of employee. "It gave us
a chance to see the bank through *their* eyes. I had no idea what
these kids would say. They blew us away." The lesson? Interactions
between senior leaders and junior employees have the greatest
community-building impact when they are two-way learning
experiences, not one-way broadcasts.

Finally, remember that the best communities are *open* communities. They integrate new members with ease and welcome back old
members with open arms. In today's Information Age economy,
companies need to accept the mobile nature of Nexus employees
and recognize that "I'm leaving" may not mean "I'm gone forever."

Keith Kocho describes the Digital Renaissance community this
way: "My philosophy is to create an open culture where people
can come and go. I believe people should stay only as long as they
are fulfilled—then go where their curiosity takes them." Placer

Dome has also tried to make its organization more open by welcoming back those who have chosen to leave for seemingly greener pastures. "Twenty years ago," says Karen Walsh, "leaving Placer Dome was an act of betrayal and heresy: you left for good. Now we recognize the importance of staying in touch and leaving the door open." Nortel's Sue Halpin also thinks that organizations should be more welcoming of returning employees. "The new knowledge and perspectives they gain on the outside can help to reinvigorate our company. And because they already know Nortel, they're in a position to apply their fresh ideas more quickly."

We believe open communities will be one of the defining features of the new workplace. An atmosphere of openness not only adapts to the reality of Nexus' desire to move and gain skills, but also helps to create a broader definition of employee loyalty, one that is better suited to the Information Age.

Code #4: Create Ownership in a Compelling Vision

The "vision thing" is a much-maligned and overused term in today's business world. Yet it is a particularly powerful way to supply Nexus the Employee with that all-important sense that work matters. Think back to Jared's words at the start of the chapter about Apple in the 1980s or Dave's comments about the revolutionary ambitions of *Wired* magazine.

The first point to make about having a corporate vision picks up on a theme that runs throughout this book: give Nexus something compelling to be a part of. Whether the vision is to put a computer on every desktop (Apple) or to make the Web as reliable as the telephone (Nortel), this generation wants to feel a sense of importance and belonging.

Jennifer Corson believes her six employees sought out Renovators ReSource because of what it stands for: the environment, women's leadership, heritage, and affordability. And their commitment to that vision, she adds, is unwavering. "A container came into our building one day with cast-iron radiators. The only day we could unload it was Sunday. Everyone came out. I didn't even have to ask." Mary Pickering, marketing manager for Greensaver, a small business that consults with homeowners on how to be more energy efficient, describes why the Nexus employees that work with her remain so loyal to the company, despite lower wages and an uncertain future: "There are other work environments with more job security, higher pay, and more benefits, but they are stifling. There is no room for change. Everything at Greensaver can be changed. It's responsive to internal improvements and it makes lasting societal improvements—all at the same time."

Second, Nexus needs to own the vision and put her stamp on it. Sometimes, ownership can be created by giving young employees a chance to interpret the company's mission. Take Blockbuster Video as an example. The overall mission of the company is to provide superior home entertainment for Canadians. But in every individual Blockbuster outlet, young employees live out that vision by creating their own wall of favourite movies (the "staff picks"). In other organizations, ownership of the vision is established by giving Nexus employees responsibility for managing a project from start to finish. This kind of ownership often allows them to see how different parts of the organization work, and how their own contributions fit into the company's overall business plan.

In addition to these informal methods of creating ownership, companies can entice Nexus employees with something more substantial: stock options. Giving young people a piece of the company connects them to the vision in a very powerful and immediate way. It inspires them to make that vision happen. But it is also worth noting that stock options may be the first real thing that a Nexus employee *owns*. A twenty-four-year-old graphic designer likely doesn't have a house, a piano, or a car. By giving her shares in the company, you're launching her into the world of ownership for the first time.

Third, a vision needs to be backed by strong leadership that can inspire Nexus to stretch. The now-legendary antics of Netscape's pioneer, Marc Andreesen, are a good example. When the company was preparing to launch the second version of its software, Andreesen gathered his young employees into an auditorium to announce a challenge: if the team was able to complete the version on time, Andreesen promised to do one of three things: 1) eat tofu; 2) buy in-line skates; or 3) wear spandex. The day that Netscape met its deadline, Andreesen rolled into the auditorium on his blades, wearing spandex, and munching on tofu.

Leadership like this need not come only once a year, or only from the mouth of the company's president. Other members of an organization are critical conduits for communicating and reinforcing the message. If Nexus sees commitment and integrity at all levels, he may just be inspired to become a visionary himself. Chris Chapman believes the success of the Operations Group recruitment effort at the Bank of Montreal owed largely to the vision that was created in the staffing team by Mary Lou Hukezalie. "She clearly articulated the direction she wanted the Operations Group to take, and then said, 'Go for it—I trust you.'" While that much freedom was difficult at times, it allowed Chris to give the vision his own creative spin. And because Mary Lou reinforced the vision with the HR team and through her own actions, Chris always had role models to follow. "The team is committed to realizing the culture shift at the bank. I wanted to match that every step of the way."

Code #5: Support Entrepreneurial Dreams

For our final code, let's come back to the entrepreneurial instincts of Nexus the Employee. When we talk with management teams inside larger companies, there's a common reaction to our observations about the Nexus Generation: "If so many of them want to be entrepreneurs, how will we ever keep them in our company?" We think Nexus' entrepreneurial spirit can be exercised in many contexts. The trick is to give this generation the freedom and support to be entrepreneurs *inside* your organization. Whether it's time off to pursue research, a special fund to back an entrepreneurial scheme, or larger-scale financing for an actual spin-off company, think about the ways in which you might act as a business partner for those Nexus employees who have a dream.

[Nexus and the Future Workplace]

We'd like to conclude this chapter with a question: Did the Boomers change corporate culture?

Most of us would agree that the workplace of today differs significantly from the environment surrounding the "organizational man" of the 1950s and 1960s. As Jay Conger observes, Baby Boomers broke through the "command model" that traditionally ruled over corporations, and introduced notions of teamwork and cross-functional cooperation. They also challenged the aura that had previously surrounded those in positions of authority, and created a movement away from "top-down" leadership. "Within the space of a single generation," he writes, "words like 'boss' and 'president' have completely changed their meanings. No longer positive signs of accomplishment and authority, they now symbolize distance from others. . . ."[34] With the introduction of women into the workforce, the Boomers also spearheaded innovations like flextime and paternity leave. There's little doubt, in fact, that Baby Boomers have made inroads into the stodginess of the corporate world. Whether it's casual Fridays, funky ties, or Dilbert-like humour, the workplace has become at least a bit more fun as a result of their presence.

An obvious follow-up question is: How will the Nexus Generation change the workplace? On first glance, it may seem as though the larger Boomer demographic will dampen any influence Nexus may have had. But on taking a second look, Nexus may have "strength in scarcity." Its skills, experience, and attributes—so crucial to surviving in the Information Age—will be in short supply. And with older Boomers retiring earlier, more positions may be vacated for the next generation of leaders. Assuming Nexus employees don't protest with their feet *en masse*, they may have a golden opportunity to define the parameters of the future of work. We believe the following few workplace trends are worth watching as the Nexus Generation moves into its working prime.

1) Hard and Soft Skills

First, this generation will help the workplace evolve towards an equal recognition of hard and soft skills, and a new appreciation for different styles of leadership. Soft skills—like collaboration, empathy, and consensus-building—were previously thought to be things that women brought to the workplace. As we move into the future, however, they will be seen as critical tools for coping with change and building support for ideas in our Information Age economy. Crunching numbers and analyzing spreadsheets won't be enough. The ability to manage human assets and facilitate collective idea-generation will be the key competencies for the next century.

2) "Real" diversity

As we progress from the dawn of the Information Age into full daylight, diversity is likely to move beyond gender and ethnic group inclusion to take on a broader meaning. Nexus the Employee will experience diversity not only through the people he works with, but also through the tasks he performs, the locations he works in, and the hours he chooses to work. Sally Helgesen, author of *Everyday Revolutionaries: Working Women and the Transformation of American Life*, uses a Starbucks' analogy to explain the more flexible world of work: the menu of options for today's employee has expanded beyond plain coffee to include espressos, macchiatos, and frappuccinos.[35] Traditional models of how, when, and where we work are giving way to a myriad of new, individualized solutions.

3) New Ways of Sharing Knowledge

Nexus the Employee will also influence how knowledge is built, stored, and transferred within organizations. As companies start to leverage the new meaning of experience, employees from different backgrounds and tenure levels will be called on to tackle complex problems, both within the workplace and in the broader global marketplace. Big ideas and innovations are unlikely to come from the mind or laboratory of one employee, but will come from the interplay of several minds from different generations. Netscape, one of the more interesting (albeit mixed) stories of the Information Age, was created through a partnership between the vision of young Marc Andressen and the business expertise of the older Jim Clark. Nexus the Employee's impatience with hierarchy and experience with teams makes her a natural for this kind of cross-generational collaboration.

4) High Touch

While high technology will continue to strongly influence how the workplace develops and shares ideas, this techno-literate generation will also be looking for more "high touch" experiences from its working life. As the hub of community for Nexus employees, the workplace will need to provide meaningful social interaction, as well as support for personal and professional growth. As long as a significant proportion of this generation remains single or childless and is looking for new community structures, the Boomer dream of the home office will have limited appeal for Nexus. Instead, we predict that this generation will try to reconcile its personal ambitions and its need for communal interaction by making the workplace more like home.

5) Let's Get Physical

If life and work for young employees are merging, then the design of physical work spaces will need to keep pace. Canadian organizations may not go as far as their neighbours in Silicon Valley, where the newest trend is to outfit high-tech firms with discount gourmet kitchens, but we expect continued advances in office architecture that will enhance both the quantity and quality of interactions among employees. Companies will need not only to provide more variation in their space—areas for teamwork, for quiet reflection, or for play—but also to ensure that office complexes are outfitted with the latest in the virtual connections that Nexus needs to the outside world.

6) Community Involvement

Finally, we forecast that Nexus employees will influence companies to take a more active part in their local and national communities, and offer increased opportunities for employee volunteership. Indeed, the whole notion of corporate citizenship is taking on a new importance as companies try to meet the changing values and demands of their more socially aware employees. In the old Industrial Age model, an employee's life proceeded through predicable stages: he studied for the first twenty years, worked for the next thirty to forty, and then gave back to the community for the last twenty. In our Information Age, that linear progression has been turned upside down; Nexus is doing everything *simultaneously*. Employees learn at several intervals during their lives, are unlikely to work for the same company for more than five years, and are seeking ways to contribute to the community at an earlier stage. Furthermore, as this chapter has demonstrated, employees are increasingly looking beyond raw compensation (i.e., bonuses) to the very nature of their working environment and what their company stands for.

[Conclusion]

The preceding pages have painted a picture of a generation that is ready and willing to contribute to the idea-based economy of the twenty-first century. The résumé of Nexus the Employee reveals high levels of education, comfort with technology, a wide range of travel and life experiences, and a relatively high tolerance for risk. The challenge for companies is to leverage this potential and adapt their workplaces to suit Nexus' learning style, entrepreneurial spirit, communal needs, work/lifestyle goals, and desire for impact. If this generation is able to fulfill its working aspirations in your organization, we believe you'll more than reap the benefits in terms of fresh perspectives and new ideas. Your workplace could look a lot more diverse—and a lot more like home—if Nexus sticks around.

You have probably noticed the conspicuous absence in this chapter of one of this country's largest employers: government. In Chapter 6, we discuss Nexus' interest in serving its country in the broader context of Nexus the Citizen.

NEXUS THE CITIZEN

We recently asked a roomful of Nexus students to join us in a little game of role-playing. Suppose you are on an airplane, travelling to your favourite vacation spot. There's a chatty fellow next to you who has already hinted that he isn't about to let you enjoy the in-flight entertainment. His English isn't great, but he insists on striking up a conversation. "Tell me about yourself," he says. What would you say? What adjectives would you use?

The responses we got were varied: a Torontonian, a francophone, an Albertan, a Western Canadian, a Jew, an Ismali, a North American, a snowboarder, a student, a Canadian. What these answers reveal is a new generation of Canadian citizens with multiple identities and loyalties. Although Nexus is the first generation of Canadians to know nothing other than the Maple Leaf as its flag, its sense of belonging to the country seems—on the surface—to be open to debate. Identifying with the Canadian nation-state is competing head to head with other powerful Nexus attachments and communities.

Our goal in this chapter is to examine what the idea of citizen means for the Nexus Generation. We'll begin by reflecting on the foundations of citizenship in Canada and considering how Nexus is currently faring in its rights and duties. We'll then move on to the relationship between Nexus and the public service, and discuss potential ways to re-engage younger Canadians in this traditional citizenship role. Next, we'll examine the opportunities that exist for Nexus citizens to contribute to the not-for-profit world, or "third sector." By way of conclusion, we'll discuss the citizenship attributes that will be critical to maintaining our caring Canadian society over the coming decades, and offer suggestions on how to inspire members of Nexus in building a better country for all of us.

[Redefining Citizenship]

Discussions about citizenship ultimately revolve around this question: what is the relationship between individuality and community membership? From the days of the ancient Greeks onward, the task of political philosophers and practitioners has been to find a way to respect individual uniqueness while at the same time create a sense of belonging to something bigger—a nation, a country, or a state. The critical piece in the puzzle is the concept of the citizen, one who can put aside his or her immediate self-interest and contribute to the "common good."

Current Challenges

Now at the peak of what should be its key citizenship years, Nexus is confronting two challenges to the definition of what it means to be a citizen. First, the boundaries of the common good are becoming fuzzy. We've described how globalization is slowly eroding the foundations of the old, insular Canadian welfare state and replacing it with a more outward-looking "competition state." For Nexus, this process is having two polarizing effects.

On the one hand, the generation has reacted to sweeping global forces by turning inward, to embellish its own personal identity with something distinct from whatever fad seems to be sweeping the world. Often, as in the case of Nexus Québécois, the inward pull manifests itself in a return to cultural identity groups, where there is a strong sense of difference. Other times, it means the creation of new and smaller tribes, where members can find an authentic sense of community. Snowboarders and squeegee kids are obvious examples. These more local attachments help to combat the feeling of "rootlessness" that globalization can bring. In the words of Nexus journalist and political commentator Irshad Manji, "As institutional and geographic borders lose their legitimacy, our search for belonging intensifies."[1]

On the other hand, Nexus is fearful of being left behind in a global economy and is therefore turning its gaze outward. Globalization is diverting Nexus loyalties to larger collectives—to North America, to the G7, or to the Western world—rather than keeping her eyes fixed on the traditional nation-state. Today, members of this generation are actively encouraged to study in the U.S. or abroad and often find themselves working in the foreign offices of global Canadian companies or for multinational corporations. Perhaps the most poignant example of shifting loyalties was the 1998 NHL All-Star Game. In what was once "Canada's game," Nexus saw *North America* pitted against the world. Another bastion of Canadianism sacrificed on the altar of global competition.

The second related challenge for Nexus is that the job description of the typical citizen seems to be changing. Some of the traditional ways of experiencing citizenship—voting or military service—are being openly questioned by many Canadians. As a result, this generation has been left wondering why and how it should contribute to the common good.

Mark Kingwell, associate professor of philosophy at the University of Toronto and author of *Dreams of Millennium*, believes globalization has not only changed the Nexus Generation's experience as consumers and employees, but also transformed its conception of rights and responsibilities. Federal and provincial governments are still the place where Nexus is supposed to secure his rights. Yet in many cases, it is private companies rather than governments that are giving him what he really needs: skills, health and dental care, and a sense of purpose or mission. Kingwell believes these trends are potentially dangerous: "Giving back to something we call Canada is less and less meaningful for young people. As a result, they are less inclined to make the necessary sacrifices for the common good." Members of the Nexus Generation, he says, have become less interested in the classic functions of citizenship that our Greek forefathers handed down: political participation, deliberation, and consensus-building.

Historical Legacies

How did we arrive at this dilemma? Earlier, we discussed how Nexus Canadians have become disenchanted with the institution of the state. To understand what this means for the future of citizenship, we need to reminisce briefly about the kind of citizen contract that was created in Canada after 1945—the fertile soil that would ultimately support the growth of Baby Boomer citizens.

At its most basic, the welfare state collectivized the key risks in Canadian society: disease, old age, unemployment, child-rearing. It moved society away from a model that threw money at the poor and towards a pool of shared community resources that anyone could draw on during their time of need. To put it simply, we were all in it *together*. For families, there were baby bonuses. For the elderly, there was the promise of pensions. For kids, there were state nurses who checked for lice and scoliosis. For the destitute, there was welfare and public housing.

At a deeper level, however, the welfare state was based on a number of important assumptions about citizenship. According to the T. H. Marshall (a prominent British sociologist whose ideas on citizenship inspired much of postwar thinking), health care, education, and social security were not merely material benefits. They were entitlements for each member of the community—part of one's identity *as a citizen*. Without the government providing these social goods, a large proportion of the population would have been prevented from exercising their more symbolic civil and political rights.[2]

Marshall's Canadian disciples—Tommy Douglas, Louis St. Laurent, and Lester Pearson—also recognized that citizenship was ultimately a contract of "gives" and "gets." The symbolic "gets," they hoped, would inspire people to give back to the community. Therefore, by securing equal rights of citizenship, the state would also be promoting national unity and loyalty.

Now it's worth remembering that the original philosophy behind the welfare state was shaped by the experience of the working class during the 1930s and 1940s. Citizenship entitlements helped to integrate this group into a common good by tackling the root cause of their exclusion—a poor socio-economic standing. Once this approach appeared to work for them, it began to be applied more generally. In the process, politicians and policy-makers began to focus less on the nuts and bolts of these entitlements, and more on how they could be used to define the qualities and values that held all Canadians together. Citizens expressed their "Canadianness" not just by buying their driveway salt at Canadian Tire or their winter boots at Eaton's, but by pulling out their health cards.

The Baby Boomers grew up under the glow of these welfare-state values. Some older members of Nexus will also remember these entitlements from their childhood. But since the early seventies, the welfare state has seen two major challenges, one economic and one political. Both have led Nexus to question the meaning of equal citizenship and the contract of gives and gets.

The first was the fiscal crisis of the mid-seventies, which the Nexus Generation experienced during its formative years. Essentially, during this period the *economic* foundations underlying citizenship in the welfare state began to erode. With growing inflation and unemployment, the ability of governments to provide the "gets" to citizens was compromised. Unfortunately, rather than addressing this head-on, Canada slid into a decade or more of deficit spending. You've all seen the graphs. For much of its lifetime, Nexus has known little else beyond the red ink.

The second blow was the political crisis of the late seventies and early eighties, which culminated in the series of key Nexus political memories we've highlighted: the rise of separatism, the Quebec referendum of 1980, and the drama surrounding the patriation of the Canadian constitution (remember Trudeau's feather pen?). These events waged a long war of attrition against the *political* foundations of citizenship in the welfare state.

The question here was whether the old approach to integrating the working class could continue to serve as a model for minority groups, such as francophones, or whether additional rights were needed. Former prime minister Pierre Trudeau clearly believed the original model was sound: integration for cultural minorities would best be achieved by guaranteeing the basic civil, political, and social rights of citizenship, not by setting up some kind of "special status." As a result, he worked tirelessly towards enshrining these "gets" into the Charter of Rights and Freedoms. The view of liberals like Trudeau was that recognizing different types of citizenship status would encourage Canadians to focus on their differences, rather than their similarities. Because of this, they might be less willing to make the mutual sacrifices and accommodations necessary for the common good.

Today, despite all the constitutional wrangling, Canada's politicians are still dealing with this political crisis. In fact, it is one of the few examples of consistency that the Nexus Generation *has* enjoyed. When Nexus turns on the TV or picks up a newspaper, she is still bombarded with stories about Quebec's aspirations to be recognized as distinct.

But while taking on the separatists remains an important task, the obsession with this second challenge is distracting political leaders from the more burning issue we outlined in the introduction: a crisis in the very fundamentals of rights, duties, and community membership. Canadian citizenship in our globalized world needs to be more than a dry, legal status defined by a set of rights. Moreover, it can no longer rely on the material entitlements that governments were able to provide during the postwar boom. To be meaningful, and to inspire Nexus, the "gives" and "gets" of citizenship need to be about something *more*. They need to tap into the values and dreams that hold members of a community together. This is the real challenge for Canada's new generation of citizens, and it is likely to resonate well into the twenty-first century.

So where does Nexus stand today in terms of its citizenship contract? We'll start by looking at the rights of protest and political participation, and then move on to consider this generation's sense of duty.

[The "Gets": Citizenship Rights]

With regard to rights, there is an interesting paradox emerging. In some ways, Nexus is also the "Charter Generation." It has had more exposure to rights talk than any other generation. Since the patriation of the constitution in 1982, Canadian society has witnessed an intense focus on rights—from equality between the sexes to the right to life and the right to die, even to the right of children to divorce their parents. In addition, the thirty-odd years of Nexus history have seen a rise in prominence of human rights on an international scale, with the signing of key United Nations declarations—like the Rights of the Child—and the activities of groups such as Amnesty International. Many within the generation experienced the rights movement through music, with concerts from the likes of pop star Peter Gabriel.

But while members of the Nexus Generation have listened (either actively or passively) to these rights discussions, the actual practice of rights by this generation has been different. Our experience suggests that many Nexus Canadians are removed from their civil and political rights of citizenship, largely because they were uninvolved in the battles that won them in the first place.

Thou Doth Protest—Too Little?

First, let's consider the example of protesting. We've argued that the vast majority within Nexus protest with their feet: if they disapprove of something, they simply opt out. An interesting illustration of this is the ongoing discussion about the future of the Canada Pension Plan. Three decades ago, for every pensioner in Canada there were 5.5 Canadians under the age of twenty who could contribute to supporting their retirement. Today, that ratio has been reduced to 2.3 young Canadians to every pensioner, and by the time Nexus reaches retirement, the ratio will be almost dead even. What does this mean for the dollars and cents of the CPP? According to economist William Robson of the C. D. Howe Institue, the math is simple: "In 30 years' time, meeting [pension] obligations will require contribution rates almost triple today's levels."[3] Since this is a burden future workers will try to avoid, the pay-out to Nexus may be much less than what it is putting in.

At d~Code, we're frequently asked by Baby Boomers why Nexus isn't "out in the streets protesting" about this "robbery" of young Canadians. A few Nexus voices in Canada, such as Preston Manning's executive assistant Ezra Levant, have predicted confrontation between Nexus and the over-thirty-five crowd because of these inequities—particularly in light of the current trend for Canadians to retire earlier at higher and higher pay-outs.[4] Yet most Nexus members we've talked to don't feel sufficiently "wronged" to demonstrate over the pension issue. Perhaps, as we discussed in the last chapter, they're too busy calculating their private RRSP investments. Research shows that almost half of Nexus-aged Canadians don't believe that the public-pension system will be there when they need it.[5]

Most theories of protest or rebellion predict that people will revolt if they are experiencing "relative deprivation," meaning that the gap between their expectations and what they actually get becomes too wide to tolerate.[6] But has Nexus crossed this line? We think the answer lies in understanding the diminished expectations of this generation, and how it has been affected by a history of recession and the current climate of do-it-yourselfism. While the Boomers may project dissatisfaction over pensions onto their younger counterparts, Canadians under the age of thirty-five have a different perception of what standard of living they are entitled to. Given the paradoxes of their formative years, it wouldn't surprise them that an entitlement isn't really an entitlement any more.

Furthermore, many in Nexus believe the Baby Boomers' actions of the 1960s proved the futility of protesting just for protest's sake. The stories of the Boomers' anti-Vietnam antics may be legendary (we like the one about naked university students making love on football fields with placards reading We Won't Pull

Out Until Nixon Does), but their effectiveness is questioned by many within the Nexus Generation. Remember the sitcom "Family Ties," where the brash young Alex makes fun of the hippy protests of his parents? While the neo-conservative political views espoused by Alex are not shared by the majority within Nexus, there is something strikingly familiar about his scepticism towards organized protest. The social security and prosperity that allowed Boomers to concern themselves with the "big" questions have been eroded for Nexus; this generation is more consumed with keeping its head above water. The absence of large-scale demonstrations by young people during the Gulf War is another case in point. Rob, a thirty-year-old member of our network, remembers the handful of protesters who came out to picket against U.S. action in the Gulf at his alma mater, the University of Western Ontario. "There were less than a dozen students out on campus. But when [the administration] threatened to shorten frosh week, there was a ton of angry voices raised and lots of traffic blocked."

This attitude towards the right of protest should not be interpreted as apathy. We think the myth of Generation X wrongly painted this generation as disaffected and underestimated its political and social awareness. Research indicates that many Nexus citizens *do* care passionately about issues, the most notable being unemployment, education, Canadian unity, deficit cutting, and health care.[7] Moreover, there are members of this generation (particularly university students) who still play the protest card, as witnessed by the recent demonstrations at the Asia Pacific Economic Conference (APEC), the sit-ins at the big banks over the student-loan program, and the uproar over the honorary doctorate given to George Bush at the University of Toronto. But according to Michael, a twenty-two-year-old d~Coder who has been active in the youth environmental movement, one of the shortcomings of these Nexus change advocates is that they are highly nomadic: they tend to jump from one issue to the next rather than defining a goal or a philosophy. "The focus is more on activism that satisfies an *individual's* identity," he says. "Yet it's really questionable if they are having a large impact in the way social movements in the past have had."

What's more interesting are the new tactics that Nexus citizens are using to raise their voices. One example is the economic boycott, a practice that grew to prominence only in the last twenty years. A recent success story was the four-year boycott of paper shopping bags organized by the Friends of the Lubicon Cree against Asian paper giant Daishowa. Their campaign was designed to support the Cree in their dispute with Daishowa, which since 1988 has been proposing to log an area of Northern Alberta that is subject to unresolved land claims and which recently tried to challenge the boycotters' right to protest in court. According to Kevin Thomas, the Toronto student who acts as a spokesperson for the Friends of the Lubicon Cree, the movement "was designed to convince fellow citizens that it was not just the Lubicon Cree's rights [that] had been threatened, but the rights of all Canadians."

Despite being an admirer of consumer boycotts, Nexus activist Duff Conacher believes this form of protest is getting harder and harder to pull off. "The whole notion of consumer power has hit a wall in Canada. Boycotts take an incredible amount of research and sacrifice, and you need to make a huge percentage of a company's market disappear before they'll notice. In other words, 'mass protest' works only if it's *really* massive." As head of Canada's Democracy Watch, Conacher takes a different and more hard-headed approach to raising his voice—one based less on placard-waving and more on education, research, and the effective use of the media. "Mass protests tend to be against things, and present no alternative solutions. At Democracy Watch, we try to be for things—like reforming the democratic process so that it reflects the concerns of people, not corporate interest groups." For democracy to work, he argues, governments need to detail the impact of corporate actions and to listen to individual citizens' concerns about protecting the public interest.

For Nexus, a generation raised on media and savvy about marketing, Conacher's pragmatic style may be a model for future protest. One thing is certain: skilful use of the media is a more efficient method than placard-waving of getting Nexus' messages out to the masses.

X Marks the Spot

But what if citizens choose not to speak up? A prominent Canadian political theorist, Will Kymlicka, has drawn up a list of citizenship qualities he sees as crucial to a healthy, democratic society. At the top of the list, he argues, is the "desire to participate in the political process in order to promote the public good and hold political authorities accountable."[8]

Here the Nexus track record also appears to be mixed. Intuitively, it would make sense that if given the chance to do something for the first time, a young person would jump in with both feet. (How many of you didn't go for a driver's test soon after your sixteenth birthday?) Yet on the voting front, this logic seems to be breaking down. Currently, only 63 per cent of eighteen- to twenty-one-year-olds vote in federal elections (compared with 88 per cent for those over fifty).[9] Furthermore, according to a 1997 Angus Reid poll, only 5 per cent of Canadians in this age group actively followed the last federal-election campaign.[10]

From the d~Coders we've talked to, two factors seem to be driving this lacklustre voting performance. First, freedom to vote is *assumed* for members of this generation. Unless they are part of a refugee family that has experienced political repression or have particular ties to political events in far-flung areas of the world, clarion calls to exercise the franchise largely fall on deaf ears. Second, many in this generation—even those who do vote—believe their act of voting won't make any real difference. Having spent most of their lives in a political environment where parties sit somewhere in the middle—and having seen political leaders like Lucien Bouchard and Jean Charest swap their party affiliations with ease—most Nexus members don't believe that an election victory for one party will mean a radical change in their lives. While recognizing that democracy is a muscle that gets weak if you don't exercise it, the voting members of our network are "working out" with very little enthusiasm. As we saw in Chapter 3, close to half of the generation is either ambivalent about government or sees it as irrelevant to their lives.[11]

To compensate for this lack of activism on the electoral front, some members of the Nexus Generation have shifted the battleground to the arena of interest groups or non-governmental organizations (NGOs). Greenpeace, for example, is an organization that has seen countless Nexus citizens move through its ranks. Many have learned the ropes inside Greenpeace and then carried on to create issue-oriented groups of their own. The key focus, however, is issues, not ideology. Few of these organizations have a broader platform or vision for Canadian society as a whole.

Other Nexus citizens are exploring more individualistic avenues for their political participation. As Irshad Manji puts it: "This is an age when institutional uncertainty exports the burden of democracy to that arena which we can directly influence: our individual constitutions and . . . our one-on-one relationships."[12] Mark Kingwell also contends that for Nexus the personal *is* the political: "This generation is making its statements not only through its attitudes about politics and society, but also through its consumption behaviour and its individual choices about life and work." One noteworthy example is the recent movement towards politically correct language, which pushes political activism down to the level of grammar. Another manifestation is Nexus' love of irony in discussions of political or social affairs. Political satire is nothing new; those unflattering cartoons of public figures date back to late-eighteenth-century Britain. Nevertheless, the "irony meter" has definitely been turned up for this generation, so much so that irony is becoming akin to a moral stance.

But as Kingwell points out, this more subtle form of protest does not mean that Nexus has written off the political sphere altogether. Rick Mercer's rants on "This Hour Has 22 Minutes" mock politicians, not the political process.

[The "Gives": Citizenship Duties]

Those are some observations on the rights side of the citizenship contract. With respect to duty, the picture is even more fuzzy. Some of the traditional paths for exercising one's citizenship duties—such as military or political service—have lost concrete meaning for the Nexus Generation.

There's No Life like It

In the last decade, the Canadian military has seen a crisis in both confidence and enrolment. As the nature of war changes from flashy, full-scale battles to surgical strikes and messy civil conflicts, the honour associated with being a soldier has diminished. And remember that the war that most registers on the Nexus radar screen, the Gulf War, seemed more like a video game (and a boring one at that) than a serious act of international law enforcement. Even the once glorious badge of peacekeeper has been tarnished by the bloody images of civilian beatings in Somalia.

It seems that those who are joining the armed forces are doing so for skill-development reasons, rather than from a burning desire to serve their country. Free tuition and a lack of viable career alternatives are also prominent motivations for today's Canadian soldier. Jamie Watson, a thirty-one-year-old former captain with the Canadian military who is now a commercial pilot, remembers the reaction of his colleagues when war broke out in 1991 in the Persian Gulf. "Everyone in the corridors was muttering, 'Hey, we didn't sign up for this!'" To explain the apparent demoralization in Canada's military (the subject of a recent parliamentary investigation), Jamie points to cut-backs and budgetary concerns. Members of Nexus who have joined the forces in junior ranks can expect not only an abysmally low paycheque (one skirting the edge of what is officially called working poor), but also run-down and shoddy housing for themselves and their young families.[13] While brass and polish were the sought-after perks of servicemen and women in the past, today, says Jamie, "The reality is that many soldiers buy their own boots."

Thirty-four-year-old Major Billy Allan, an aerospace engineer who currently resides with his family in Cold Lake, Alberta, insists the current malaise in the military stems from a deeper problem with societal values. With a decade and a half of service under his belt, Allan still feels the loyalty and pride that attracted many young men and women to serving in uniform in the past. However, he has seen three-quarters of his graduating class of the Royal Military College in Kingston leave for apparently greener pastures. "The values demanded by military service are not valued today by our broader society, " he explains. "Things like sacrifice and commitment are unpopular things. In my opinion, no one will sign up to anything for nine years [the typical minimum]—not to a marriage, a job, or a bank account. So why would the military be any different?" In years past, those in the armed forces believed their commitment would be matched by a long-standing military tradition to look after their interests, but that unwritten contract has now broken down. "Before, it was enough for us that there was a 'they' out there to speak on our behalf. Now, there are more than enough examples to show that there is no 'they.' By necessity, the leadership today is preoccupied [with] building business cases to prove to Canadians that the maintenance of peace and security has financial value."

It's hardly surprising that the Canadian Armed Forces has launched an impressive national ad campaign—which includes subway posters and clips in movie theatres—to sell the positive features of a career in the military. Interestingly enough, it may be the domestic activities of the army that will turn Nexus perceptions around. During the 1997 Manitoba flood and the recent ice storm in Ontario and Quebec, military servicemen and -women were greeted with gratitude and enthusiasm by most of their fellow citizens.

Unlikely Candidates

Next, let's examine the political aspirations of this generation. A key point to re-emphasize about Nexus citizens is their extreme scepticism towards politicians. Research shows that 47 per cent of young Canadians believe that "politicians don't listen to young people."[14] Further, when asked in the *Building Bridges* survey to rank careers they saw as desirable, only 6 per cent of respondents chose politician—just ahead of commissioned salesperson but well below occupations such as filmmaker and entrepreneur.

In discussions with our d~Coders and other members of the generation, we have observed this lack of respect for political leaders. It's not that those in this generation don't know what a good leader is. Quite the contrary. We hear a number of leadership qualities consistently mentioned by Nexus as being attractive, qualities that mirror their consumer expectations and preferences: humility, honesty, courage, vision, and humour. However, when asked to name a political leader they admire, many of them come up empty. Jean-François, a twenty-nine-year-old d~Coder from Montreal, sums it up best: "I don't think the verb 'admire' applies to the feelings I have for any politician. I can't say there are any I admire. Just some that don't disappoint me as much as others."

The political leaders that are mentioned tend to include larger-than-life figures like René Lévesque, Malcolm X, and Nelson Mandela. The latter, in particular, is seen by many within this generation as a leading political figure of the twentieth century. "In a universe where most politicians and leaders seem to lack anything resembling a moral centre," says Maged, a twenty-six-year-old d~Coder from Winnipeg, "Mandela is a rare breed of person."

One of the current Canadian politicians who does appear to hold promise for this generation is Quebec Liberal leader Jean Charest. Members of Nexus we've talked to almost universally applaud Charest's seemingly selfless decision to put his dedication to Canada ahead of his own personal fortunes (at least temporarily). As a one-time minister of Youth and minister of the Environment, the former federal Tory leader also has experience in issues near and dear to Nexus hearts. In the province of Quebec, Charest's ratings show he is popular with all age groups—and especially young people. Patrick, from Montreal, offers this explanation: "Charest is the first politician from Quebec who's not afraid to say he's proud to be Québécois *and* Canadian. He may be the one who can communicate a fresh, positive vision of Canada to young Québécois."

The critical attitudes shown towards politicians are not unique to Nexus. Instead, they reflect a steady erosion in support for political leaders that has occurred during the life-span of the generation (roughly since 1970).[15] Nevertheless, they do raise fundamental questions as to where the next generation of political leaders is going to come from.

Indeed, when you look at the participation of young Canadians in partisan activities, the message is much the same. Less than 5 per cent of those in the eighteen-to-twenty-four age range have actively worked in a political party.[16] One reason for this is that ideology has become less meaningful; you no longer distinguish what you're about by joining a left-wing or a right-wing party. Another explanation is that the policy-development processes of traditional political parties have closed them off to grass-roots ideas. Unless you're prepared to compromise a ton—or manage to join a party at the very top—it's tough to make a difference. "If a young person wants to know what it is like to be marginalized," says Duff Conacher, "he or she should join one of the major political parties."

There are two interesting exceptions to this. The first is the Reform Party, where members of the Nexus Generation are driving many of the new ideas behind the party platform. According to twenty-nine-year-old Calgary Southeast MP Jason Kenney, the younger members of Reform have greater "moral authority" than they do in Canada's older parties. Perhaps that's why the party has been able to attract members of the under-thirty crowd to its ranks. "Most people graduating from high school today heard about Reform during their education," explains Kenney. "They're attracted to the fact that we aren't tied to political traditions as many of the mainstream parties are. In addition, the Reform Party has spoken about generational equity and the degree to which policies such as the CPP have compromised the future of this generation. This generation has been looking for a spokesperson for them, and Reform fulfills this need."

The sovereigntist parties inside Quebec—the Bloc Québécois and the Parti Québécois—have also seen high levels of Nexus participation. Both are significantly influenced by the passions and dreams of young francophones. Elise, a twenty-three-year-old d~Coder and PQ supporter, offers this rationale: "I loved the leadership of Jacques Parizeau, for the same reasons I like the PQ. Strong ideas and a clear project to be part of." Polls taken soon after the 1995 referendum consistently showed that support for sovereignty in Quebec tends to be higher among those eighteen to thirty-four (57 per cent) than among those over sixty-five (28 per cent).[17]

In both of these cases, the attraction for Nexus relates back to some of its youthful generational genes: the Reform Party represents an opportunity to be part of something new and non-establishment, while the BQ and PQ represent an association with a compelling vision (an independent state of Quebec). Neil Nevitte, author of *The Decline of Deference*, makes the same observations about the attitudes of youth towards political change: "The young are always significantly more likely than the old to prefer new ideas."[18]

In closing, it's worth keeping in mind that Nexus citizens already constitute close to 40 per cent of Canada's voting population. As we approach 2001—the likely year of the next federal election—the political attitudes and engagement of young Canadians could have a profound impact on the shape of government and society. As Jason Kenney observes, "2001 will have over two million first-time voters—the largest segment since 1957. This signals a demographic shift in politics in favour of a new generation. Younger people should not be shy about the political muscle they can flex." If the Nexus Generation wants to be heard, it will be. If it continues to opt out, it's agreeing to be governed by someone else.

[Nexus and the Public Service: A Noble Pursuit?]

The forces that have redefined Nexus' citizenship contract have also affected this generation's view of the career of public servant, whether provincial or federal. For example, 1997 statistics indicate

231

that only 8 per cent of Canada's approximately 187,000 federal public-service employees are under the age of thirty (the average age is forty-three).[19] In a country where a professional, non-partisan public service has been instrumental in building democracy and prosperity, these numbers are worrying, to say the least.

There are three reasons why members of Nexus are such an important resource for Canada's public service. First, we argued in the previous chapter that our economy is increasingly being driven by knowledge and ideas, rather than the hard inputs of production. In order to cope with this transition, the Information Age skills and experience of Nexus are as useful to the public sector as they are to the private sector.

Second, the current demographic skew within the public service towards older employers is making this institution less and less astute in meeting the needs of a more diverse Canada. During the last two decades, there has been a widening gap between the profile of the Canadian population and that of the public service. The Nexus Generation brings not only a younger perspective, but also a composition that is ethno-culturally and linguistically diverse.

Third, as those within the public service begin to retire, there is a serious risk that institutional memory will be lost. As of January 1, 1998, twenty-three thousand federal public servants were eligible to retire (12 per cent of the total public-service population). Many more are leaving to take up lucrative positions in the private sector. Unless knowledge can be transferred and mentorship programs put in place for young rising stars, this mass exodus could have serious repercussions on the quality of policy development in the years ahead.

The 1997 La Relève Task Force, initiated by the Public Service Commission in Ottawa, is meant to tackle these burgeoning problems. La Relève—which suggests a "changing of the guard"—is dedicated to building a more dynamic public service that fully uses the talent of its people and can better adapt to the future needs of Canadian society. In the words of Jocelyne Bourgon, clerk of the Privy Council, in her 1998 report to the prime minister: "[To] build a modern and vibrant professional, non-partisan public service, it is necessary to commit as much time and energy to human resources management as to policy development or service delivery . . . to retain, motivate and attract a corps of talented and dedicated public servants requires profound change."[20]

The La Relève report rightly points out that the current crisis in the public service is partially driven by hiring freezes and downsizing. But for Nexus, the issue runs much deeper than this. The bottom line is that a career in the civil service has become unattractive for many of Canada's young professionals. Trevor Bhupsingh, a thirty-year-old analyst who works in the Policy, Research and Communications Branch of the Public Service Commission, describes the magnitude of the recruiting challenge: "Our problem is that the public service is facing massive competition for skilled labour from the private sector. And we are competing with three strikes against us: limited opportunity, limited remuneration, and a perceptual crisis about government. It's hard for us to appeal to this new generation when we're not yet sure where we're going."

The Push Factors

At the root of the crisis is the fact that the mission of the public servant has lost its cachet. Remember the heady decades of the 1960s and 1970s, when Canada's best and brightest flocked to Ottawa to serve the public good? The prestigious title of civil servant was a magnet for many Canadians. Moreover, the challenges awaiting these eager minds—health care, multiculturalism, education reform, the constitution, industrial policy—were truly noble pursuits. For Nexus the Citizen, the picture has been much different.

She grew up in the era of "bad government," debts, and scandals. Furthermore, she saw many of the projects that politicians sponsored during the eighties and early nineties—such as the Meech Lake and Charlottetown accords—crumble. This lack of credible success stories has made a government career seem less and less appealing. Tim Barber, who has been working in Ottawa for the last five years (most recently as an assistant to Canada's trade minister, Sergio Marchi), sums up the contrast between then and now: "Three decades ago, the limits of government programs were the limits of your imagination. The public service could offer the bright young minds of Canada an exciting, creative career in re-designing government. Now, policy is being developed by politics, with very little front-end thinking. And most of it lacks the impact and substance that it had in the past."

The recent war on the deficit has contributed to Nexus' perception that government is no longer about big ideas. Everywhere Nexus looks—whether it is to the federal Liberals or to Ralph Klein's Tories in Alberta—slashing deficits has been the dominant sport. In fact, it's surprising just how many young people, when asked about the priorities of government, still reel off the well-used phrase "reducing the deficit." Many within this generation don't recognize their government in any other capacity.

While debt management has been crucial to the resurgence of our Canadian economy, there's clearly a downside to all this talk about slashing: it's *uninspiring*. Paul Corriveau, a thirty-one-year-old consultant who formerly developed policy in the Prime Minister's Office, believes the wartime analogies used by finance ministers were off the mark: "When I listened to Ernie Eves announcing the slashes of the Harris government, he spoke in a celebratory tone. He didn't speak with any sadness or shame about the mistakes of his predecessors. And he showed no recognition of the permanent damage that has been done to government and its image—damage that his own rhetoric was exacerbating." For the Nexus Generation, which wants to build rather than destroy, it's little wonder that a career as a public servant has been an unattractive proposition.

As Corriveau's words suggest, deficit reduction is not a creative exercise that you can sink your teeth into. Moreover, it's not an inclusive process that draws on input from multiple constituents. It's important to remember that deficit-cutting was something done behind closed doors, with high-level ministry officials bargaining with the Treasury Board over which program should be axed. Most young people in government weren't privy to the process. Brian Humphreys, a provincial public servant in the Saskatchewan NDP government, describes another exclusionary aspect—a structural one—that faced many of his Nexus peers: "Understandably, deficit-cutting has kept young people out structurally. Because of downsizing, the system has become backed up and most younger public servants can't get into a position of real influence."

A further drawback of the public service for Nexus is its maze of bureaucracy. To a generation accustomed to rapid change and eager to take risks, the clumsy policies, procedures, and acronyms of government departments are an unnecessary evil. Indeed, the Nexus workplace priorities we've identified—flexibility, challenge, skill development, and opportunities for impact—have been especially difficult to realize in this environment. Stephane Letourneau, who left the Department of Foreign Affairs three years ago for a job in the private sector, felt he was compromising his creativity and freedom to keep the enormous machinery of government moving. "For me, the public service became a professional waste of time. I was too impatient and too restless to sacrifice my most creative years with the hope of advancement somewhere down the line." Other young public servants we spoke to complained about pushing paper, begging for budget dollars to support their projects, and diverting their energies into work that ultimately didn't go anywhere.

This brings us to another difficult aspect of government for Nexus: its traditional view of experience. The dominant ethos of the public service has been that younger employees need to pay their dues in lower-level work—regardless of their level of education or other experiences—before rising to positions with greater responsibility. But for the majority of Nexus, this long range contract is no longer tenable. If career expectations involve at least three or four job shifts over an adult lifetime, then years of waiting for real challenge and impact seem too high a price to pay. "The problem with our generation," says Tim Barber, "is that if you do the same thing for more than five years you're viewed as a loser."

Unfortunately, over the coming decades, the public service will continue to carry the stigma of the cut-back years of the early 1990s. Although younger people had previously been willing to accept less money to serve the public good, Nexus now believes the public service can offer precious little by way of job security or, more important, career development. Government bureaucracies, caught in their own soul-searching exercises, need to offer something more substantial to fresh and bright-eyed university graduates. Ben Farmer, who works with the Public Service Commission, puts the question this way: "Do we make a commitment to the public service, and accept a lower wage, even if we aren't sure that we will ever reach our goals or potential?" For many in this generation, the proposition is too risky: they want their experience and contributions valued *today*.

Farmer also hints at a related conundrum: the hidden ageism that pervades the public service. While La Relève has instigated efforts to make the public sector more "horizontal," and to increase the amount of teamwork across generations, many older public servants are more interested in maintaining the status quo. The overwhelming majority of managers in the federal bureaucracy are Baby Boomers, some of whom have children as old as those in the Nexus Generation. As a consequence, many find it difficult to treat Nexus employees as equal colleagues, or to give equal weight to their ideas. To add fuel to the fire, they are holding the positions that Nexus covets and are paranoid (justifiably) about being phased out. These factors have converged to shut off the knowledge-transfer taps within the public service. The more senior are reluctant to share information with the more junior, for fear of jeopardizing their own positions. As long as tenure is the trump card, Nexus is facing a losing game in this sector.

To retain the best and the brightest of the Nexus Generation, we believe the designers behind La Relève should take heed of the codes of conduct set out in our last chapter: create an environment for continuous learning, provide a more meaningful system of rewards, build a stimulating and supportive community, communicate a compelling vision, and allow Nexus to exercise its entrepreneurial spirit. Yes, we need to take care of those Canadians who have given their sweat and tears to the public sector for twenty to thirty years. But we also need to give younger Canadians a reason to come to the public service, and more important, a reason to stay.

Failure to address the Nexus Generation's aversion to the public service could have an impact beyond the institution of government itself—it could lead to a breakdown in the spirit of partnership between the private and public sectors that has built our country into what it is today. If the public service continues to age and young Canadians continue to flock to the private sector, we may see a widening gulf between government and business. Rather than collaborating to solve social and economic problems, the private and public sectors will create a new version of the "two solitudes" in Canada. Over time, Canadians could see more of the bold moves, such as the recent wave of bank mergers, that disregard government altogether. The business community will keep forging ahead, complaining that government is trying to hold it back.

An alternative scenario would see successful partnerships between government and business, like the recent Team Canada trade missions, continue to flourish. But as any politician or public servant will attest, an initiative such as Team Canada requires extremely thorough groundwork and preparation. Without the best talent on *both* sides of the table, the rationale for collaboration will be much less compelling.

The Pull Factors

So how do we re-engage Nexus in thinking about the public sector as a place to learn and contribute? One possibility is to harness the energy and ideas of those Nexus civil servants who *are* inspired by serving the public good. Brian Humphreys insists that government was the best avenue available for him to contribute something back to the community and country: "I not only learned about how government works," he explains, "but also understood the positive role it can play. I saw firsthand how nimble and powerful government can be when good people have great ideas. If given a meaningful role, a young public servant truly can make a difference."

Chris Alexander, who at the age of twenty-nine is deputy director (Russia) in the Eastern Europe Division of the Department of Foreign Affairs and International Trade, wouldn't dream of trading in his experiences for the economic gain of a private-sector position. His time in the public service has offered him a variety of benefits, including national and international travel, a better work/life balance, language skills, and a chance to shape the bigger picture. "As a lawyer," says Alexander, "would you like to help two companies merge or would you like to draft new law that will potentially affect all Canadians? In the public service, you can really leave an imprint on society."

In marketing the public service to the Nexus Generation, we recommend drawing on the themes of transparency and differentiation we discussed in Chapter 5. First, as Alexander suggests, the public service needs to start highlighting the opportunities for advancement and skill development that *do* exist for Nexus. "Because there are so few young people in the civil service, they are treasured as a resource by those who take the long view. As the decade comes to a close, our 'new world experience' will be a crucial resource for governments." In fact, he contends that 1998 is a perfect year for members of this generation to check out the public service. "There is a balanced budget now, and priorities have shifted so that new program development is on the horizon. It's possible to dream again."

In addition, the public service needs to trumpet the value only it can offer younger Canadians. Ultimately, this "sales pitch" to Nexus will depend more on intangibles than on money or status. As Trevor Bhupsingh puts it: "The public sector offers diverse issues, political excitement, and the opportunity to work for the public interest. The private sector is all about the bottom-line profit motive." Chris Alexander agrees: "There are lots of things you can do here that you can't do anywhere else—romantic things and big-picture issues. Young people by their very nature have a potent sense of idealism that needs an outlet."

But before the public service can provide that outlet, two things need to occur. Within the public sector itself, a challenging environment needs to be created so Nexus can contribute to its full potential and select from a variety of career paths. And within society at large, respect for the role of the public servant will need to be re-established. In short, Canadians must believe again that government matters.

Liberal MP John Godfrey thinks that Canada needs new and compelling national projects that will demonstrate to Canadians, particularly those who have grown up in the deficit era, what government is capable of. By "national project," Godfrey means a problem or issue that is too complex to be handled by one sector of society alone; instead, it requires the collaboration of many. In the past, examples might have included putting a man on the moon or (in Canada) the creation of a national health service. Today, candidates might be a national program to enhance early child development or a commitment to connect every grade-school child to the Internet. By creating a collective purpose around a key issue, and having government play the role of facilitator, Godfrey believes we may be able to elevate the stature of government in the eyes of younger generations. "Government shouldn't be in the business of merely executing transactions," he claims. "Instead, the role of government is to step back, take a wider or systemic view, and rally Canadians together around the values that are most important to them." As Godfrey points out, prior to 1967 health care wasn't a national value.

Does Nexus the Citizen want government and the public service to play that broader role? The evidence suggests that she does. While the formative years of this generation make it sympathetic to a reduced role for government, it is clear that "less government" does not mean "no government." Despite proclamations from the Reform Party about the right-wing bent of younger generations, research conducted by Environics in early 1998 (after the release of the Liberal government's balanced budget) shows that Canadians between eighteen and thirty-four were the *most likely* age group to believe that fiscal surpluses should be directed towards funding programs and services, rather than used for tax cuts.

Which of these do you think is most important? (Percentage response)

	18–24	25–34	35–44	45–54	55–64	65+
Cutting taxes	24	23	21	19	21	19
Paying down the federal debt	33	38	45	42	42	42
Increasing or restoring funding to programs and services	43	38	33	37	34	34

Source: Environics, Fiscal Issues Survey (February 1998); sample size: 1,534

When asked which areas should get that funding, Nexus indicated that health care, student loans, the unemployed, employment training, and the working poor were the top five priorities, while some of the traditional functions of government—such as repairing roads and highways or maintaining the armed forces—fell further down the list. These figures indicate that although members of Nexus expect a more focused set of activities for government, they also support a public-policy agenda that will enhance the health and economic well-being of Canadians. The real task is to inspire them to get involved in shaping it.

[Nexus and the Third Sector: From Philanthropy to Citizenship]

As governments redefine their place in Canadian society in a post-deficit era, the responsibility of individual citizens to contribute to the common good is taking on a new importance. In the realm of health and social services, where governments previously backed core operations, non-governmental organizations and private citizens are stepping in to donate money, time, and energy to ensure that Canada remains a country that cares about those who might otherwise fall through the cracks. In other areas of society—such as the arts, culture, or amateur sports—groups of Canadians have become more aggressive in their fund-raising approaches in order to keep these important threads of our national fabric in place.

Organized activities such as these fall under the umbrella of what has come to be known as the third sector. This sector meets a variety of citizen needs that either are not fulfilled by commercial, for-profit businesses or cannot be run directly by governments. Patrick Johnston, president and CEO of the Canadian Centre for Philanthropy (CCFP), claims that every single day, millions of Canadians enter in and out of the third sector without even knowing it. "It happens when they drop their kids off at day care; when they go for a lunch-time workout at the YMCA; when they visit art galleries and museums; when they write their notes on the stationery they bought from the UNICEF boutique." Furthermore, there are countless Canadians who work within the third sector, either as volunteers or as paid employees. Research undertaken by the CCFP concluded that there were approximately forty thousand community- based charities and foundations in Canada in 1993—and they employed just over half a million part-time and full-time employees.[21]

Despite all of this activity, the third sector is a relative unknown to Canadians, particularly those in the Nexus Generation. Johnston believes there are several reasons for the lack of awareness. To start with, there is very little public discussion about this important piece of Canadian society. "Media stories relating to the 'third sector,' when there are any, are usually consigned to the Lifestyle section of the newspapers," Johnston claims. In addition, until recently there has been very little academic attention devoted to the third sector, and young citizens are rarely educated about the possibilities for employment and volunteership. Finally, as Johnston explains, the third sector tends to be defined in negative terms. "It encompasses organizations that are not-for-profit and non-governmental. Beyond that, there is little, if any, consensus about its boundaries. It may be that the term *invisible sector* or *no-name sector* is a more appropriate description."

Given the scepticism of Nexus citizens towards partisan politics and the public service, the relatively unknown third sector may in fact offer the greatest immediate opportunity to engage them in their duties as citizens. For Nexus, the third sector offers at least four kinds of citizenship possibilities: private donations, volunteerism, corporate citizenship, and paid employment. We'll touch briefly on the opportunities and challenges of each.

A New Kind of Donor

To begin, let's go back to our discussion of Nexus' disposable income. For many in this generation, the capacity to donate to charitable causes is substantial—especially in light of the extended freedom zone. Coupled with this financial capacity is what appears to be a strong philanthropic motivation running through this generation of citizens. In *Reconnecting Government with Youth,* 56 per cent of Nexus respondents strongly agreed with the assertion that "helping others and giving to charity is an important part of being Canadian." Furthermore, 43 per cent strongly *disagreed* that "all you have to do is pay your taxes and vote to fulfil your obligations as a Canadian."[22]

Nevertheless, there are two obstacles for not-for-profit organizations that seek to make a play for the wallets of Nexus citizens. First, donors in this generation are harder to find. For large-scale fund-raisers like the United Way, the formula used to be quite simple: appeal to young donors in the annual workplace campaign. Today, however, many members of Nexus are in non-traditional workplaces or have struck out on their own. Appealing to this fragmented mass is a much more daunting task, and requires more sophisticated fund-raising techniques. Second, Nexus donors have a much wider choice when it comes to charitable causes. That means that many of them want to see and feel the impact of their dollars. Gone are the days when a donor would put funds into a discreet box or respond to guilt-ridden messages. Anne Golden, president of the United Way of Greater Toronto, believes that today's charities need to "help donors manoeuvre their way through the myriad of worthy causes by demonstrating how and why their money will address community problems." This means providing Nexus donors with a firsthand, interactive experience with a social-service agency.

The "New Age" Volunteer

d~Code's experience with members of the Nexus Generation indicates that they have both the time and the inclination to give back to their communities through volunteerism. Indeed, the *Building Bridges* research reveals that while many Canadians between the ages of eighteen and thirty-four are disenchanted with the formal political process, 64 per cent believe they will volunteer in the community at some point in their lives.[23] Moreover, while only 8 per cent feel good about the future of Canada, 33 per cent claim that they feel good about their community. These results demonstrate that Nexus is not "checking out" of society; she is simply defining her role and contribution in new ways.

Although statistics like these point to a strong community spirit within the generation, there are significant obstacles to activating it. First, we should keep in mind that the Nexus Generation will put as many demands on the voluntary sector as it does on any other: it will not be content to play the role of "envelope licker." According to Stoney McCart, president of *TG Magazine*, "Many young people feel that they are continually waiting in the wings for their big break—whether it's in the workplace or at a not-for-profit organization. Whatever it is you ask young people to do, be it paid or volunteer, it has be *meaningful*—both to them and society at large." Nexus volunteers want to be involved on the ground floor, in the design of community activities and programs. They also want their views represented on the board of directors. And when not-for-profits seem in need of some shaking up, Nexus volunteers want the opportunity to exercise their entrepreneurial spirit.

It's also important to acknowledge that given the realities of the competitive job market, Nexus views the not-for-profit world as an environment in which to gain skills and experience. Some in the voluntary sector lament the self-interestedness of these "New Age" volunteers, claiming that younger generations have lost their spirit of altruism. Others, like Gordon Floyd, the Canadian Centre for Philanthropy's director of public affairs, believe not-for-profit organizations need to look beyond the motivations for involvement and focus on the rewards a volunteer needs to keep coming back. "The next generation of volunteers," he claims, "holds the key to continuing the improvement of our quality of life here in Canada—but only if we can provide them with the opportunities to act out their values, to experience growth through self-improvement, and to see the difference that they can make." In other words, we should leverage the Nexus Generation's current interest in the third sector—whether that interest is motivated by social obligation or the desire to build personal competencies—and provide its members with a context in which to act out their citizenship.

Finally, there are few inspiring role models of volunteerism or philanthropy that Nexus can identify with. Stoney McCart thinks this deficiency can be traced to the Boomers, "who tended to have more celebrity-oriented role models growing up." As a result, she explains, "there has been a gap in the younger generations as far as communicating the value of contributing to society. It's the great paradox of our age of communications. We are connected to more and more people, but we have no mechanisms for collaborating on specific community projects." Without the examples or the means to connect this generation to the causes it cares about, the vast potential of the Nexus volunteer may not be realized.

A Career in the Not-for-Profit Sector

A positive experience as a volunteer could lead some members of this generation to consider the not-for-profit world as an option for paid employment. As shown earlier, close to half a million Canadians have already made the third sector the focal point for their careers. And writers like Jeremy Rifkin believe this sector holds the key to addressing chronic problems of unemployment that have marred the transition from the Industrial Age to the Information Age. Says Rifkin, "As the private and public sectors play a less prominent role in the day-to-day lives of citizens, the 'power vacuum' will likely be taken up by greater participation in the third sector."[24]

How does Nexus view its employment prospects in this sector of society? *Building Bridges* helps to shed some light on the subject. Eighteen per cent of respondents saw being the director of a nonprofit as a desirable career—ranking it ahead of stockbroker, politician, and commissioned salesperson, and just below doctor and lawyer.[25] We think this attraction to the third sector is likely a result of Nexus' desire to be "part of something" and its search for a cohesive and supportive environment in the workplace.

Despite young Canadians' seemingly positive opinion of this sector, three major hurdles remain. First, until very recently most people thought of and described the third sector as the "voluntary sector." The notion that the not-for-profit world could be a source for paid employment or entrepreneurship was, and still is, foreign to a great number of people. Therefore, the option of working in the third sector as a full-time employee has not been actively presented to members of this generation—particularly those university graduates who are visiting the flashy career booths of private-sector organizations. While the modest efforts at recruitment are partly a product of cut-backs in the sector, they are also a reflection of some old thinking about employment in the not-for-profit world.

Second, many organizations in this sector are not yet ready to adapt to the attitudes and expectations of the Nexus Generation. Rod Lohin, a thirty-four-year-old consultant who recently joined Manifest Communications after spending five years in the third sector, claims that the philosophy underpinning many not-for-profit organizations doesn't match the orientation of many young Canadians. "The attitude that dominates the not-for-profit world is a 'to be' attitude. Our work is a reflection of who we are and what we stand for. So the biggest question that needs to be answered is 'What do we believe?' By contrast, the attitude that dominates the private sector is a 'to do' attitude. The focus is on the action that needs to be taken, and the biggest question that needs to be answered is 'Did we get there or not?' My experience is that younger people want a balance between 'to be' and 'to do.' If all you do is talk about your beliefs, you don't accomplish as much— having a cause doesn't mean having an effect. On the flip side, if all you do is focus on results, you can lose sight of what's important. Younger people want to do the right thing, but they are much less likely to be dogmatic and more likely to question processes."

A final point is that the third sector has not thought systematically about the future leadership potential of the Nexus Generation. According to Patrick Johnston, many of the senior leaders in

Canada's not-for-profit world have worked exclusively for charitable and voluntary organizations for years (if not decades), and therefore do not fully reflect the demographic diversity of Canada. Moreover, the leadership skills required today are very different than those required of third-sector leaders even a decade ago. Reduced government funding, increased demand for the sector's services, and the evolving role of partnerships with the private sector have created the need for new competencies and experiences—many of which the Nexus Generation may be able to provide. To Johnston, this suggests the need for a conscious campaign of "succession planning" for the not-for-profit world: "If the third sector is to continue to play a strong role in strengthening civil society—alongside the private and public sectors—we all need to ensure that skilled and entrepreneurial young Canadians continue to see it as an attractive place for a long-term career." As with the public and private sectors, engaging Nexus in a career with the third sector will depend not only on creating opportunities for skills development, challenges, and task variety, but also on providing members of this generation with a *real* chance to make a difference.

Jay Godsall, a thirty-year-old "social entrepreneur" who is chairman of the Environmental Vision Exchange (EVE), dedicates his energies to getting members of his generation out of their comfortable, TV-watching environment. "The Baby Boomers have shut down," Godsall claims. "They no longer have the time or the interest to be optimistic about getting out there and 'helping.' We are better at adjusting to change and have the raw stuff to be creative about solutions to community problems. We also grew up during the 1980s, when Mulroney, Thatcher, and Reagan all championed the concept of self-reliance. That means we see the image of the entrepreneur as cool—in both the private and the not-for-profit world." EVE, a non-profit new-ventures company, acts as an idea broker for other Nexus social entrepreneurs. According to Godsall, it was born out of the tendency for Nexus' ideas to be rejected by older generations as unfeasible or impossible. "We encourage young Canadians to remove the mental obstacles to making their ideas happen, and then we help them gather the resources. We treat community-development ideas as if they are venture capital."

Corporate Citizens

A good way to bring the entrepreneurialism and voluntarism of Nexus together is through corporate citizenship. While the leaders of Canada's blue-chip companies debate over what percentage of profits they should give to charities—or whether they should give anything at all beyond taxes—a new generation of Canadian business leaders, like Jennifer Corson of the Renovators ReSource, are engaged in a host of creative initiatives that are having a real impact in their towns and cities. For Corson, corporate citizenship is a broad concept that includes community involvement, environmental responsibility, and progressive employment practices. "When I think about it, corporate citizenship wasn't an explicit goal; it was inherent to the purpose of the company. I am running a company within and for the community. There is no distinction between 'us' and 'them.'" Keith Kocho of Digital Renaissance shares that view. "The health of my local community is integral to the success of my business," he says. "It just makes *sense* to get involved."

For young entrepreneurs like Corson and Kocho, the rationale for corporate citizenship has never been more compelling. First, given the changes in the role of government and the fall-out from the transition to a new economy, the private sector is being called on to help devise innovative solutions to new social problems. Young entrepreneurs are already driven by a commitment to new ideas in their business environment. A golden opportunity exists to transfer this innovative capacity to the area of social development.

In addition, as we discussed in Chapter 5, there is a new model of corporate responsibility emerging to match the realities of the Information Age, one where working and giving back have become simultaneous rather than linear phenomena. Why wait until you're fifty to start contributing your business skills and knowledge to the community? Nexus entrepreneurs have lived through this transition from one economic model to another, and should be well poised to act on the implications. Finally, young entrepreneurs understand better than any business owner the difficulties in attracting and retaining Nexus employees. Corporate citizenship is one way of demonstrating that a company stands for something. It also offers new possibilities for skills development and team-building within the workplace.

In spite of this new potential for corporate citizenship, there are significant challenges to connecting with Canada's young entrepreneurs. Through research that d~Code and the Angus Reid Group conducted for the Canadian Centre of Philanthropy in February 1998, we found that young business leaders in this country are split on whether companies should be expected to give to charities or support community causes. The overwhelming priorities for today's young entrepreneurs are growing or maintaining their businesses and hiring more staff. Only 16 percent reported corporate citizenship as a major priority, and three in four agreed that their current level of involvement ($400 a year on average) was sufficient. There also appear to be few examples for young entrepreneurs to follow in the area of corporate citizenship. One in two respondents were unable to identify a single company that exemplified good corporate citizenship, and two in three were unable to come up with any inspiring examples of philanthropic or community activity.[26]

We believe there are three key factors to successfully raising awareness about corporate citizenship among Nexus entrepreneurs. First, a new definition and a new language are needed, tailored to individual business leaders rather than big corporations. The message must be delivered by fresh faces and spokespersons who share "cool" examples of corporate citizenship from organizations of all shapes and sizes. Second, corporate citizenship needs to be aligned clearly with professional and business goals. While often cynically perceived of as a public-relations stunt, corporate philanthropy does lead to business benefits such as new contacts, networks, and skills. Altruism will drive some young business leaders to become more active in their communities, but most will need these additional incentives. Finally, any effort to inspire young entrepreneurs to do more as corporate citizens must include an educational component. As mentioned above, community needs are changing and intensifying. Connecting young small-business leaders to the organizations and the people who need their help will ensure that when they are ready to act, they will know where to go.

[The Attributes of Citizenship]

Thus far we have presented a "good news–bad news" story about the citizenship potential of the Nexus Generation. Nexus is embarking on its "citizen career" at a time of profound change and uncertainty. Allegiances are shifting, and the idea of "Canada" is competing with other powerful loyalties. Rights and duties are taking on a new meaning, and can no longer rest on the material comforts provided by our postwar system of entitlements. Furthermore, Nexus citizens appear to be reinterpreting the contract of "gives" and "gets," and are less inspired by some of the traditional channels for exercising citizenship, such as military service, participation in partisan politics, or a career as a public servant. Even the third sector, perhaps the area with the greatest potential for re-engaging Nexus citizens, is in danger of being passed over by this generation unless it can create more meaningful opportunities for Nexus to contribute to the common good.

Does this mean that you, as fellow citizens of Nexus, should be worried about the fate of Canada under the stewardship of this generation? We don't think so. As we look at the citizenship attributes that will be critical to maintaining a compassionate and prosperous country in the decades ahead, three in particular stand out: tolerance, self-restraint, and a commitment to Canada. Fortunately, signs of all three are present in the Nexus Generation.

Tolerance

If we go back to the ideas of Will Kymlicka, one of the pivotal citizenship features he highlights is the "ability to tolerate and work together with others who are different from themselves."[27] Tolerance and multiculturalism have long been the hallmarks of Canada's positive reputation around the world, and will be even more important as the effects of immigration and globalization multiply. So how does Nexus fare in this area?

Throughout this book, we have highlighted the fact that Nexus is the most diverse of any Canadian generation to date. Its primary, secondary, and post-secondary years have been marked by constant interaction with multiple cultures and alternative lifestyles, and its participation in the workplace has been no different. These conditioning experiences have seeped through the consciousness of Nexus to produce a level of tolerance that surpasses that of previous generations of Canadians. Pollster Allan Gregg, chairman of the Strategic Counsel, speaks to this trend in his commentary on the 1997 *Maclean's*/CBC Year-End Poll. What's surprising about younger Canadians, he writes, "is that, far from fitting the conflicting stereotypes of despair and alienation on the one hand, or steely, buttoned-down calculators of self-interest on the other, they are, if anything, rock-ribbed social liberals. Not only are they the most comfortable of all generations with wearing the liberal label, their acceptance of a diversity in lifestyles, mores and social behaviour is truly breath-taking."[28] In the year-end poll, 65 per cent of eighteen- to twenty-four-year-olds characterized themselves as liberal (the highest level of any age group); conversely, this segment was the least likely to describe itself as conservative. The *Building Bridges* research echoes Gregg's findings. When asked to describe their values, the majority of Nexus Canadians between the ages of eighteen and thirty-four (55 per cent) agreed that they are more comfortable with diversity than their parents.

Self-Restraint

Kymlicka also argues that progressive societies require citizens who are willing to show self-restraint—both in the economic demands they place on government and in the personal choices that affect their health and environment. As the population on our planet increases and the resource base to support it becomes stretched, an ability to curb individual excesses for the greater good will become an even more important attribute of citizenship. So how does Nexus score in this category?

On the question of economic demands, the news appears good. As we have argued, the Nexus Generation has reduced expectations of the Canadian state as stable provider, and is already taking a self-reliant approach to planning its financial future. At the same time, its attitudes about how to allocate the impending fiscal surplus reflect a long-standing Canadian commitment to providing social security for the less fortunate and minimizing income disparities. In the words of Allan Gregg, "for all the worrying that cold-hearted policies and attitudes are threatening the traditions that make Canada the kindest and gentlest of all nations, the newest generation of adults will not allow that to happen without a fight."[29]

In terms of environment and health, there are also glimmerings of hope. We have shown how Nexus was exposed to the reality of scarcity early in its formative years, and how it grew up in a culture of recycling, conservation, and environmental activism. Today, eighteen- to thirty-four-year-olds are more concerned about living in a sustainable fashion, and are more likely than other age groups to believe that individuals, rather than governments, should take responsibility for environmentally friendly behaviour.[30] In the same way, although Nexus continues to engage in many unhealthy behaviours—such as smoking and alcohol and drug abuse—there are signs that this generation is taking a more holistic approach to its health. In the 1997 *Maclean's*/CBC Year-End Poll, Nexus-aged Canadians ranked being physically fit as their third most important value—just behind being in a relationship and having a fulfilling job, and well ahead of making money.[31] A concern for mind, body, and soul is leading many Nexus members to step off the workaholic treadmill of the 1980s and carve out a new work/life balance. While the generational gene of recklessness still influences Nexus' choices and behaviours, some members of this generation are developing a healthy respect for limits.

A Commitment to Canada

Finally, let's revisit the major preoccupation of those responsible for citizenship policy-making: the quest for a stronger Canadian identity. Whether it's Heritage Minister Sheila Copps's efforts to distribute thousands of Canadian flags or the Reform Party's flag-waving and anthem-singing antics in the House of Commons, there seems to be an obsession these days with in-your-face "Canadian-ness."

But do we really need to sort out, for once and for all, *the* Canadian identity? What's wrong with something a little more subtle, that still allows for diversity and creative interpretation?

These loud displays of Canadian patriotism are trying to stamp out a reality that many Nexus citizens have become quite comfortable with: the reality of *multiple* identities. Yes, this new generation has many attachments, both local and global. But does that make it any less committed to Canada? Mark Kingwell believes that for members of younger generations, "the Canadian identity no longer trumps all other identities." In our view, the jury is still out. Currently, the overwhelming majority of Nexus citizens (except those in the province of Quebec) strongly agree that they are "proud to be Canadian."[32] Moreover, 40 per cent strongly agree that they would like to learn more about Canada's history and heritage.[33] Increasingly, we think the greatest skill a Canadian citizen can possess is an ability to balance different allegiances without compromising his obligations to the common good. The Nexus Generation seems to have an excellent head start, provided it can find meaningful ways to contribute to Canada.

[Conclusion: Engaging Nexus Citizens]

We recognize that the task of re-engaging Nexus citizens is a daunting one. We also know that it is not a task limited to this generation alone. Ever since the failure of the Charlottetown Accord in 1992, politicians, public servants, and not-for-profit leaders across the country have been investigating new ways to connect to Canadians—be it through public consultations, round tables, or the use of the information highway. We don't have all the answers, but we do have ideas. Our codes of conduct for connecting with Nexus the Citizen come from our experiences working with young

Canadians and from the lessons learned by many of our d~Coders. The advice is straightforward: communicate and engage.

Code #1: Treat Nexus as a Valued "Customer"

The volume of information directed at young Canadians today is truly staggering. In our work with government departments, we have stressed the importance of approaching communications strategies with much the same mind-set as a marketing manager in the private sector. That means the secret to communicating with Nexus citizens draws on many of the same recommendations we provided for Nexus consumers: be authentic, make them part of the story, and provide multiple-access points for your message. One powerful illustration of this approach is a recent anti-smoking campaign from Health Canada, which selected television commercials from hundreds of submissions by young Canadians. One of the winners shows a young woman sitting in the hallway of her school, talking about all of the big events of her life that her mother, who had died of cancer, would not be around to share with her. There is no hype. There are no burning cigarettes. It is straight stuff, right from the source.

Code #2: Touch Emotional Trigger Points

Above all, communication efforts should strive to reach the emotional trigger points of Nexus citizens. While rational arguments can move the Nexus Generation, the most powerful messages are those that dig deeper, to seek out their dreams and aspirations. Perhaps the most obvious example of emotion vs. rationality was the 1995 referendum campaign in Quebec. The Parti Québécois enjoyed phenomenal success with young francophones, largely because it was able to touch the emotional core of this generation. (Who can forget the TV shots of young Québécois crying and waving their flags as the results of the vote were announced?) The initial federalist strategy, by contrast, spoke about *numbers*—numbers of jobs lost, numbers of businesses moving out of Quebec, numbers of basis points lost on the value of the Canadian dollar. The better approach, we believe, is to position Canada in a positive and more visionary light, using a range of different spokespersons. Most important, we need to demonstrate that narrow-minded nationalism is unimaginative and passé. The exciting project of building Canada is all about finding a new way to ensure that diverse cultures and citizens can work together.

Code #3: Use a Pack Mentality

Civic engagement is a new area of involvement for many members of the Nexus Generation. That means that despite being do-it-yourselfers in the consumer and working worlds, they may be uncomfortable striking out on their own. Too often, public-policy or third-sector initiatives fall short by having only one token youth on their planning committees. One of two things happens: 1) the young person talks too much (bearing the burden of having to speak for *all* young people); or 2) the young person talks too little (suffering from a complete lack of confidence). A better strategy is to think about how to involve "packs" of Nexus citizens. Increasing their numbers will not only build greater confidence in the participants, but also ensure a more creative outcome.

TG Magazine's Stoney McCart pursued this line of thinking in the run-up to the 1997 Asia Pacific Economic Co-operation (APEC) leaders' meeting in Vancouver. Rather than having one or two youth representatives participate, *TG* and the Students' Commission were asked to create a parallel youth program for all of the APEC ministerial meetings held in Canada during the year. More than one thousand youth gave direct input to APEC. "The goal was to showcase the fact that young people do have a contribution to make," Stoney explains. "Our youth participants were often able to cut across the political/cultural differences within the groups better than their older counterparts." The involvement of Nexus Canadians at APEC led to a number of new policy ideas and educational initiatives, as well as an electronic sourcebook for use by youth throughout all eighteen APEC economies. Youth from Malaysia, the host of the next APEC gathering, are planning to copy the formula.

Another example of the pack approach that is currently being used by some government departments is the creation of "youth round-tables" to advise on, and participate in, policy development. We generally applaud these kinds of endeavours. However, a word of caution is in order. When assembling such tables, don't obsess about representativeness or political correctness. While diversity is a key component of democratic accountability, an equally important objective is to find energetic, bright Nexus citizens who can work well as part of a team. To capture quality input and ideas, look for younger Canadians who are devoted to the overall policy goal and not just their individual regions or organizations.

Code #4: Appeal to Altruism and Self-Interest

We have argued that the raw material for good citizenship does exist within the Nexus Generation. Nevertheless, the most successful engagement strategies are those that can tap into both altruism and self-interest. In other words, offer Nexus the opportunity to develop skills and knowledge while doing good.

One exciting example of this strategy is NetCorps, an initiative launched by Prime Minister Chrétien at the Santiago summit in April 1998. The objective of the program is to use the energy and technological know-how of Nexus-aged Canadians to encourage all countries in the Americas to become full participants in the Information Age. NetCorps participants will be placed for six to twelve months in an organization or business to help them get connected, by building networks, configuring software, and offering computer training. In return, the interns will learn professional and personal skills that will help prepare them for entry into the international workforce. By March 1999, it is hoped that more than thirty-five hundred young Canadians will have taken advantage of the program.

The United Way of Greater Toronto's Build Yourself—Build Your City initiative also illustrates how altruism and self-interest can be married. Targeted at university and college students, the campaign introduces young Torontonians to the needs of their community and the myriad ways that they can give something back. However, it also stresses the tangible benefits that can be gained through volunteering and establishes a system whereby the United Way provides employers with letters of recommendation for young volunteers that speak to the time they dedicated and the valuable skills they acquired.

Code #5: Prove to Nexus That It Is a Valuable Partner

With so many interest groups currently dotting the landscape of Canadian society, we think it may be counter-productive to create yet another one based around youth. In the words of Mike, a student activist in our network, "Age as a vehicle for social action is limited by its inherent fluid nature. Unlike identity—[which is] based on sex or race—age is constantly in transition. In addition, age as defined by youth activists renders any other groups or individuals, even if they are allies in a social cause, as the oppressive 'adult other.'" Our belief is that Nexus Canadians should rally around issues—not age—and cooperate with other like-minded citizens of multiple generations.

Similarly, it seems as though members of the Nexus Generation have become sceptical about programs for young people because of the "dog and pony show" phenomenon. To put it simply, they can see the photo opportunity coming a mile away. Politicians or civic leaders just love to be snapped standing next to a bunch of young people.

So how do you prove to Nexus that it is more than a stage prop? The best way is to try something different: let *them* run it. Nexus citizens will fulfil your expectations if you give them something meaningful to do. Provide them with the parameters, and then let their creativity take off.

This was the philosophy behind Generation 2000, a not-for-profit organization whose mission was to get the next generation of citizens involved in Canada's development. Each year, forty Nexus-aged Canadians were recruited to create a "road show" about the national issues that mattered most to them—health, the environment, education, and national unity. There was no pre-defined program or agenda; the content of the message was up to them. After three weeks of intensive training, the group split into teams of five and traversed the county, talking and listening to high-school students about their hopes and concerns for the future and educating them about the ways in which they could get involved in their communities. Between 1991 and 1995, Generation 2000 visited twelve hundred schools across Canada and spoke to 750,000 young people.

Unlike so many of the national-unity initiatives of the past decade—which have deliberated over how to re-balance the federal/provincial relationship, how to interpret the meaning of "distinct society," or how to define the Canadian identity—Generation 2000 adopted a community-service model as its starting point. At d~Code, we're convinced that any "big picture" agenda will fail unless it is accompanied by these kinds of small steps. If Nexus citizens get involved in their country at a grass-roots level, they are far more likely to feel the impact. Only then will they be inspired to *do more*.

CONCLUSION: BUILDING BRIDGES

By now it should be pretty clear that Nexus is not Generation X. Although members of Nexus are sceptical, restless, and at times elusive, they are also savvy, optimistic about their future, and aspire to some familiar—almost traditional—goals.

We know that Nexus is relatively young (in an era where people seem to be staying young longer), with attributes that can be traced back to a few standard generational genes. Just as past generations were when they were young, the Nexus Generation today is a little reckless, a little rebellious, and a little naïve. These traits are nothing new—they are simply part of growing up. In fact, some members of Nexus are poised to do just that. Many will marry, have children, and buy homes, albeit much later in life and perhaps in a different way than past generations. Over time, as their stability gene kicks in, they will seek out more security, although this concept is being defined a new way. Success is also important to Nexus, though increasingly it is less tied to money or a job title. It is more about accumulating experiences, being connected with people and ideas, and balancing work, life, and play.

In as much as Nexus is a do-it-yourself generation, it still looks to institutions to help provide the stability, security, and success that it craves. Family and community (however they are defined) still offer support and a sense of belonging to members of this generation. The state will continue to supply a measure of economic and personal security, as well as an attachment to a larger national identity. The workplace will remain an important arena for Nexus to be rewarded for its skills and creativity. But Nexus is also putting the heat on traditional institutions to change, by opting out, by creating new institutions, and by acting as an agent for change from the *inside*. Nexus is looking for new outlets to satisfy its spiritual desires and its appetite for learning, though these outlets may not be the established church or the ivory tower as we know them.

We also know that Nexus has experienced some powerful generational conditioning that has left it decidedly unique. It is the only generation to straddle the Industrial and the Information ages, and as such comes rigged with a potent and relevant set of skills to take into the future. Most important among these are Nexus' command over technology, its sophisticated style of media-consumption, and its adaptation to global forces—all compliments of a steady diet of "chips and pop" over its formative years. Also, by virtue of its particular place in history, Nexus is charged with an important generational role: it acts as a buffer between the Baby Boom and subsequent generations. Members of Nexus look a little bit like the Boomers, a little bit like the Boomers' kids, and a little bit like no other generation in history. Understanding Nexus means understanding both its "uniqueness" and its "sameness."

For those interested in marketing, human resources, or public policy, the "uniqueness" and "sameness" of Nexus presents a myriad of challenges and opportunities. We have demonstrated, for example, that Nexus already has significant disposable income and invests in the future, but at the same time insists on consuming experience and enjoying the small luxuries of life. We've discussed how Nexus espouses entrepreneurialism, thirsts for challenging work, and as the consummate "free agent," prefers to leave its options open. We have seen not only how Nexus treats the workplace as a hub of community, but also how it will protest with its feet when the equation of "gives" and "gets" fails to balance. We find that while Nexus distrusts national governments and feels part of a global village, it seems comfortable juggling multiple allegiances and is starting to redefine its citizenship rights and duties.

To assist you with the challenges of understanding the Nexus Generation, we have furnished a series of codes of conduct that revolve around the themes of authenticity, inclusion, multiple-access points, customization, diversity, and emotional triggers. In fact, you have probably noticed a continuous thread running through each of the three chapters in Section II. Many of the people and the organizations we cited as illustrative examples appeared in all three areas—consumer, employee, and citizen. This is no accident, since our ultimate code asks you to think about Nexus in a *holistic* way, regardless of the functional hat you might wear. Clearly, the task of connecting with this generation straddles the vertical silos known as marketing, human resources, and public policy; so, naturally, do the solutions. Nexus isn't just your employee; he's also consuming any number of products and services (which may include your own) and shares with you the responsibility for maintaining a healthy community and prosperous country.

When we solicit help from our d~Coders, we don't ask them to think only like marketers or to work only on human-resource projects. Rather, we assume they can wear several hats at the same time and create a coherent story with all of them. Organizations that can follow this lead and coordinate their Nexus approach will enjoy more meaningful and lasting connections with the generation. This means sharing information, communicating success stories, collaborating on strategy, and delivering a consistent message.

Remember: media-savvy Nexus is watching you from all sides and all angles. Our best advice is to observe it in the same way.

As we stated in the Introduction, however, our ultimate goal at d~Code goes beyond helping people sell more products, hire better people, or mould better citizens. It is to help build bridges across generations. Today's news is brimming with stories steeped in generational conflict—the federal debt and pension plans, unemployment, the environment, health care, and education among them. When it comes to addressing these issues, doom and gloom abound; the solutions are too often thin, if not absent altogether. We think the prescription for mitigating generational conflict has two steps.

Step 1 is to achieve a deep level of intergenerational understanding, a fundamental reason why we wrote *Chips & Pop*. Owing both to lingering stereotypes and the lightning speed of change, our society has generational understanding gaps that need to be bridged. These gaps are not just about Nexus. The Boomers are struggling to understand their kids, while both the Depression and the Second World War generations are questioning whether their knowledge and value systems are still relevant at the dawn of a new century.

We think understanding involves more than just comprehension or tolerance; understanding must also include *intergenerational learning*. Both recent and not-so-recent history provide examples where success was tied to the ability of different generations to collaborate. Consider the phenomenal industrial success of early North America, which can be traced to the mix between a highly productive labour force of young immigrants and the proven methods of industrial organization and expertise inherited from Europe (without the complacency and bureaucracy that tends to befall more mature industries). North America (and particularly the United States) soon built on its advantage and became an industrial powerhouse in the world economy.[1] Modern farming offers another interesting illustration. Today's farmer must understand engineering, chemistry, finance, public policy, and even futures trading to stay ahead in a competitive marketplace. Younger farmers tend to bring the latest information and skills in these areas. Yet without the more instinctive knowledge of the weather, the soil conditions, and the changing seasons—knowledge passed down from members of older generations—the farmer cannot succeed.

Contrary to popular perceptions, Nexus thinks it has much to learn from other generations. In the 1997 *Maclean's*/CBC Year-End Poll, 62 per cent of Nexus-aged Canadians disagreed with the statement "The world has changed so much in the last 20 years that people over 40 can teach those under 25 very little about the world." What is more interesting, from the same survey, is that close to 60 per cent of Canadians older than sixty-five actually *agreed* with this statement.[2] Members of Nexus are eager to learn, but older generations must also be willing to teach. Similarly, we hope we've made the case that Nexus has a great deal to offer to other generations. The idea of reverse mentorship is not something to be practised in isolation—it should be considered a learning partnership across *all* generations.

Step 2 in mitigating generational conflict is to generate good ideas. After a speech we gave in early 1998, one audience member predicted that our society would soon be bereft of good ideas because the highly mobile younger generations no longer specialize in anything. His argument was that individual expertise and dedication are the key factors in solving complex problems. We could not disagree more. Instead, we believe that innovation is more dependent than ever before on multiple minds and multiple perspectives.

Take, for example, the Canadian Institute for Advanced Research (CIAR), which has been leveraging diversity to solve problems for a decade and a half. CIAR's philosophy is to bring together leaders from a multitude of disciplines to work on complex societal problems. Its work in population and health draws on medicine, sociology, anthropology, and mathematics to build important frameworks of understanding. Rather than equating innovation with deep knowledge, CIAR seeks to create the right mix of different experiences and to profit from the exchange of perspectives.

If placed in this kind of context, Nexus has the potential to be a highly innovative generation—a potential that stems from its exposure to diversity, its ability to parallel process, and its comfort with multiple information sources. Putting Nexus in situations where it can cooperate with members of other generations will bring yet another dimension into the mix. This requires us to move beyond merely protecting the stake we all have in our post-millennium society. It means combining the different skills and viewpoints we can all bring to bear on the issues, and being clever about the solutions.

As a final word, we'd like to pass on some observations to the parents of Nexus, since family is still one of the most basic areas where generations need to coexist. We hope we've contributed to, or at least verified, your own understanding of the Nexus Generation. In particular, the concept of the extended freedom zone and the changing definition of success will be important for you to keep in mind as your relationship with your Nexus kids evolves. Nexus may question the institutions you hold near and dear, but that doesn't mean she won't take part in their evolution. Nexus may be more open to diverse moral codes than you are, but that doesn't mean he has no values. Nexus may expect to change jobs more frequently than you did, but that doesn't mean she isn't willing to work hard. And while Nexus may take a different approach to creating support structures, that doesn't mean he doesn't want or need them. Many within this generation have left their original nesting places to become part of this large global economy, but they find quiet comforts in their friends (who always seem to be changing), in the pictures they have on the walls of their cramped apartments, and in the corner coffee shops they frequent—no matter where they happen to be.

By recognizing the generational genes in your Nexus-aged children, and appreciating the impact of their generational conditioning, you're well on your way to becoming an honourary d~Coder. Now treat yourself to some chips and pop.

ACKNOWLEDGMENTS

———

As you might imagine, a book project involving three very different and strong-willed authors is bound for the odd stretch of "bumpy road." But thanks to the support of a great many people who provided everything from inspiration to veritable slave labour, we managed to finish *Chips & Pop* while still enthusiastic and relatively unscathed.

We begin by thanking Robert's original co-conspirators, Andy Heintzman and Sabaa Quao, without whom d~Code and the idea to focus on the generation would not exist. For giving this generation its distinctive Nexus name, we acknowledge the always-clever Chris Barnard (see, we didn't forget!).

We are especially grateful to the d~Code Toronto core, who helped out with *Chips & Pop* on numerous occasions, encouraged us during our trials, and managed to keep the business afloat at the same time. Many thanks to Hollis "Talking to the Hand" Hopkins, Jared "Data Hound" Landry, and Natalie "Love the Shoes" Lacey for performing the thankless tasks of data collection and quotation verification. We also thank Amy "Barbara Walters" Halpenny for her interviewing prowess, and Camran "I Can't Print" Baig for building us the perfect beast on which to write. Too bad we weren't able to rig up the Voice Recognition Software after all.

269

We also owe our entire d~Code network a debt of gratitude for their responses and creative ideas, which helped to animate many parts of this book. d~Coders Jonathan Ehrlich, Mike Marcolongo, and Karen Wright deserve special mention for turning a critical eye to particular chapters, as do Ryan Bigge and Jacquie Manchevsky for their timely insights and reflections. *Chips & Pop* simply reinforces our belief, which has always been at the heart of d~Code, that innovation comes through diversity.

To our many clients through the years: thank you for allowing us to work on *your* problems, which has helped us build *our* intellectual capital. It has been a privilege to work alongside you.

A number of inanimate and "virtually" inanimate objects also made critical contributions to *Chips & Pop*. Among them are the Internet, MetaCrawler, smoked salmon, Labatt 50, Jen's sun deck, Mike Orkscrew, Beck's Taxi, the late Michael Hedges, 102.1 The Edge, acid jazz, *Fast Company* magazine, and Kenny from Winnipeg. Thanks are also due to the many establishments that patiently fed and watered us while we worked—Loftus Lloyd, Kensington Kitchen, Bangkok Paradise, Monsoon, Solo, By the Way Café, Serra, Peter Pan—it was *really* good.

Finally, a special tribute to our new friends—those from the book world—who helped ease our foray into "author-hood." Gordon Robertson accommodated our font fickleness and designed a book cover to match the moods of our many audiences. The razor sharp editing of Janice Weaver—who managed to distinguish the blue marks from the red—saved us from potential embarrassments, such as the legendary first-date reference. Most of all, we extend our thanks to our agent, Beverly Slopen, who enlightened us with her road-kill stats, and our publisher, Malcolm Lester, who calmly (but firmly) dealt with the designated caller's eleventh-hour pleas. Without their blind faith, *Chips & Pop* might never have seen the light of day.

NOTES

CHAPTER 1: *The Stereotypes of Generation X*

1. Douglas Coupland, *Generation X: Tales for an Accelerated Culture* (New York: St. Martin's Press, 1992).
2. See Billy Idol's Web site at www.roughguides.com/rock/index.html.
3. David K. Foot, with Daniel Stoffman, *Boom, Bust & Echo: How to Profit from the Coming Demographic Shift* (Toronto: Macfarlane, Walter and Ross, 1996), 21.
4. Michael Adams, *Sex in the Snow: Canadian Social Values at the End of the Millennium* (Toronto: Viking, 1997).
5. William Strauss and Neil Howe, *13th Gen: Abort? Retry? Ignore? Fail?* (New York: Vintage, 1993).
6. Karen Ritchie, *Marketing to Generation X* (New York: Lexington Books, 1995), 16.
7. Foot and Stoffman, *Boom, Bust & Echo*, 19.
8. Cited in James E. Côté and Anton L. Allahar, *Generation on Hold: Coming of Age in the Late Twentieth Century* (Toronto: Stoddart Publishing, 1994), xi.
9. Ibid.
10. Adams, *Sex in the Snow*, 106.
11. Rick Mercer, *Streeters: Rants and Raves from This Hour Has 22 Minutes* (Toronto: Doubleday, 1998), 80.

271

12. "1000 Voices: Lives on Hold," *Toronto Star*, 6 December 1997, A1.

13. Statistic taken from the Statistics Canada Web site at www.statcan.ca/english/Pgdb/People/Population/demo10a.htm.

14. Don Tapscott, *Growing Up Digital: The Rise of the Net Generation* (New York: McGraw Hill, 1997).

15. Ezra Levant, *YouthQuake* (Vancouver: The Fraser Institute, 1996), 9.

16. Angus Reid Group and d~Code, *Building Bridges: New Perspectives of the Nexus Generation*, prepared for the Royal Bank of Canada (Toronto, April 1997).

17. "Year-End Poll," *Maclean's* 110, no. 52 (December 29, 1997–January 5, 1998): 16.

18. *Building Bridges*.

19. "Year-End Poll," *Maclean's*, 26.

20. *Building Bridges*.

21. *Building Bridges*.

CHAPTER 2: *The Making of a Generation*

1. Carla J. Shatz, "The Developing Brain," *Scientific American*, September 1992.

2. Thomas J. Bouchard, Jr., "Whenever the Twain Shall Meet," *The Sciences*, September/October 1997, 52–57.

3. William Strauss and Neil Howe, *Generations: The History of America's Future, 1584–2069* (New York: William Morrow, 1991).

4. Bill Gates, *The Road Ahead* (New York: Penguin, 1995), 17.

5. Ritchie, *Marketing to Generation X*, 87.

6. Francis Fukuyama, *The End of History and the Last Man* (New York: Free Press, 1992).

7. Nathan Rosenberg and L. E. Birdzell, Jr., *How the West Grew Rich: The Economic Transformation of the Industrial World* (New York: Harper-Collins, 1991).

8. Douglas Rushkoff, *Playing the Future: How Children's Culture Can Teach Us to Thrive in an Age of Chaos* (New York: HarperCollins, 1996), 2.

CHAPTER 3: *The Institution of Change*

1. Alanna Mitchell, "Family Values a Big Hit with Boomers Kids," *Globe and Mail*, 17 March 1998, A1.
2. Vanier Institute of the Family, *Profiling Canada's Families* (Ottawa: January 1994), 39.
3. Statistic from the Department of Housing, Family and Social Statistics, Statistics Canada.
4. Census of Canada, 1996.
5. *Profiling Canada's Families*, 39.
6. Ibid., 47.
7. Ibid., 51.
8. *Building Bridges.*
9. Statistics Canada, *Canadian Social Trends* (Spring 1998): 8.
10. Ibid., 8.
11. Mitchell, "Family Values."
12. *Canadian Social Trends*, 4.
13. Ibid., 3.
14. Statistic from the Department of Housing, Family and Social Statistics, Statistics Canada.
15. *Canadian Social Trends*, 4.
16. Ibid., 4.
17. Angus Reid Group, *Housing Study,* prepared for the Royal Bank of Canada (Toronto, 1998), 140.
18. Royal Bank of Canada, *Fourth Annual Canadian Homeownership Survey* (Toronto, 1997), 43.
19. Canada Mortgage and Housing Corporation, *Household Income Facilities and Equipment Survey*, 1994.
20. *Housing Study*, 51.
21. Ibid., 49.
22. *Building Bridges.*
23. Ibid.
24. The Rotary Club allowed only one member from each employment classification; the Kinsman and his father were both plumbers, so only one could be a Rotarian.

25. "The American Dream, Virtually," *The Economist*, 21 March 1998, 81.
26. Cited on the *Fortune* magazine Web site at www.pathfinder.com/fortune/1997/970707/c004.html.
27. Cited on the company's Web site at www.tripod. com.
28. Clifford Stoll, *Silicon Snake Oil* (New York: Doubleday, 1995).
29. Ibid., 24.
30. Ibid., 57.
31. "God Decentralized: A Special Issue," *New York Times Magazine*, 7 December 1997.
32. Based on the segment of the population that believes God is a relative concept in today's world.
33. Reginald Bibby, *The Bibby Report: Social Trends Canadian Style* (Toronto: Stoddart Publishing, 1995), 125.
34. Angus Reid Group, *Canada/U.S. Religion and Politics Survey*, (Toronto, 1996), 88. This does not include weddings, funerals, or baptisms.
35. Ibid., 47.
36. Ibid., 77.
37. Bibby, *The Bibby Report*, 133.
38. Adams, *Sex in the Snow*, 102.
39. Lila Sarick, "Flash, Lingo Beat Fire, Brimstone," *Globe and Mail*, 11 April 1998, A2.
40. Philip G. Czerny, "Globalization and Other Stories: The Search for a New Paradigm for International Relations," *International Journal* 51, no. 4 (Autumn 1996): 633.
41. *Canada/U.S. Religion and Politics Survey*, 49.
42. Bibby, *The Bibby Report*, 113.
43. Environics Research Group, *Fiscal Issues Survey*, prepared for the Canadian Broadcasting Corporation (Toronto, 1998).
44. Angus Reid Group, *Reconnecting Government with Youth*, prepared for the Canada Information Office (Toronto, 1997).
45. Ibid.
46. Statistics Canada, *Education in Canada* (1996): 21.
47. Ibid., 20.
48. Ibid., 20.
49. Census of Canada, 1996.
50. *Education in Canada*, 158.

51. Côté and Allahar, *Generation on Hold*, 36.

52. Alanna Mitchell, "Women Jump to Head of Class," *Globe and Mail*, 15 April 1998, A8.

53. *Education in Canada*, 21.

54. Statistics Canada, *Education Quarterly Review* 4, no. 2, (Summer 1997): 27.

55. Ibid., 15.

56. Ibid., 16.

57. David S. Kinahan and Harold Heft, *On Your Mark: Getting Better Grades Without Working Harder or Being Smarter* (Toronto: Macmillan, 1997).

58. Ibid., 2.

59. Ibid., 23.

60. Douglas Rushkoff, *Media Virus: Hidden Agendas in Popular Culture* (New York: Ballantine, 1994), 4.

61. *Canada/U.S. Religion and Politics Survey.*

62. *Building Bridges.*

63. Ibid.

64. Statistics Canada, *Periodical Publishing Survey* (1994).

65. This phrase was coined by advertising executive Leslie Perkins.

66. *Reconnecting Government with Youth.*

67. *Building Bridges.*

68. Robert Owen, *Gen X TV: The Brady Bunch to Melrose Place* (Syracuse, NY: Syracuse University Press, 1997).

69. Statistic taken from the Statistics Canada Web site at www.statcan.ca/daily/english/980205/d980205.htm#ART/.

70. Douglas Rushkoff, *Playing the Future: How Children's Culture Can Teach Us to Thrive in an Age of Chaos* (New York: HarperCollins, 1996), 39.

71. Ibid., 39.

72. Mercer, *Streeters*, 30.

73. Taken from the official Seinfeld homepage at www.nbc.com/tvcentral/shows/seinfeld.

74. Rushkoff, *Media Virus*, 110.

75. *Reconnecting Government with Youth.*

CHAPTER 4: *Nexus the Consumer*

1. Klaus Rohrich, "Forget the Kids," *Marketing* (September 22, 1997): 22.
2. Ritchie, *Marketing to Generation X*, 3.
3. Revenue Canada, 1995.
4. Revenue Canada, 1995. See also *Profiling Canada's Families*.
5. Revenue Canada, 1995.
6. Ibid.
7. *Building Bridges*.
8. Eric Weiner, "Banks Slack on Gen-X Market: Poll," *Globe and Mail Report on Business*, 13 August 1997, B13.
9. Cited in Tibbett L. Speer, "College Come-Ons," *American Demographics*, (March 1998): 42.
10. Jennifer Nicholson, "Generation Debt," *Monday Magazine* 24, no. 13, (March 26–April 1, 1998): 8.
11. Print Measurement Bureau/J. C. Williams Group National Retail Report (Ottawa, April 1997). This survey was conducted on a sample size of 20,145 Canadians; 5,676 were from the eighteen to thirty-four age group.
12. Patti Summerfield, "New Amex Card Shoots Younger," *Strategy* (January 19, 1998): 1.
13. Speer, "College Come-Ons."
14. Derek Holt, "Will Generation X Benefit from an Inheritance Windfall?" *Financial Industry Monitoring Service* (December 1997): 2.
15. PMB/J. C. Williams National Retail Report, 1997. The average for all age groups was 54 per cent and 52 per cent, respectively.
16. *Building Bridges*.
17. Twenty-two per cent of eighteen- to thirty-four-year-olds bought sports clothing in the last twelve months, compared with 18 per cent for thirty-five- to forty-nine-year-olds, 13 per cent for fifty- to sixty-four-year-olds, and 7 per cent for those over sixty-five. PMB/J. C. Williams National Retail Report, 1997.
18. PMB/J. C. Williams National Retail Report, 1997.
19. Rushkoff, *Playing the Future*, 15–16.
20. PMB/J. C. Williams National Retail Report, 1997.

21. Amy Schrier, "Editor's Note," *Blue: A Journal for the New Traveller*, no. 2 (Winter 1998).

22. Ben Malbon, "Clubbing: Consumption, Identity and the Spatial Practices of Every-Night Life," in Tracey Skelton and Gil Valentine, eds., *Cool Places: Geographies of Youth Cultures* (London: Routledge, 1998), 266–88.

23. Ibid., 267.

24. Ibid., 277.

25. PMB/J. C. Williams National Retail Report, 1997.

26. Shane Peacock, "Crème Brûlé," *Shift* (May 1998): 34–35.

27. PMB/J. C. Williams National Retail Report, 1997. This is particularly true of younger members of the generation. Sixty-four per cent of eighteen- to twenty-four-year-olds and 57 per cent of students agreed with the first statement (compared with 67 per cent of fifty- to sixty-four-year-olds). In terms of the second statement, 36 per cent of eighteen- to twenty-four-year-olds were likely to pass up their favourite brand for something on sale, compared with 34 per cent for fifty- to sixty-four-year-olds.

28. See Abraham Maslow, *Motivation and Personality*, 2d ed. (New York: Harper and Row, 1970). Maslow believed that the hierarchy of needs ran as follows: basic physiological needs (food, water, sex, etc.), safety, love, self-esteem, and self-actualization.

29. Jean-Marie Dru, *Conventions and Shaking Up the Marketplace* (New York: John Wiley and Sons, 1996), 127.

30. Strauss and Howe, *13th Gen*, 103.

31. PMB/J. C. Williams National Retail Report, 1997.

32. Gill Valentine, Tracey Skelton and Deborah Chambers, "Cool Places: an Introduction to Youth and Youth Cultures," in Skelton and Valentine, *Cool Places*, 1–32.

33. For a further discussion of the limitations of focus groups, see Doug Saunders, "Getting into Focus," *Globe and Mail*, 10 January 1998, C1.

34. Don Peppers and Martha Rogers, *The One-to-One Future: Building Relationships One Customer at a Time* (New York: Doubleday, 1993).

35. *Building Bridges*.

36. PMB/J. C. Williams National Retail Report, 1997.

37. Ritchie, *Marketing to Generation X*, 137.

38. Darby Romeo, ed., *Retro Hell: Life in the '70s and '80s, from Afros to Zotz* (Boston: Little Brown and Company, 1997), xii.

39. Ibid., xii.

40. PMB/J. C. Williams National Retail Report, 1997.

41. Ibid.

42. Ibid. Seventy-six per cent of eighteen- to twenty-four-year-olds buy their clothing at specialty stores and 45 per cent buy at department stores. The numbers for thirty-five- to forty-nine-year-olds are 67 per cent and 53 per cent, respectively.

43. *Retro Hell*, 120.

44. Bonnie Sherman, "Losing the Fear of Spending On-Line," *Marketing* (March 16, 1998): 16.

45. Gayle MacDonald, "The Internet Is Overrated," *Globe and Mail*, 3 July 1997, B9.

46. PMB/J. C. Williams National Retail Report, 1997. Thirty-two per cent of eighteen- to twenty-four-year-olds agreed with the statement "I am willing to pay a little extra to save time shopping," compared with 37 per cent for thirty-five- to forty-nine-year-olds.

47. Simon Houpt, "Compact Discs Get Personal on the Net," *Globe and Mail*, 28 March 1998, C29.

48. PMB/J. C. Williams National Retail Report, 1997. Thirty-six per cent of eighteen- to twenty-four-year-olds and 31 per cent of twenty-five- to thirty-four-year-olds agreed with the statement, compared with 29 per cent of Boomers (thirty-five- to forty-nine-year-olds).

49. William C. Taylor, "Permission Marketing," *Fast Company*, no. 14 (April/May 1998): 200.

CHAPTER 5: *Nexus the Employee*

1. William Bridges, *Job Shift: How to Prosper in a Workplace without Jobs* (New York, Addison-Wesley, 1994).

2. Cited in Jeremy Rifkin, "After Work," *Utne Reader*, no. 69, (May–June 1995): 52–63.

3. Thomas Davenport, "The Fad That Forgot People: Why Re-engineering Failed," *Fast Company*, no. 1 (December 1995): 70.

4. Charles Baillie, "The Changing Nature of Work," notes for remarks given to the Canadian Club, Orillia, Ontario (May 2, 1997).

5. Royal Bank Financial Group, *State of Employment* (Toronto, May 1997).

6. Peter C. Newman, "A Revolutionary Young Economist," *Maclean's* 111, no. 13 (March 30, 1998): 46.

7. Thomas Stewart, *Intellectual Capital: The New Wealth of Organizations* (New York: Doubleday, 1997), xiii.

8. Jay A. Conger, "How 'Gen-X Managers' Manage," *Strategy and Business*, no. 10 (First quarter, 1998): 29–30.

9. Bill Taylor, speech given to the Retail Council of Canada, Eighth Annual Marketing Conference (November 1997). See also Daniel Pink, "Free Agent Nation," *Fast Company*, no. 12 (December/January 1998): 131–47.

10. *State of Employment.*

11. Statistic taken from the Statistics Canada Web site at www.statcan.ca/.

12. David Foot, "Youth Unemployment: A 'Bust' Priority," *Globe and Mail*, 14 October 1997, A17.

13. *State of Employment.*

14. *Building Bridges.*

15. Ibid.

16. "Two Cheers for Loyalty," *The Economist*, 6–12 January 1996, 49.

17. Conger, "How 'Gen-X Managers' Manage," 27.

18. *Building Bridges.*

19. For an overview of the survey's findings, see Helen Wilkinson, "It's Just a Matter of Time: Twentysomethings View Their Jobs Differently Than Boomers," *Utne Reader*, no. 69, (May/June 1995): 66–67.

20. Catalyst and the Conference Board of Canada, *Closing the Gap: Women's Advancement in Corporate and Professional Canada* (Toronto, December 1997).

21. *Building Bridges.*

22. Douglas Coupland, *Microserfs* (New York: Regan Books, 1995), 4.

23. Pam Withers, "What Makes Gen X Employees Tick?" *B.C. Business* (March 1998): 24.

24. *State of Employment.*

25. David Berman, "Who's Hot? You Are," *Canadian Business* 70, no. 15, (November 14, 1997): 40–52.

26. Kevin Cox and Patrick Brethour, "Know a High-Tech Worker? You Could Pocket $1,000," *Globe and Mail*, 12 March 1998, A1.

27. *State of Employment.*

28. *Reconnecting Government with Youth.*

29. Marc Prensky, "Twitch Speed," *Across the Board* (January 1998): 14.

30. Ibid., 17.

31. Alfie Kohn, *Punished by Rewards: The Trouble with Gold Stars, Incentive Plans, A's, Praise and Other Bribes* (New York: Houghton Mifflin, 1993), 134.

32. *Building Bridges.* Seventy-six per cent of eighteen- to thirty-four-year-olds said that basic dental/medical benefits were a "very desirable" workplace benefit.

33. Conger, "How 'Gen-X Managers' Manage," 31.

34. Ibid., 25.

35. Sally Helgesen, *Everyday Revolutionaries: Working Women and the Transformation of American Life* (New York: Doubleday, 1988) and Polly LaBarre, "The Starbucks Sisterhood," *Fast Company*, no. 13 (February/March 1998): 66.

CHAPTER 6: *Nexus the Citizen*

1. Irshad Manji, *Risking Utopia: On the Edge of a New Democracy* (Toronto: Douglas and McIntyre, 1997), 11.

2. T. H. Marshall, "Citizenship and Social Class," in *Class, Citizenship and Social Development* (New York: Anchor, 1965).

3. William B. P. Robson, "Putting Some Gold in the Golden Years: Fixing the Canada Pension Plan," *Commentary* 76 (January 1996).

4. Levant, *YouthQuake*, 67–82.

5. *Reconnecting Government with Youth.*

6. See James C. Davies, "Towards a Theory of Revolution," *American Sociological Review* 6, no. 1 (February 1962): 5–19.

7. *Reconnecting Government with Youth.*

8. Will Kymlicka, *Multicultural Citizenship: A Liberal Theory of Minority Rights* (Oxford: Clarendon Press, 1995), 175.

9. Cited in Levant, *YouthQuake*, 69.

10. Statistic taken from the Angus Reid Group, 1997.

11. *Reconnecting Government with Youth.* As discussed in Chapter 3, this research estimates that the "ambivalent segment" comprises 25 per cent of sixteen- to thirty-year-olds, and the "dissatisfied independents" (who see government as irrelevant) make up 21 per cent.

12. Manji, *Risking Utopia*, 156.

13. Jeff Sallot, "The Malaise in Canada's Military," *Globe and Mail*, 25 April 1998, D2.

14. *Reconnecting Government with Youth.*

15. Harold D. Clarke, Jane Jenson, Lawrence LeDuc, and Jon H. Pammett, *Absent Mandate: Interpreting Change in Canadian Elections* (Toronto: Gage, 1991). These authors show how every political leader in Canada has experienced a decline in popular support from the moment of their first successful election (with the brief exception of former NDP leader Ed Broadbent).

16. While the overall percentage is 4.1, the numbers are slightly higher for Quebec youth (6.2 per cent) than non-Quebec youth (3.4 per cent). Print Measurement Bureau, 1996.

17. See, for instance, the October 1996 Leger and Leger poll. This is raw data, calculated before distribution of the undecided vote.

18. Neil Nevitte, *The Decline of Deference: Canadian Value Change in Cross-National Perspective* (Peterborough, Ont.: Broadview Press, 1996), 99.

19. Statistic from the Canadian Treasury Board, January 1998.

20. Jocelyne Bourgon, clerk of the Privy Council and secretary to the Cabinet, *Fifth Annual Report to the Prime Minister on the Public Service of Canada*, (Ottawa, 1998), 3.

21. Statistics from the Canadian Centre for Philanthropy and Revenue Canada, 1993. The total number of registered charities in Canada (when you include places of worship, hospitals, and teaching institutions) is approximately seventy-five thousand.

22. *Reconnecting Government with Youth.*

23. *Building Bridges*. Strauss and Howe also observe that Generation X volunteers in significant numbers. See *13th Gen*, 132.

24. Jeremy Rifkin, *The End of Work: The Decline of the Global Labor Force and the Dawn of the Post-Market Era* (New York: G. P. Putnam's Sons, 1995), 249.

25. *Building Bridges*.

26. Angus Reid Group and d~Code, *Redefining Corporate Citizenship: The Path for Canada's Young Entrepreneurs*, prepared for the Canadian Centre of Philanthropy (Toronto, March 1998).

27. Kymlicka, *Multicultural Citizenship*, 175.

28. Allan Gregg, "A Confident Nation," *Maclean's* 110, no. 52 (December 29, 1997–January 5, 1998): 17.

29. Ibid.

30. See "Young Canadians and the Environment: Review of Recent Public Opinion Polls," *Environmental Monitor* (1995). Martin Lagace's research shows that eighteen- to thirty-four-year-olds are more likely than the general population to make lifestyle sacrifices to help the environment.

31. Joe Chidley, "Defining Qualities," *Maclean's* 110, no. 52 (December 29, 1997–January 5, 1998): 29.

32. *Reconnecting Government with Youth*. The numbers of those who strongly agreed, by region, were as follows: British Columbia (79 per cent), Alberta (90 per cent), Saskatchewan/Manitoba (89 per cent), Ontario (87 per cent), Quebec (45 per cent), and Atlantic Canada (94 per cent).

33. Ibid.

CONCLUSION: *Building Bridges*

1. See John Kenneth Galbraith, *A Journey Through Economic Time: A Firsthand View* (New York: Houghton Mifflin, 1994), 3–4.

2. Chidley, "Defining Qualities," *Maclean's*, 30.

INDEX

Consumption trends, 136–40
Continuous learning, 191–96
Copps, Sheila, 254
Corporate citizenship, 210–11
Corporate concierge, 197–98
Corriveau, Paul, 234
Corson, Jennifer, 136, 164–65,
  204–205, 249
Côté, James, 15
Coupland, Douglas, 9, 10, 14, 17, 32,
  123, 178
Customization, 145

Darveau-Garneau, Nick, 145
Data visualization, 195
Database marketing, 133–34
Deficit reduction, 83, 112, 227,
  234–35
Democracy Watch, 223–24
Demos, 176
Digital Renaissance, 161, 178,
  183–84, 203
Diminishing returns, 159
Discount stores, 140, 141
"Discovering the rituals," 133
Disengaged Darwinists (Adams), 16
Diversity, 19, 79, 131–35, 162–63,
  208–209
Divorces, 51–52, 59, 63–64, 65–66
Do-it-yourselfism, 83, 102, 131,
  137–38, 144–45, 165, 167
Downsizing and re-engineering,
  157, 173
Dru, Jean-Marie, 129
Drucker, Peter, 157
Duties of citizenship, 226–31

Early childhood experiences, 28
Echo Generation, 2, 19–20

Eco Challenge, 121
Economist, 173
Education, post-secondary. *See*
  Universities and colleges
Employers:
  recruitment strategies. *See*
    Recruiting Nexus employees
  retention strategies. *See* Retaining
    Nexus employees
  views on ideal employers, 155–56
Employment equity, 163
Energy crisis, 57–58
Entrepreneurialism, 22, 164–65, 169,
  171, 206–207
Environics, 240–41
Environmentalism, 58, 121, 136–37
Eves, Ernie, 234–35
Experience, search for, 117–22,
  124–25, 141
Experimentation, 117–22, 126–29, 154
Extended family, 67–68
Extended freedom zone, 69–70, 111,
  180
Extra-curricular experiences, 162
Exxon Valdez spill, 57–58

Family values, 62–70
  break-ups, 51–52, 59, 63–64, 65–66
  marriage. *See* Marriage
Farmer, Ben, 236
Fast Company magazine, 151,
  157–58, 163–64
FastLane Technologies, 182
Feedback, 193
Films, 52, 54, 55, 56, 57, 139–40, 153
Financial services:
  concern with investments, 112–14
  and the Internet, 145–46
Floyd, Gordon, 245